Communicating for Development

SUNY Series, Human Communication Processes
Donald P. Cushman and Ted J. Smith, III, Editors

Communicating for Development

A New Pan-Disciplinary Perspective

Andrew A. Moemeka,
Editor

STATE UNIVERSITY OF NEW YORK PRESS

Published by
State University of New York Press, Albany

© 1994 State University of New York

For information, address State University of New York
Press, State University Plaza, Albany, N.Y., 12246

Production by E. Moore
Marketing by Dana E. Yanulavich

Library of Congress Cataloging-in-Publication Data

Communicating for development : a new pan-disciplinary perspective /
  Andrew A. Moemeka, editor
      p.   cm. — (SUNY series, Human communication processes)
    Includes bibliographical references and index.
    ISBN 0-7914-1833-2 (alk. paper). — ISBN 0-7914-1834-0 (pbk. :
  alk. paper)
      1. Communication in economic development. 2. Communication in
  community development.   I. Moemeka, Andrew A.   II. Series: Suny
  series in human communication processes.
  HD76.C64   1994
  302.2—dc20   93–3456
                                                              CIP

10 9 8 7 6 5 4 3 2 1

Contents

Preface

This book has two main objectives. The first is directed toward critically discussing conceptual and theoretical bases of building the communication component into development and social change activities. The second, which is an extension of the first, is to critically examine approaches, methods, and strategies that are utilized in the process of trying to ensure that the integration of communication into development plans and execution is efficient and effective.

The practice of development communication is discussed from the interpersonal as well as the mass media perspectives but not without some insightful references to the importance of traditional channels and the role of folk media. The wide and varied experience of the contributors, and the variety of the backgrounds from which they write, imbue the book with a unique quality. Furthermore, the book discusses the place of communication in development as it pertains not only to the "developing" world (the traditional arena for discussing development communication) but also the "developed" world, where economic advancement and social change or the reduction/elimination of the dysfunctional effects of physical development have become national issues.

One aspect of this volume that needs explanation is our decision not to follow the practice in certain quarters of interchangeably using the terms *development communication* and *communication development*. We stand convinced that even though their ultimate aim—improvement of human conditions of living—is the same, they are not synonymous. The former refers to the use of communication to improve the processes of planning and execution of development projects; the latter is mainly concerned with technological improvements of communication infrastructure. We agree completely with the Institute of Culture and Communication, East-West Center, Honolulu[1] that:

A distinction should be made between two aspects of communication

1. *Communication Infrastructure*, which deals with the development of communication systems (Communication Development), and
2. *Communication Operation*, which is concerned with the uses of communication elements and contents for development objectives (Development Communication).

STRUCTURE OF THE BOOK

The book is divided into four parts with a total of twelve chapters. The contributors are specialists in different disciplines who write with background experiences from different parts of the world, including Canada, China, India, Nigeria, and the United States of America.

Part I covers historical background, conceptual bases, and theoretical underpinnings. The place assigned to communication in the process of development has passed through three basic stages: from when communication was considered merely tangential (Communication in Support of Development) through when it was seen as important (Development Support Communication) to now that it is recognized as crucial (Development Communication). It is noteworthy that communication's role has also gone through stages. Here, however, the specific role assigned has been dictated by extant economic development theories ranging from Dependency through Marginality and Trickle Down to Self-help, Basic Needs, and Self-reliance.

Chapter 1 gives a brief history of how communication has been used in the service of development since the early 1960s, the failure of early attempts because of the materialistic perspective of development, and the movement toward better understanding and conceptualization and redirection of efforts. It also discusses the conceptual framework of the new development and communication paradigms, as well as the interface of development and communication. Chapter 2 discusses old myths and new realities about the role of communication in the development and social change process. It draws attention to the resurgence of the importance of the economic factor, pointing out certain preconditions necessary for active participation in world trade, which it sees as the key to economic, and therefore, social development. The basic thrust of this chapter is that solutions to social problems are difficult, if not impossible, without viable economic conditions. Social problems cannot be solved unless economic problems are first solved.

Chapter 3 examines old and existing theoretical formulations, pointing out defaults in both conceptualization and application. It ends with a detailed discussion on emerging perspectives and how these could be implemented, with a view to reaching some consensus on formulating a more comprehensive theory of development communication. Chapter 4 discusses approaches to and planning strategies for effective development communication. Using existing theoretical perspectives, it examines different approaches, methods, and planning strategies and points to the inevitable impact of cultural, socioeconomic, and political contexts in development communication.

Part II deals with the influence of the mass media on development and social change. The three chapters in this section—chapters 5, 6, and 7—discuss the three most important media of mass communication (radio, television, and newspapers) and the role or roles they can and have played in both physical and sociocultural developments, and suggest new strategies, methods, and tactics to improve their effectiveness.

It is true that the mass media, in reality and by their very nature, are instruments of mass information rather than of mass communication. It is also true, as research has shown, that they are not very effective in changing people's attitudes; their greatest potential is in reaching out easily to audiences far and wide. This quality of wide area coverage becomes a great advantage when the mass media are turned from being merely instruments of information to being channels of communication. This obtains when the mass media work through a nexus of factors—standardized and/or creative—that help build the interpersonal component into their communication endeavors. How this can and has been done to advantage using television, radio, and the newspaper is the focus of this second part of the book.

In Part III the book examines some aspects of industrial organizations vis-à-vis industrial and economic development. Traditional development communication studies, in strong aversion to the heavy economic orientation of communication in the task of development in the 1960s, tend to ignore to a large extent the economic factor in development. The argument usually is that human and social development are the key to national development because without them economic development would not be put to profitable ends. For example, it is good and fitting to provide pipe-borne water in a village, but for it to be managed and utilized successfully, the villagers must be educated to understand and value this amenity. This, of course, should not mean that the economic conditions that are necessary to produce or buy the materials and tools needed for the pipe-borne water are not important. Human and social development would not survive unless they are supported by and subsequently lead to improvement in economic conditions.

Chapter 8 discusses the relationship between multinational corporations and their host countries in the face of improved high-speed management and organizational communication. With appropriately relevant examples, the authors discuss not only the critical forces favoring rapid economic development but also models for positive capitalization, effective use of communication to develop continuous organizational improvement programs, and multinationals that have stimulated national economic development. Chapter 9 focuses on the importance of industrial peace in the effort to achieve economic development. It sees public relations as the major tool for achieving and maintaining such industrial peace. The chapter outlines the limitation of models for Third-World development and presents public relations strategies for attaining industrial peace and development. Based on a shift from industry-driven economic development to government-generated economic growth, the author points out and discusses two major contributory roles of public relations—institutional-sociopolitical stability and institutional-sociostructural Integration.

Part IV contains case studies that provide practical and theoretical insights into the application of development communication techniques to the processes of national development. The chapters show in various ways that strict vertical feedforward communication strategy is not only a hindrance to effective development communication but also a wedge in the cog of the wheel of social change and development. The studies, in different words, affirm the importance of knowledge of the sociocultural contexts of target audiences, the key role of audience participation and, the crucial nature of content relevance.

Chapter 10 is a study of a Canadian experience. It examines the impact (or the lack of it) of Canadian television on Canadians in general and young Canadians in particular because of "cultural imperialism." It also discusses the impact of geographic contiguity on the relationship between the United States and Canada in such issues as media technology, media economics, and media content. After reviewing the 1991 Canadian Broadcasting Act—which it describes as a strong instrument for changing the status quo and for minimizing the invasion of foreign culture and, therefore, the effect of media imperialism—it strongly recommends the Canadian model to other countries, both developed and developing.

Chapter 11 discusses the impact of the mass media in a health campaign. It is a study of the immunization campaign to eradicate six deadly infantile diseases from rural communities in Nigeria. The study confirms the limitations of a campaign predicated almost exclusively on using only the mass media, in spite of their outreach abilities, to significantly change people's attitudes, especially on such personal and intimate issue as health. It makes a number of suggestions as to how to improve the effectiveness of the mass media, such as through integration with interpersonal channels.

Chapter 12 is a case study from India. It, also, is a study of a campaign that did not work as expected, but this time because of the neglect of sociocultural realities and disregard of key communication factors in development activities. The chapter discusses in detail the reasons why a family planning campaign in three Indian villages did not succeed and notes that the government (in the light of the new development and communication paradigm) has revised its communication strategy, taking into account many factors, including recipient group participation, relevance of messages to community contexts, and the need for increased motivation.

NOTE

1. *An Introduction to Development Communication Teacher's Resource Manual* 85

Part I

ANDREW A. MOEMEKA

1

Development Communication: A Historical and Conceptual Overview

HISTORICAL BRIEF

Although the concept of development communication has been with us for a long time, recognition of its importance for sociocultural, economic, and political development, and utilization of its approaches and methods (see chapter 4) did not gain public and academic acceptance until the early 1960s. Its development, problems, and potentials, outlined and critically examined in this text, reflect the thorny road it has traveled. It has been subjected to intellectual skepticism and public doubts and has been misinterpreted and misapplied; recently, questions of its relevance to developed societies have been raised. Chapter 3 shows how the road has been or is being cleared, and points out that contrary to widely held views, especially in the developed societies of the world, development communication is a universal need—a development imperative without which concrete economic and social developments would be difficult to achieve

The place of communication in the development process was given a boost when Lerner (1958) wrote his famous treatise, *The Passing of the Traditional Society*, in which he acknowledged that mass media growth was one of the three phases of democratic political development. He pointed out that the mass media had the power to create opportunity for empathy which "disciplined western men in skills that spell modernity." A further boost was given by Klapper (1960) with his book *The Effects of Mass Communication* which discussed the impacts that the mass media have on society. Although couched in general terms, such impacts included increase in general and specific knowledge which cannot but affect development—both human and socioeconomic. In more specific terms, Schramm (1964), in what many have classified as the best known exposition of the relationship between the mass media and national development in the 1960s, lists twelve areas of influence for the mass media in the task of national development. They include widening horizons, focusing attention on relevant issues, raising aspiration, creating a climate for development, helping change strongly held attitudes or values not conducive to development, feeding interpersonal channels of communication, conferring status, broadening the policy dialogue, enforcing social norms, helping form tastes, affecting attitudes lightly held and canalizing stronger attitudes, and helping substantially in all types of education and training.

These pioneers in the field of communication and development, though basically concerned with mass media communication, showed such strong faith in communication's power to help cause development that they succeeded in winning the support of researchers in other disciplines, especially in political science. Almon and Verba (1963) agreed that communication was essential in political integration. Pye (1963) thought that the problem of political development is one of cultural diffusion and of adapting and adjusting old patterns of life to new demands. Such diffusion, adapting, and adjusting can only be done through communication. Because communication is the web of society, its flow determines the direction and pace of dynamic social development. In more emphatic words, Deutsch (1964) pointed to communication as a prerequisite for successful political democracy. And Cutwright (1964) asserted the importance of communication in development by holding that communications development is the strongest socioeconomic correlate of political development.

Important though these pioneering attempts to expose the power of communication in development are, they fell prey to the paradigmatic environment in which they were made. The conception of "communication" with which the researchers worked was not significantly different from the discredited Bullet (or Hypodermic Needle) theory that treated the mass media as an all-powerful institution. Emphasis was on what communication can do and/or the effect it can have on literacy, aspiration, empathy, attitudes, agricultural production, health, and so on. Very little or no attention was given to the cultural and socioeconomic realities of the communities studied. The social and historical contexts of the variables they used were not studied. Neither was sufficient thought given to how the variables were logically linked with one another. The researchers would appear to have believed that the social structure of recipient villages or communities was not important; that the type of interest groups and social relationships and the economic, political, educational, and social institutions within the communities were not relevant to the influence of communication. As Golding (1974) points out, the old paradigm of communication's role in development conceives the "developing countries as emerging from static isolation, requiring an external stimulus to shake them into the twentieth century." Does this sound familiar with regard to the conception of communication's role in social change activities in the so-called developed societies? In bemoaning this lack of sensitivity toward the realities of recipient communities and therefore the absence of relevant data, the Commission on Health Research for Development (1990) refuted the claim that research was a luxury in countries struggling to meet basic human needs, pointing out that research is essential for these countries precisely because of the need to empower those who must accomplish more with fewer resources.

Not only was the old paradigm of communication unilinear it was also "transportational." It assumed that communicating to or informing the elite, the well-to-do, the articulate, and the educated was all the impetus needed to ensure communication effectiveness; that the "inevitable" benefits deriving from the responses of these highly placed members of the communities to the communication would, of necessity, trickle down to the masses. Of course, this did not happen. In a 1974 report, the World Bank said, inter alia: "These efforts at using the mass media in development did not appreciably affect, in positive ways, the lives of the people in the developing countries." Many reasons have been given for this failure. Among the most important (Moemeka, 1985) are the complete neglect of the sociocultural environment in which the mass media were supposed to function effectively as well as the equation of the mass media with Communication and the complete absence of audience-oriented feedback.

Because the dominant development paradigm in the 1960s was predicated on industrial growth and increased GNP, the pioneer researchers in the field of development communication saw economic growth as the final goal of development and geared all their efforts toward using communication to help achieve this goal in the developing societies. But, as research has shown, their efforts left much to be desired. By the early 1970s, it was clear that the vast majority of people in the developing countries were not benefiting from the numerous capital-intensive, industrial growth-based, unilinear communication-supported development programs executed in their communities. The Green Revolution programs directed toward increased agriculture production and the various health and family welfare programs seemed to be producing adverse effects (Beal and Jussawalla, 1981; and Stewart and Streeten, 1976). In fact, the attempt at industrialization caused large-scale migration from the rural areas; technology fostered greater dependency rather than self-reliance; and Western values and behaviors (e.g., high degree of self-interest and individualism) successfully threatened indigenous cultures and social institutions. A simplistic approach to communication in support of development, which was a natural counterpart of the simplistic model of economic development that held sway in the 1960s, had failed.

This failure led to a decline of emphasis on bare economic growth. It also helped to expose the limitations of UNESCO's quantitative approach contained in the celebrated "norms" for developing countries—ten daily newspaper copies, twenty radio sets, and two cinema seats per 100 people—which ignored the important issues of media content, the context of media messages, and access to mass media channels and utilization capacities and patterns. As a result, a slow but conscious realization began to emerge that development for each country has to be seen in terms of that country's own needs, which, in turn, must be related to its unique circumstances of climatic, historical, cultural and social conditions as well as human and physical resources. Attention to variability, Bebe (1987) pointed out, was expected to lead to new extension approaches that present people with options that they can adapt to their existing systems as opposed to packages of technology or ideas that they are expected to adopt in place of their existing systems.

The immediate result of such rethinking was manifest in sensitivity to the structural and cultural constraints on the impact of communication, in addition to conscious awareness that the mass media were just a part of the total communication infrastructure. It became evident that successful and effective use of communication in any community requires adequate knowledge of the availability, accessibility, relationships, and utilization of communication infrastructure and software in that community. Because this calls for a holistic understanding of the communication environment, ethnocommunication (Eilers and Oepen, 1991), that is, the description and study of communication means, structures and processes in a cultural unit, was advocated. Three studies are relevant here. Donohue et al (1975) studied the phenomenon of Information Gap, and pointed out some of the effects of community structure on the role of communication. Rogers (1976a), in a review of past studies, noted the weaknesses in the study of diffusion (e.g., psychological bias ignoring the social structural variables and a reliance on the individual as the unit of analysis). Halloran (1981) called for critical, problem/policy-oriented research concerned with questioning the values and claims of the system, applying independent criteria, suggesting alternatives, and exploring the possibility of new forms and structures.

What might be described as the real turning point for the study of communication in the service of development was the 1975 experts conference held in Honolulu, Hawaii to review the use of communication in economic and social development. At the conference, the two best known pioneers in this area of study—Lerner and Schramm—admitted that the model of "trickle down" communication in development (the unilinear approach) had been proven ineffective. This admission gave the impetus for making concerted efforts toward finding alternative approaches that would be efficient and effective. Many studies were conducted. Some of the better known were published in a book edited by Rogers (1976b) titled *Communication and Development: Critical Perspectives*. A sample of the articles (chapters) includes "New Perspectives on Communication and Development"; "Alien Premises, Objects and Methods in Latin American Communication;" "How Communication Interfaces with Change"; and "Communication and Development: The Passing of the Dominant Paradigm." These articles examine critically the dominant paradigm of communication in development and propose a new development model based on the ideal of social equality rather than economic growth. The following is a summary of backgrounds and contents of the emergent alternatives as compared with the dominant paradigm (Rogers, 1976):

Table 1.1
Emergent Alternatives to the Dominant Paradigm of Development

Main Elements in the Dominant Paradigm of Development	Emerging Alternatives to the Dominant Paradigm	Possible Factors Leading to the Emerging Alternatives
1. Economic growth	1. Equality of distribution	1. Development weariness from the slow rate of economic development during the 1950s and 1960s
		2. Publication of the Pearson Report
		3. Growing loss of faith in the "trickle down" theory of distributing development benefits
2. Capital-intensive technology	1. Concern with quality of life	1. Environmental pollution problems in Euro-America and Japan
	2. Integration of "traditional" and "modern" systems in a country	2. Limits to growth
	3. Greater emphasis on intermediate-level and labor-intensive technology	3. The energy crisis following the 1973 Yom Kippur War
3. Centralized planning	1. Self-reliance in development	1. The People's Republic of China experience with decentralized participatory self-development (known elsewhere after 1971)

(continued)

Table 1.1 (*Continued*)

Main Elements in the Dominant Paradigm of Development	Emerging Alternatives to the Dominant Paradigm	Possible Factors Leading to the Emerging Alternatives
	2. Popular participation in decentralized self-development planning and execution (e.g., to village level)	
4. Mainly internal causes of underdevelopment	1. Internal and external causes of under-development	1. The rise of "oil power" in the years following the energy crisis of 1973–74
		2. Shifts in world power illustrated by the voting behavior at the United Nations
		3. Criticism of the dominant paradigm by radical economists such as Frank and other dependency theorists

Source: Everett M. Rogers; *Communication and Development: Critical Perspectives* (Beverly Hills: Sage Publications, 1976) 132.

The new development paradigm repudiates the one-dimensional approach of the old paradigm which was predicated solely on economic growth or increases in the gross national product. It takes a multidimensional approach that incorporates equity, social justice, and economic growth. In addition, it addresses the relationship among these four sets of variables: social structural variables; communication potentials and tasks; the psycho-cultural factors of the social actors at both the individual and societal levels; and the socioeconomic goals of development. Congenial to this new paradigm of development, the new model (concept) of development communication sees development not only in physical (economic growth) but also in sociocultural (human) terms. It stresses access to the media of communication, participation in communication activities, and relevance of communication content to sociocultural contexts.

CONCEPTUAL FRAMEWORK

The new and culturally relevant role assigned communication in the task of development under the new order required a redefinition of development communication. In 1973, when opinions were molding in support of equity, social justice, access, and participation, a working committee of the International Broadcast Institute meeting at Cologne on "Communication in Support of Development" defined the key concepts of the paradigm thus:

Development: The improvement of the well-being of the individual and the betterment of the quality of his/her life

Communication: The transfer of information between individuals or groups of individuals by human or technical means

Development Support Communication: The systematic use of communication in the planning and implementation of development.

While these definitions would appear to capture the central issues of these key concepts, they are not operational enough. They fail to provide the framework for explanations and/or demonstrations to enable in-depth understanding and realistic and practical application. Hence, specialists, especially those from developing countries who know "where the shoe pinches" set themselves the task of fashioning more appropriate definitions that are operationally relevant to the new paradigm. What follows is a discussion of some of the definitions of the concepts.

Development

Even at the time when the world was still basing all hopes of development on industrialization and economic growth, Inayatullah (1967: 101) drew attention to what development meant in reality to developing countries. His aim was to identify the specific roles which development should play, giving it a holistic perspective. Thus, he defined the concept as "change toward patterns of society that allows better realization of human values, that allows a society greater control over its environments, and over its own political destiny, and that enables its individuals to gain increased control over themselves." In support of Inayatullah, and to show that his views about development have changed in line with the new paradigm, Rogers (1976b: 345) redefined development as "a widely participatory process of social change and material advancement (including greater equality, freedom and other valued qualities) for the majority of the people through their gaining greater control over their environment."

These two definitions show clearly that development is a multifaceted concept. This is why it generally means different things to different people, and in different disciplines. In discussing the concept, most psychologists, for example, lay emphasis on such individual or personality variables as self-reliance, achievement motivation, self-worth, and self-actualization. For the sociologist, the concept of development tends to revolve around the process of differentiation that characterizes modern societies. The political scientist is mainly concerned with developing a capacity to innovate change, increase political awareness, and improve the ability to resolve conflict in political situations. The communication specialist (the development communicator) tends to see development as the acquisition of new knowledge and skills, increased self-confidence, control over oneself and one's environment, greater equality, freedom, ability to understand one's potentials and limitations, and willingness to work hard enough to improve on existing positive conditions.

These different angles from which development is viewed are, of course, not exclusive; they are interwoven. Together, they stress the fact that development is a normative concept in that it assumes that existing conditions are no longer conducive to human dignity and socioeconomic advancement, and therefore should be changed for the better. Therefore, though seen from different perspectives, development means one basic thing in all perspectives and to all people—a change for the better in the human, cultural, socioeconomic, and political conditions of the individual and consequently of the society. It is not solely a matter of technology or of gross national product; more importantly, it is a matter of increased knowledge and skills, growth of new consciousness, expansion of the human mind, the uplifting of the human spirit, and the fusion of human confidence.

Communication

Communication is the exchange of ideas. It is not the mechanical transfer of facts and figures as the mathematical model of communication (Shannon and Weaver, 1949) would appear to indicate. It is also not talking at people. It is instead an interactive process that works in a circular, dynamic and ongoing way (Hiebert et al,1985). It is talking with people—a process with no permanent sender and no permanent receiver. In the process of communication, the roles of sending and receiving change hands depending on who is talking and who is listening. This implies freedom, equality, and shared interest.

Communication defined this way departs from what Beltran (1974: 13) has identified as "the classical mechanistic-vertical model," which sees communication as a process of transmission of modes of thinking, feeling, and behaving from one or more persons to another person or persons. In this classical model, the paramount goal of communication is persuasion, and the element of feedback is important chiefly as a message-adjusting device to enable the communicator to secure the performance of the expected response from the receiver. This is the model which assigns an actively predominant role to the communicator, and a very passive role to the communicatee—a sort of one-way communication in which emphasis is on the effects that communication can have on people or on ways in which *messages can use people*. The new concept of communication—the humanized democratic-interactive model (Beltran, 1974)—places emphasis on how *people use communication or messages*. It stresses genuine dialogue, or free and proportioned opportunity to exert mutual influence and rejects the idea that *persuasion* is the chief role of communication. In this new order, *understanding* is the crucial factor; it is recognized as the chief role of communication. Because of this, audience-oriented feedback is imperative; its importance lies in the opportunity it creates for understanding the receiver's point of view, and therefore, for ensuring co-orientational influence.

Development Communication

In a very concise way, development communication is the application of the processes of communication to the development process. In other words, development communication is the use of the principles and practices of the exchange of ideas to achieve development objectives. It is, or should be, therefore, an element of the management process in the overall planning and implementation of development programs. In a very broad sense, development is "the art and science of human communication applied to the speedy transformation of a country (economic growth, modernization, industrialization, etc.) and the mass of its people (self-actualization, fulfillment of human potentials, greater social justice, etc.) through the identification and utilization of appropriate expertise in the development process that will assist in increasing participation of intended beneficiaries at the grassroots level" (Rosario-Braid, 1979).

Because it is communication with a social conscience, development communication is heavily oriented toward the human aspects of development. This means that physical and economic growth are important only in so far as they help to improve the human condition, that is, if functionality of physical conditions does not produce dysfunctions in human conditions. Even though development communication is primarily associated with rural development and the developing societies, it is also concerned with urban and suburban problems, as well as with social problems in developed societies. It plays two broad roles. The first is the transformation role through which it seeks social change or development in the direction of higher quality of life and social justice. The second is the socialization role through which it strives to maintain some of the established values of society that are consonant with development and social change. In playing these roles, development communication tries to create an enhancing atmosphere for exchange of ideas that produces a happy balance in social and economic advancement between physical output and human interrelationships (Moemeka, 1987).

INTERFACE OF COMMUNICATION AND DEVELOPMENT

A close examination of the basic tenets of the new development paradigm (Rogers, 1976) and of the ultimate requirements of the new communication approach to development (Beltran, 1974) would reveal very close similarity between them. To begin with, participation is the key variable in the new development paradigm, just as it is for the new communication approach to development. In broad terms, the ultimate objectives of national development (urban and rural) are economic growth, equitable distribution of facilities and of benefits, national cohesion, and human development. These are also, in broad terms, the ultimate objectives of development communication, even though, because of the importance attached to intelligent understanding of development issues, development communication gives the pride of place to human development. In order to achieve these ultimate objectives, both the new development paradigm and the new communication approach stress the need for the following which Rogers (1976) identified as the key characteristics of the new order:

- equality of the distribution of social and economic benefits, information, and education
- popular participation in development planning and execution, accompanied by decentralization of activities to local levels
- self-reliance and independence in development with emphasis on the potential of local resources
- integration of traditional with modern systems, so that development is a syncretization of old and new ideas, with the exact mixture somewhat different in each locale

However, further demands are made from communication for specific actions that are necessary to smooth the path to the above goals. At the International Conference on Communication Policies for Rapidly Developing Societies held at Mashad, Iran (UNESCO, 1975), a working group identified specific activities that development communication must strive to accomplish if it is to contribute effectively to development. These include:

- determination of the needs of the people and the provision of sufficient citizen access to the communication systems to serve as effective feedback to the government
- provision of horizontal and vertical (interactive) communication linkage at all levels of society and communication channels through which people at all levels of society and in all regions and localities have the capability to communicate with one another in order to accomplish coordination necessary for human and material development
- provision of local community support for cultural preservation, and provision of local media to serve as effective channels
- provision of relevant information
- support for specific development projects and social services
- raising people's awareness of development projects and opportunities and helping to foster attitudes and motivations that contribute to development

Development communication is not merely a matter of transmitting information about how things can be done better by using available resources and facilities. It is much more than the exchange of problem-solving information. It also involves the generation of psychic mobility or empathy, raising of aspirations and willingness to work hard to meet those aspirations, teaching of new skills, and encouragement of local participation in development activities. In addition, it performs the broader function of helping people to restructure their mental framework in interpreting specific events and phenomena and to relate to the broader world beyond their immediate environments. To be effective in doing this, communication activities in development must be interwoven with sociocultural, economic, and political processes.

True and effective community development requires the participation of every segment of the nation—rural, urban, city, suburban; and every sector—government and private and public business. These groups and sectors must establish new social relations with one another before they can collectively be effective. It is the task of development communication to facilitate the growth and development of such human relationships. But it cannot perform this role effectively unless it is incorporated into the total development process. Such deliberate incorporation also helps put communication in a favorable position to positively affect the achievement of the four cardinal elements without which no development activity can succeed, that is, to provide the information and intellectual environment that will help the people to

know *what* to do
know *how* to do it
be *willing* to do it, and
have the *resources* to do it.

If any of the four elements is missing from the equation, development will not occur. But each of them could very easily be left out, intentionally or not, unless communication, whose primary duty it is to ensure the first three and which is also expected to help create the climate in which the fourth can obtain, is well integrated into the planning and execution of development projects.

These four cardinal elements emphasize the all-important and pervasive nature of communication in human development efforts and they stress its important role in the planning and implementation of development and social change programs. Of course, recognition of the place of communication in development is not new. There have been calls, since the mid-sixties for the integration of communication into development plans. The International Commission for the Study of Communication Problems

(McBride, 1980) re-echoed this call emphatically when it called on nations to incorporate communication policies into development strategies "as an integral part in the diagnosis of needs, and in the design and the implementation of selected priorities." Unfortunately, not much has changed. As Servaes (1991) points out, existing national communication policies are characterized by fragmentation and by uncoordinated and sometimes contradictory objectives, thus creating a wide gap between what is advocated and the reality of the ad hoc nature of national communication policies, especially in most of the developing world.

Also stressed by the four elements is the importance of economic or material resources without which development efforts cannot go beyond the ideas and willingness stages. The new development paradigm, no doubt, attempts to reorient development toward models that can truly "put people first, and poor people first of all" (Jamieson, 1991), but it also does not lose sight of the importance of economic (physical) resources. In today's world, it is foolhardy to talk about development without reference to technology and industry and the goods and services they produce to make the sociocultural and human environments worthwhile. "Money speaks," says an Igbo adage. Indeed, Money speaks, in the development arenas of the world. Hence the importance of economic development.

It is true, as a number of researchers have shown (Chen et al, 1990; Gupta and Ball, 1990; Kjelostrom and Rosenstock, 1990; Romieu al, 1990; FASE, 1991; Masironi, 1988; Takeichi, 1992; Rowley, 1986; Todaro, 1977; Kumar, 1980; Beal and Jussawalla, 1981; Stewart and Streeten, 1976) that most economic development outcomes, even though successful economically, bring with them numerous social, health, human, environmental, and even economic problems. For example, the Green Revolution and similar large-scale agricultural development programs of the 1970s achieved dramatic increases in food production in the core areas of many parts of the world (e.g., Central Thai plain, East and Central Java). But the success of such enterprises (Jamieson, 1991) has served to divert resources from and impede the creation of techniques that can help resource-poor farmers in the hinterland, characterized by extreme cultural and ecological diversity, and has served as (Moemeka, 1987) a disincentive to grow more crops among rural farmers in Nigeria. However, it is also true that economic development makes it possible to solve many of these problems by creating the financial environment in which resources can be made available to meet community and national needs. Therefore, it is now admitted that the physical (economic) and sociocultural (human) aspects of life are complementary in the process of development; that unless they are effectively integrated in both the planning and the implementation of development programs (a task which communication is well suited to do) they would each be a drag on the other.

Two concepts that have become very important in the application of the new development paradigm are privatization and interdependence. This aspect of the new paradigm attempts to combine economic (material) development with social justice. Privatization attempts to restructure economic and industrial activities within the nation in order to make them more efficient in operation and more effective in meeting the human and social needs of the population. Interdependence stresses the fact that no country can exist and survive on its own without any interaction—social or economic—with any other country. Because every country has some problem or problems—social, economic, political, or cultural—which it cannot solve by itself, cooperation between and among countries is imperative for survival. It aims at maximizing the strengths of individual countries and minimizing their weaknesses, thereby strengthening the overall economic output of the participating countries to the greater advantage of all.

Examples of the impact of privatization on the economic and social life of citizens abound in both the developing countries and in the newly industrialized countries (NIC). The first attempts at privatization by regional governments in Nigeria turned heavily indebted government transport companies into profitable ventures. This gave an impetus to the establishment of a national Technical Committee on Privatization and Commercialization (TCPC) charged with the responsibility of selling state-owned ventures to private organizations. Here, privatization is as much geared toward efficiency and profitability as it is toward spreading ownership of industrial ventures to as many Nigerians as possible. In the newly industrialized countries known as the Four Dragons—Singapore, Korea, Hong Kong, and Taiwan—privatization is directed at consolidating healthy industrial ventures in the hands of private citizens who can afford to buy them. This is the type of privatization that is also seen as a major factor in Mexico's rebounding economy (Perry, 1992). In the Commonwealth of Independent States (CIS), privatization appears to be directed toward the sale of state ventures to foreign nationals and organizations. The existing variability in privatization strategies is dictated by the realities of each country's socioeconomic condition. And the fact that each has succeeded where it has been applied is a reflection of the importance of *relevance*, which generally obtains as a result of genuine dialogue and discussion, effective communication, and understanding.

Interdependence (inter-state and/or regional cooperation) has also taken different forms depending on the socioeconomic and political realities of each country or region. In Africa, and against the advice of the World Bank that "export-led" development programs (more intensive export of tropical products and minerals to pay for manufactured and industrial goods from outside) should be intensified, the Organization of African Unity has opted for "Collective Self-Reliance" (Browne, 1992). At the Heads of State Summit (Abuja, 1991), African leaders unanimously agreed to focus their energies on producing the products that Africa consumes, and committed themselves to working toward the integration of their economies, first on a subregional and later on a continent-wide (African Economic Community) basis.

In Saudi Arabia, internal capital and external technology and expertise have joined to produce the "wonders" of Jubail and Yanbu (*Development Review*, 1990 and 1992). These are two entirely new cities built in the desert and provided with every modern amenity—schools, hospitals, water, electricity, supermarkets, housing—as well as modern commercial and industrial ventures—iron and steel, methanol, petrochemical, gas, polyprophylene, etc.

In Asia, where Japan is seen as the "guiding hand that uses aid to coordinate the region's economy" (*Wall Street Journal*, 1990; *The Economist*, 1991), interdependence would seem to be aimed at "teaching how to fish" rather than "giving fish." The Japanese provide the financial capital and the technical know-how used within each country by the nationals of these countries. In the process, education and training is not only improved but also expanded within each of these participating countries. These countries are now moving toward closer ties among themselves. For example, Singapore, Malaysia, and Indonesia are trying to forge a "Growth Triangle" (*Business Times*, 1991), and Brunei, Indonesia, Malaysia, Singapore, the Philippines, and Thailand have put together plans for a Southeast Asia Economic Integration (Pura, 1990).

These seemingly pure economic development programs would certainly not have succeeded to the extent that they did if there had been no effective communication component built into the programs, and if the results deriving therefrom had not included social and cultural benefits. It was the effective communication component that created the climate in which discussions and dialogues led to understanding of the ramifications of the development projects and to the full and active participation which made the projects successful. The truth of this appears to have been summarized in the comment by Worthy (1991) on the success of Japan both within and outside her borders: "Their products (and influence) seem to be everywhere, but not because of innovative marketing techniques. The real reason: good information, personal relationships and patience . . . (effective communication)."

REFERENCES

Almond, G., and Verba, S. 1963. *The Civic Culture: Political Attitudes and Democracy in Five Nations*. Princeton, N.J.: Princeton University Press.

Beltran, L. R. 1974. Rural Development and Social Communication: Relationships and Strategies. *Communication Strategies for Rural Development*. Proceedings of the Cornell-CIAT International Symposium, March 17–24, New York State College of Agriculture and Life Sciences, New York.

Beal, G., and Jussawalla, M. 1981. Old and New Paradigms of Development: Concept and Issues. Paper presented at the Conference on Communication Policy for Rural Development. Dhmibol Dam, Thailand.

Bebe, J. 1987. Rapid Appraisal: The Evolution of the Concept and the Definition of Issues. Proceedings of the 1985 International Conference on Rapid Rural Appraisal (pp. 47–68), Khon Kaen University, Thailand.

Browne, R. S. 1992. The Lagos Plan: Revising Africa's Last Hope. *Emerge (International)*, Vol. 3, No. 10, Sept., pp. 12–13.

Business Times. 1991. An Asian 'Growth Triangle'. Section 3, Oct. 13.

Chen, B. H. et al. 1990. Indoor Air Pollution in Developing Countries. *World Health Statistics Quarterly*, Vol. 43, No. 3, pp. 127–38.

Commission on Health Research for Development. 1990. *Health Research: Essential Link to Equity in Development.* New York: Oxford University Press.

Deutsch, K. S. 1964. Communication theory and Political Integration. In Jacob, P. E., and Tascano, J. V. (eds.), *The Integration of Political Community.* New York: Lippincott.

Donohue, G. A., et al. 1970. Mass Media and the Knowledge Gap: A Hypothesis Reconsidered. *Communication Research 2 (1),* January.

Eilers, F., and Oepen, M. 1991. Communication and Development: Mainstream and Off-Stream Perspectives—A German View. In Casmir, L. (ed), *Communication in Development* Norwood, N.J.: Ablex Publishing Corporation. 305.

FASE. 1991. Exporting Banned and Hazardous Pesticides. *FASE Reports* 9(1):51–58.

Golding, P. 1974. Media Role in National Development: a Critique of a Theoretical Orthodoxy. *Journal of Communication 24(3),* Summer.

Gupta, P. C., and Ball, K. 1990. India: Tobacco Tragedy. *Lancet* 335:594–95.

Halloran, J. 1980. The Need for Communication Research in Developing Countries. *Media Asia,* Vol. 7, No. 3, pp. 137–44.

Hiebert, R.E., et al 1985. *Mass Media IV: An Introduction to Modern Communication,* Longman, New York, pp. 31–32.

International Broadcast Institute 1975. Communication in Support of Development. IBI Annual Meeting: *Report of Working Committee I* (Mimeographed). See also Working Committee I: Development Support Communication. *Intermedia,* (IBI) 3, No. 2, p. 5.

Inayatullah. 1967. Quoted in Hamdan bin Adnan et al (1985). The Nature of Development. In Clayton, V., and Simmons, J. (eds.), *Development Communication: A Resource Manual for Teaching,* p. 4. Singapore: Asia Mass Communication Research and Information Centre.

Jamieson, N. 1991. Communication and the New Paradigm of Development. In Casmir, Fred L. (ed.). *Communication in Development . . .* p. 31.

Kjellstrom, T., and Rosenstock, L. 1990. The Role of Environmental and Occupational Hazards in the Adult Health Transition. *World Health Statistics Quarterly,* Vol. 43, No. 3, pp. 186–96.

Klapper, J. T. 1960. *The Effects of Mass Communication.* Glencoe, Ill.: The Free Press.

Kumar, K. (ed.). 1980. *Transnational Enterprises: Their Impact on Third World Societies and Culture.* Boulder, Colo.: Westview.

Lerner, D. 1958. *The Passing of the Traditional Society.* Glencoe, Ill.: The Free Press.

Masironi, R. and Rothwell, K. 1988. Smoking Trends and Effects World-wide. *World Health Statistics Quarterly* 41: 228–41.

McBride, S. (ed.). 1980. *Many Voices, One World: Communication and Society, Today and Tomorrow.* Paris: UNESCO.

Moemeka, A. A. 1985. Communication in National Development: The Use of the Mass Media in Rural Development. *Informatologia Yugoslavica*, Vol. 17, Nos. 1–2, pp. 171–85.

————. 1987. *Rural Radio Broadcasting and Community Health Practices in Nigeria: A Case-Study of Radio O-Y-O On the Move.* Ph.D. Dissertation, State University of New York, Albany.

————. 1987. Integrated Rural Development in Bendel State: The Role of and Strategy for Mass Media Communication. In Omu, Fred A. I., and Makinwa-Adebusoye, P. K. (eds.), *Integrated Rural Development in Nigeria and Women's Role*, pp. 131–42. Heineman Educational Books (Nig) Ltd.

Perry, N. J. 1992. What's Powering Mexico's Success. *Fortune* Feb., p. 109.

Pye, L. W. (ed.). 1963. *Communication and Political Development.* Princeton, N.J.: Princeton University Press.

Rogers, E. M. 1976a. Where are We in Understanding the Diffusion of Innovations. In W. Schramm and D. Lerner (eds.), *Communication and Change: The Last Ten Years—And the Next*, Honolulu: 204–22. The University Press of Hawaii.

————. (ed.) 1976b. *Communication and Development: Critical Perspectives.* Beverly Hills, Calif.: Sage Publications.

Romieu, I., et al. 1990. Urban Air Pollution in Latin America and the Caribbean: Health Perspectives. *World Health Statistics Quarterly*, Vol. 43, No. 3, pp. 153–67.

Rosario-Braid, F. 1979. A User-Oriented Communication Strategy. In Rosario-Braid (ed.), *Communication Strategy for Productivity Improvement.* Tokyo: 34. Asian Productivity Organization.

Rowley, C. D. 1986. *Recovery: The Politics of Aboriginal Reform.* Australia: Penguin Books.

Royal Commission for Jubail and Yanbu. 1990. Jubail Industrial City. *Jubail Development Review*, Vol. 5, No. 1, June. Kingdom of Saudi Arabia.

————. 1992. Flaring Economy. *Jubail Development Review*, Vol. 7, No. 1, June. Kingdom of Saudi Arabia.

Schramm, W. 1964. *Mass Media and National Development.* Stanford, Calif.: Stanford University Press.

Servaes, J. 1991. Towards a New Perspective for Communication and Development. In Casmir, Fred L. (ed.), *Communication in Development . . .* 52.

Shannon, C. E., and Weaver, W. 1949. *Mathematical Theory of Communication.* Urbana, Ill.: University of Illinois Press.

Stewart, F., and Streeten, P. 1976. New Strategies for Development: Poverty, Income Distribution and Growth. In C. K. Wilbur (ed.), *The Political Economy of Development and Underdevelopment.* New York: Random House.

Takeichi, H. 1992. *Environmental Pollution and Japan (The Japanese—Their Possibilities).* Tokyo: Veritas Shuppansha.

Todaro, M. P. 1977. *Economic Development in the Third World: An Introduction to Problems and Policies in a Global Perspective.* New York: Longman.

UNESCO. 1975. *Report of the Meeting of Experts on Communication Policies for Rapidly Developing Societies, Mashad, Iran.* See also, UNESCO (1975). *Report of the Meeting of Experts on Communication Policies and Planning in Asia, Philippines*, Oct. 4–8, pp. 5–10.

Wall Street Journal. 1990. The Guiding Hand—Using Aid to Coordinate Asia's Economy. (Eastern Edition) Aug., p. 1.

Worthy, F. S. 1991. Keys to Japanese Success in Asia. *Fortune (Special Report)*, Oct., p. 157.

World Bank. 1974. *Rural Development: Sector Working Paper.* Washington, D.C.

SARAH S. KING
DONALD P. CUSHMAN

2

Communication in Development and Social Change: Old Myths and New Realities

It is "old and bad news" that one-fifth of the world's population live on less than one dollar per day (World Bank, 1991). The"new and good news" that another one-fifth of the world's population who had annual incomes of between $2,000 and $5,000 per year have over the past twenty years watched their annual income double and in some cases triple and quadruple (World Bank, 1991). What exactly is the difference in economic development between these two groups?

The April 1992 issue of *Asian Business* pictured a bullock laden with straw baskets of goods and paraphernalia with the caption "The Road Out of Poverty . . . Leads to Market." Why? Because over the past twenty years world trade has increased three times as fast as gross domestic produce (*The Economist*, Nov. 7,

1977:17). That means that those nations involved in world trade could grow three times more rapidly than those involved in internal sales. This single fact has led several nations to move from underdeveloped to developed national status within the time span of ten to twenty years. This has led also to a new model for economic development based on "a new alliance between national governments, private sector multinational organizations and their participation in trade within global competitive markets which have led to the effective allocation of a nation's economic and natural resources" (Cushman and King, 1993). This single fact has led to several new perspectives on the role communication must play in economic development.

In this chapter we will (1) analyze what is necessary for rapid economic development in the latter part of the twentieth century; (2) discuss when communication is necessary for development; and (3) what are the old myths and new realities regarding development communication.

ECONOMIC DEVELOPMENT IN THE LATTER HALF OF THE TWENTIETH CENTURY

Models of economic, political, and cultural development are numerous, and over time have been highly debated, particularly in their political and cultural contexts. The 1970s and the 1980s were marked by such controversies. However, in the latter half of the 1980s and early 1990s, the debate has narrowed and focused. In hindsight, historians as indicated in an article in *The Economist* (January 4, 1992) may select 1983 as the probable watershed for the articulation of a new model for rapid economic development. This theory was outlined in a dissertation written by Paul Romer, now at the University of California at Berkeley, and was titled "Dynamic Competitive Equilibria with Externalities, Increasing Returns and Unbounded Growth" (*The Economist*, January 4, 1992:15).

This theory modified classical economic theory which argued that economic growth was based on the appropriate use of *land* or natural resources, *labor*, and *capital*. The new theory puts forward four major factors of economic growth: *capital*, *labor*, *practical knowledge* or how to make things, and *new ideas* as measured by patents. Mr. Romer thought this theory could explain rapid economic development as it exists in the world today where such small island nations as Japan, Hong Kong, Singapore, and Taiwan who had experienced very rapid growth yet had little land or natural resources. This theory has several unique features which warrant further discussion.

First, the new theory recognized that knowledge of how to make things or practical knowledge is central to economic development which can raise dramatically the return on investment. In addition, it recognizes that education and/or new ideas which cannot be translated into practical knowledge have only a limited or delayed effect upon economic growth and will retard the payback on investment.

Second, such knowledge is a factor of production which must be paid for by foregoing consumption and investing in practical knowledge training, generation, and diffusion. Education as such must be broadened from a liberal arts base to a practical and technological knowledge base. More significantly, it elevates practical knowledge of production processes to an equal status with professional and scientific knowledge. The discovery and diffusion of such knowledge, as well as training in the use of practical knowledge, is as likely to take place at work as in a formal education system. Thus, multinational corporations are becoming the laboratory for discovery of and the teaching and diffusion of such knowledge to work at all levels of formal education, and even for those who have little or no formal education.

Third, investment in the use of such knowledge over extended periods of time will spur rapid national growth while investment at the same time will spur the further accumulation of practical knowledge.

Finally, a sustained investment in practical knowledge can permanently raise a country's growth rate while at the same time driving down the price of such products to one's own citizens, and raising their overall quality of life.

In order to gain the benefits which follow from the application of this new model of economic development to the global economy, a nation, or more specifically a nation's government, must produce some rather specific governmental policies.

"Over the past forty years a single model of governmental economic policy has emerged for all nations who wish to participate in this increase in world trade" ("Explaining the Mystery," Jan. 4, 1992:15). The generalization of such a model does not imply that all governments or all economies are alike; it merely suggests broad central tendencies in the economic policies of most nations as they begin to participate in the world economy. This model includes seven general features: (1) control of inflation through fiscal austerity and monetary restrictions; (2) reduction of labor costs as a percentage of product cost; (3) increased productivity and profitability through the effective use of information and communication technology; (4) restructuring of industrial and service sectors by disinvesting from low profit areas and investing in high growth, high profit areas; (5) privatization and deregulation of some aspects of the economy by withdrawing from state ownership and control in favor of open market forces; (6) relative control over the pricing of raw materials and energy assuring the stability of pricing systems and exchange flows; and (7) opening up gradually to world markets and increased internationalization of economies (Castells, 1986; Macrae, 1991; Cushman and King, 1993).

In short, to pursue rapid economic development, a nation needs three things: (1) access to world trade; (2) access to practical knowledge; and (3) access to the investment capital necessary to create the infrastructure for the application of practical knowledge to global markets. Such access has led Mexico, Argentina, Spain, Portugal, Indonesia, Malaysia, Thailand, Hong Kong, Singapore, Taiwan, China, and South Korea to experience rapid economic growth along with an appreciable increase in the quality of life for their citizens.

CONTRIBUTION OF COMMUNICATION TO DEVELOPMENT

A criticism of the old dominant paradigm model of the role of communication in development is that developing countries were perceived as ". . . emerging from static isolation, requiring an external stimulus to shake them into the twentieth century" (Golding 1974). Inayatullah in 1967, in an attempt to identify the role of development, defined the concept as ". . . change toward patterns of society that allows better realization of human values, that allows a society greater control over its environments, and over its own political destiny, and that enables its individuals to gain increased control over themselves." Rogers reaffirmed this approach in 1976 by defining development as ". . . a widely participatory process of social change and material advancement (including greater equality, freedom and other valued qualities) for the majority of the people through their gaining greater control over their environment." No one of these approaches is in variance with models which capitalize on economic opportunities for a country and its people. If, as we assert in chapter 8, that an increase in economic development for a country can be synonymous with an increase in the quality of life factors for its people (education, health, resources), then those of us working in development communication should have an intense vested interest in economic development as well.

But when does the contribution of communication to development become a necessary element in the process? Let us examine three models of development in order to answer this question the diffusion model, the national corporation model, and the model which is based on participation in world trade.

The Diffusion of Innovation Model

As early as 1976, Everett Rogers advanced his "diffusion model" which invoked controversy not so much regarding development and the role that communication should play in it, but in the way in which he characterized the stakeholders within the social system, in particular the periscope through which the adopters might be perceived by the proponents of the innovations. He defined change as the result of the diffusion of an innovation through channels over time throughout a social system. These innovations were perceived as "good" ways in which to improve the quality of life of the individuals within the social system. Changes in the social system in the diffusion model were the result of changing the individual behaviors of those within that system, and the communication of influence played an integral role in this. This is the type of change or development which the United Nations attempted in sending troops to oversee the distribution of food in Somalia, with no assurance that the action would contribute to the future well-being of the individuals involved. But there was an immediate, albeit perhaps not lasting, effect without the commitment to stay on and reinforce the peacekeeping role that the United Nations took upon itself. In the diffusion model, communication plays a major role in informing and persuading the recipients of the aid to participate.

The National Corporation Model

In the early 1970s and throughout portions of the 1980s, many nations sought to improve economic development by nationalizing private sector corporations and bringing them under government control. The tendency was pronounced even in developing societies in Western Europe and even more pronounced in most of the underdeveloped and developing countries of the world. This movement failed for a number of reasons.

First, government control led to waste mismanagement and political interference which prevented economic development. Second, this led national governments to look within the country for solutions to economic problems rather than developmental trends across countries. Third, this prevented trade rather than encouraging it. Later, when the system was abandoned, trade would become the great engine of growth.

By the mid 1980s and early 1990s, governments that had pursued this policy began to escape the stranglehold of these organizations on their economies by privatizing them and making them subject to market forces as a means of improvement.

Over the past thirty years, world trade has grown three times faster than the average growth in national GNP. This means that rapid economic growth is tied not to increases in national GNP development but to becoming a major player in world trade. More specifically, nations involved in world trade can grow three times faster than nations not actively engaged in such processes.

The Participation in a World Trade Model

However, before a nation can become an active player in world trade, a nation's people and its government must first transform themselves into a global competitor. Communication is central to this process. Communication between a government and its people must function to reduce inflation, develop a convertable covering, put in place an infrastructure, and diffuse practical knowledge on how to be world class in making things. This type of communication has been central to the development process in Hong Kong, Taiwan, Singapore, South Korea, Malaysia, Spain, Mexico and Argentina. Once this has been accomplished, organizational communication is central to the development, production, distribution, and sales of a nation's products throughout the world.

In examining the establishment of the Asian Development Corridor, Masaru Saito (July 1990) discusses the new trends and developments of practical knowledge transfer in Asia which are changing the structures of the "international division of labor, foreign direct investment (FDI), technology transfer, and economic development." He cites such instances of technology transfer trends and developments as diversification of technological needs to such areas as high-tech software, the development of support industries, and prevention of pollution, and to the more active behavior of multinational companies. He lists the main factors in technology transfer as

1. good communications between transferor and transferee, and effective information systems
2. mutual trust
3. research & development capabilities
4. innovation
5. a coupling of innovation and entrepreneurship (Saito, 1990:52)

Most interesting is that Saito defines this corridor as ". . . a communication infrastructure among growth-leading regions." It is composed of transportation systems, communications systems, and interchange systems such as economy, politics, culture, education, science, etc. There is an interaction effect and a mutual adjustment and cooperation effect. The objective is to increase economic development and decrease economic gaps in development by spanning developed and developing countries, reducing the gap between them (Saito, July 1990).

OLD MYTHS ABOUT DEVELOPMENT AND DEVELOPMENT COMMUNICATION AND THE NEW REALITIES

There are a number of old myths about development communication which may be laid to rest by considering the new realities. First let us examine the old myths which die hard because they are ingrained in a set of liberal values which seeks to explain a lack of development by concentrating blame on a third party or a political or economic system, rather than on seeking causes and remedies within the developing nation itself.

The new realities which puncture these myths point the way to economic development as the key to the realization of the quality of life factors. The iron rice bowl is not a myth and when the stomach is empty it is difficult indeed to be concerned with anything but appeasing the hunger.

Culture matters: The assumption has been that political and cultural change must lead economic change. In the latter half of the nineteenth and twentieth centuries, we now know this is false.

We know that when people have a higher standard of living, that their political and economic views change automatically. (For example, China, South Korea, Mexico, and Spain have all witnessed massive cultural and political change due to rapid economic growth.)

Table 2.1
Old Myths Die Hard

Economic and Political Myths	Communication Myths
a. Culture matters	a. Mass media matters
b. Democracy matters	b. Government can use communication to set agenda
c. Government control matters	c. News flow matters
d. Economic development cannot fuel political and cultural development	d. People want local cultural communication

Democracy matters: Economic development must meet the preconditions outlined previously. Contemporary experience suggests that such an evolution of economic development takes place equally well, no matter what the governmental structure, as long as we meet the preconditions. (For example, Korea, Taiwan, Hong Kong, and Singapore are respectively military, political, or dictatorship regimes.)

Government control matters: Again in the latter half of the twentieth century, government control in the matters of production has been less important than governmental investment in infrastructure and knowledge creation and governmental privatizations has been substantial in all nations.

Economic development: Numerous examples exist where political discrimination within and without the country have been overcome due to strong economic ties between nations involved in trade. (For example, Germany and France, Mexico and the U.S., Japan and China.) However, where economic growth did not fuel political and economic change as in parts of Eastern Europe and Africa, old political hatreds emerged as the guiding factors in economic decline. (For example, Yugoslavia, Sudan, Ireland, and the Middle East.)

Communication Myths

Mass media matters: The dominance of mass media as an agenda-setting tool in economic development has given way to the rise in information technology (computers, Fax, integrated manufacturing, etc.) as a means of integrating interpersonal, organizational, and mass communication into a viable developmental force.

Government control matters: Development agendas are no longer set by governments but by the availability of practical knowledge and the growth of private sector markets throughout the world.

News flow matters: Again, the debates regarding the one- and two-way flow of news have evaporated as information transfer in regard to practical knowledge becomes more important than political or ideological frameworks.

People want cultural communication: The interest in local customs is less in demand than the emerging global interest in music, entertainment, and the arts.

THE NEW REALITIES

How does this new model for development communication translate into practice? Let us list a few of the ways.

a. Access to world trade is the necessary entry behavior for a rapid increase in economic growth.
b. A steady increase in the growth of practical knowledge is the basic fuel for the energies of economic growth.
c. Investment in the creation and diffusion of such knowledge spurs growth, which in turn spurs the accumulation of practical knowledge.
d. A sustained investment in such knowledge can permanently raise a country's standard of living.
e. A sustained increase in practical knowledge will cause prices to fall while quality, practicality, and profits rise, thus lifting a nation's quality of life and future economic growth.

Thus, communication functions to expand a nation's infrastructure to attract investment, sell products, improve management, diffuse practical knowledge, and maintain competition.

REFERENCES

Castells, M. (1986). "High-Technology, World Development and the Structured Transformation: The Trends and Debate, *Alternatives*, 11:297–342.

Cushman, D.P. and King, S.S. (1993). "Communication and Management in the Global Economy." In King, S.S. and Cushman, D.P. (eds), *High-Speed Management and Organizational Communication in the 1990s: A Reader.* Albany: SUNY Press.

Cushman, D.P. and King, S.S. (1992). High-Speed Management: A Revolution in Organizational Communication in the 1990s. In Deetz, S. (ed), *Communication Yearbook 16*, pp. 209–236.

"Economic Growth: Explaining the Mystery," *The Economist*, January 4, 1992, pp. 15–17.

"Explaining the Mystery," *The Economist*, January 4, 1992, pp. 15–17.

Golding, P. (1974). "Media Role in National Development: A Critique of a Theoretical Orthodoxy," *Journal of Communication*, 24.

Inayatullah (1967). Quoted by Hamdan bin Adnan, et.al (1985). "The Nature of Development." In Clayton, V. and Simmons, J. (eds), *Development Communication: A Resource Manual for Teaching.* Singapore: AMIC.

Kraar, L. (October 5, 1992). "The Pacific Rim: Asia 2000," *Fortune*, pp. 111–113.

Labate, John (July 27, 1992). "The World Economy in Charts," *Fortune*, pp. 61.

Macrae, N. (December 21, 1991). "A Future History of Privatization, 1992–2022," *The Economist*, pp. 15–18.

Pollack, A. (February 1, 1992). "Technology Without Borders Raising Big Questions for the U.S.," *The New York Times*, A1.

Ramamurti, Ravi (1992). "Why Are Developing Countries Privatizing?," *Journal of International Business Studies*, pp. 225–245.

"Remembering the Unthinkable," *The Economist*, November 7, 1992, p. 17.

Rogers, Everett M. (1976). "Communication and Development: The Passing of the Dominant Paradigm." In Rogers, Everett M. (ed.), *Communication and Development: Critical Perspectives.* Beverly Hills; Sage Publications.

Rogers, E. M. with F. Shoemaker (1971). *Communication of Innovations: A Cross Cultural Approach.* New York: Free Press.

Saito, M. (July 1990). Establishment of Asian Development Corridor, *TOKYO Business Today*, pp. 52–54.

Schumacher, E.F. (1973). *Small Is Beautiful: Economics As If People Mattered.* New York: Harper & Row.

World Bank (1991). *World Development Report*, 1–300.

3

Communication and Development: Some Emerging Theoretical Perspectives

Academic interest in the potential role of communication for promoting national development surfaced shortly after the Second World War. The United States had found itself to be the dominant world power following the defeat of Germany and Japan and the war devastation of Great Britain and France. This new American role emerged at a time of worldwide movements of national independence when many of the former colonies of European powers began to raise their demands for sovereignty and economic prosperity. The Soviet Union. though preoccupied with consolidating its positions in the newly gained satellite states in Eastern Europe, was already showing signs of aggressively reaching out to Asia, Africa and Latin America in a bid to expand the influence of Communism while keeping its own doors tightly closed to prevent outside intervention. It was in this context of uneasy confrontation in the wake of a ruinous world war that the political slogan of "Iron Curtain" was coined by Winston Churchill to signify the beginning of a protracted Cold War.

In its new leadership role in the free world, the United States was immensely interested in promoting economic development in the newly independent countries. This desire partly reflected the historical concern of the United States for the welfare of the underdeveloped nations. The United States itself grew out of an independence movement. This position was also engineered to counter the expansionist moves of the Soviet Union. If a nation was able to build a foundation of economic sufficiency, it was argued, the perils of a Communist revolution would be greatly reduced.

It was in this historical context that massive economic aids were pumped by the United States into many of the developing nations in the postwar years. The American foreign aid policy at that time seemed to be in part influenced by the theoretical writings of such masters as John Maynard Keynes and Joseph Schumpeter, based on their analyses of Western countries. To Schumpeter (1934), the economic development of the Western world gained its impetus from profit-making and thrived on entrepreneurship. Keynes (1936) saw Western economic development as primarily resulting from investment—the pooling of resources for productive activities. If this was how economic development happened in the West, some American policymakers believed, countries in the underdeveloped world could fruitfully use it as a blueprint. These nations were now freed from the burdens of their former colonial rulers. They had the will to develop their economy. The major ingredient that was missing seemed to be the pooling of resources. Once that was made available, by way of economic aid if not raised domestically, these countries would soon be on the road toward economic development.

It did not take long, however, for American policymakers to recognize that the results of U.S. economic aid programs were, to say the least, disappointing. Shiploads of supplies and materials, as well as huge amounts of monetary aid, did not seem to make a dent in the poverty and sufferings of the aid recipient countries. Why? In search for an answer, some American scholars, perhaps influenced by the work of such prominent British anthropologists as A. R. Radcliffe-Browne in Africa, discovered that something was lacking in the indigenous cultural values among the people in these new nations. Certain cultural values that were prominent in

Western societies, such as the Protestant work ethic, achievement motives, and pragmatic concerns in economic decision-making, seemed to be weak or even absent. Bert Hoselitz (1952) and Everett Hagen (1962), among others, proposed their thought-provoking hypothesis that economic development is not merely a matter of pooling resources or investment, but must be built on the foundation of supportive cultural values and social organizations. An important component of these cultural values was what David McClelland (1961) called the achievement motives. The question then became one of cultivating those cultural values and fostering those social organizations where they did not exist. But how?

EARLY CONCEPTS

One answer came, almost by way of serendipity, from a sample survey in six Middle East countries. This pioneer survey was conducted in 1950 and 1951 by the Columbia University's Bureau of Applied Social Research, under the general direction of Charles Glock, using a questionnaire developed with the help of Paul Lazarsfeld and Robert Merton. The primary objective of the survey, covering some 300 respondents in each country, was to assess their habits with regard to mass media of communication, their attitudes toward foreigners, and their general outlook on life. After an initial report was filed, the data were kept in Columbia University until Daniel Lerner began to analyze them in depth and published in 1958 his classic *The Passing of Traditional Society* (Lerner, 1958). This book could be considered a milestone for the study of communication in national development. While others had presented research findings on communication and political awareness (e.g., Damle, 1952; Hirabayashi and Khatib, 1958), it was Lerner who, in a manner that caught the imagination of the academic world, identified participation in mass media as a major factor of modernization along with literacy, urbanization, and political participation. Lerner used the Middle East survey data as support for his theory of modernity, particularly for emphaty as a key element of what he called a mobile personality. Participation in mass media can be a mobility multiplier, Lerner theorized, and can contribute to empathy as a trait of modernity.

Lerner's ideas were further developed by Wilbur Schramm. Schramm (1963) published a brief but thoughtful article that set the research agenda for communication and development for the next ten years. Schramm recognized the importance of economics as a primary mover of development. But he also saw a key role for communication as a mover. He proposed the following:

1. Communication must be used to contribute to the feeling of nation-ness.
2. Communication must be used as the voice of national planning.
3. Communication must be used to help teach the necessary skills.
4. Communication must be used to help extend the effective market.
5. As the plan develops, communication must be used to help prepare people to play their new roles.
6. Communication must be used to prepare the people to play their role as a nation among nations.

Creative research on communication and development was already proceeding in a number of Third World countries. Many of the more important findings were summarized and synthesized by Everett Rogers (1969). A year after his 1963 article, Schramm organized a conference with Lerner at the East-West Center in Honolulu to assess the field (Lerner and Schramm, 1967). New research findings from Asian countries, including initial findings from China (Yu, 1967; Barnett, 1967), were intensely discussed. Even at that 1964 conference, critical voices were raised, primarily by scholars from Asia (Dube, 1967; Inayatullah, 1967), who pointed out the inadequate attention Schramm and Lerner paid to institutional barriers to development, which mass communication alone would not be able to overcome.

In retrospect, it should be pointed out that Schramm never meant communication to be a sufficient condition for development (Schramm, 1964). He saw communication as a mover, but not a prime mover. Both he and Lerner apparently considered communication to be either a necessary or a contributing condition for development, although neither specifically made it clear which way they were leaning. In fact, in his 1963 article Schramm was clearly aware of the institutional and even the international perspectives of development when he discussed the roles of communication in fostering an effective market, and in preparing people to play their new roles as citizens and as a nation among nations. These issues went beyond the individual perspective of research in communication and development which was prevalent among American academicians at that time, partly because the quantitative methodology they employed was meant for an individual mode of analysis. Nevertheless, the theoretical concepts of structural analysis were not prominent in the thinking of either Schramm or Lerner until the mid-1970s.

STRUCTURAL PERSPECTIVES

For Schramm and Lerner, that change of research conceptualization again came in Honolulu, at the 1975 conference which they organized at the East-West Center (Schramm and Lerner, 1976) as a follow-up endeavor of their 1964 conference. Everett Rogers discussed at the conference his ideas of a new paradigm of research which he later published in his much cited article (Rogers, 1976) on the passing of the dominant paradigm. Godwin Chu presented initial findings of his work on the use of communication by Mao Zedong as an instrument of bringing about radical structural change as a necessary step toward his vision of national development. The China research was extensively discussed because it examined an approach to development entirely different from the dominant paradigm (Chu, 1976; Durdin, 1976; Oshima, 1976). The transferability of the China experience was carefully evaluated (Schramm, Chu, and Yu, 1976). Chu's work, later published in *Radical Change Through Communication in Mao's China* (1977), remains to this day one of the few empirical research efforts that examined the roles of communication in both micro and macro perspectives as a nation went through the agonizing processes of major structural change on its road toward development.

It would not be inappropriate to say that the study of communication and development started with imaginative, thought provoking research, such as Lerner's work on The *Passing of Traditional Society*, without waiting for a well developed theoretical foundation. Generally, this is how a new field begins. And the study of communication and development is no exception. Robert Hornik (1988) has provided a succinct historical overview. Other than Chu's research on China, Lerner's pioneering work of assessing the roles of communication in the process of development in six Middle East countries is one of the few macro studies, although the data were originally collected for a different purpose.

Most research in the 1960s and 1970s evaluated the effectiveness of communication strategies in development projects, either for adoption of agricultural innovations or for promoting modern health practices and better nutrition (Rogers, 1969; Hornik, 1988). This type of research, following primarily an individual perspective within the context of a specific development project, has made important contributions. At the risk of oversimplication, the implicit theoretical premise is: When given relevant information about a new practice, be it a high-yielding seed, chemical fertilizers, a family-planning device, or nutritious food, the audience will likely abandon the old in favor of the new, provided that the new practice is seen to be more rewarding and that the adoption can take place in an atmosphere of social support. In other words, the input of new information in our existing life space, if we may use that term, will prompt us to reassess our alternatives and change our behavioral patterns and their attached attitudes. The research question is how to develop the most appropriate messages and communication channels in order to get the information to the audience and how to cultivate a social environment in support of the behavioral or attitudinal change. While specific strategies may be modified and refined for different types of audience and practices, on the whole, our cumulative research has demonstrated the effectiveness of communication for accomplishing the project objectives, as Hornik has cogently documented.

If we define development in this focused context, then much of the basic knowledge we are looking for in the field of communication and development would appear to be within our reach. But is this what development is about as some have asked (Hedebro, 1982)? A good argument can be made in favor of this concept of development primarily in terms of adoption of innovation. But if we go basic to the larger concerns expressed in the 1950s and 1960s, concerns that questioned the effectiveness of U.S. aid programs, clearly development means more than the successful implementation of specific projects. In the minds of many thoughtful scholars, development should be cast in the larger perspective of modernization, even though that term itself seems to defy definition. Schramm, as we recall, included in his conception of development such objectives as cultivating a feeling of nationness, the extension of effective market, the learning of new citizen roles, and even participation in national planning. Lemer appeared to be fascinated by the psychological aspect of modernity, which he called empathy. McClelland's concern was with achievement motives. What these founding fathers had in mind was something much broader, and much more encompassing than the effective use of communication strategies for successful project implementation. What they had in mind, it seems clear in retrospect, was fundamental social transformation and possibly even basic cultural change. Lerner, in particular, was keenly concerned with both.

MODERNIZATION VERSUS DEPENDENCY SCHOOL

In that sense, the gulf that separates the thinking of Lerner, Schramm, and others in what has become known as the "modernization school," and their critics who are generally identified as the "dependency school," may not be as large as it seems on the surface. There is definitely some common ground between the two. Both recognize the need for social transformation as a primary goal. The difference lies in their ideological approaches in the means to achieve the goals. As pointed out by Frank (1967, 1969), one of the major exponents of the dependency school, those in the modernization school tend to see development within the confined context of a Third World nation itself. They see something missing within the socioeconomic system of that nation, such as lack of supportive cultural values and social organizations. But they fail to give due attention to the fact that no socioeconomic system exists in isolation but must function in interaction with other socioeconomic systems in the world, which a Third World nation is heavily dependent upon because of its meager resources.

Those in the dependency school (Dos Santos, 1971; Foster-Carter, 1973; Bolmstrom and Hettne, 1984) argued that a solution was in breaking the bondage of dependency. Internally, they were in favor of accomplishing the necessary social transformation through a Marxist mode of revolution, similar to what happened in Mao's China. The use of communication to promote agricultural and health-related innovations seemed to be a secondary concern. This thinking was particularly popular in Latin American universities in the 1960s and 1970s, before the disastrous consequences of Maoist revolution became known to the outside world. Externally, they demanded an end of the de facto colonialism and foreign dominance, which they saw as a major obstacle to development.

The recent breakup of the Soviet Union and the collapse of communism in Eastern European states should be sufficient evidence that the Marxist solution is not feasible. Even China has found it necessary to abandon Maoism in practice while still holding on to Marxism in name. If recent trends are an indication, Beijing's eulogy of Marxism may not last very long either. As Deng Xiaoping put it during his tour of the Special Economic Zone in Shenzheng on the other side of Hong Kong in the spring of 1992, as long as a policy works in the sense of improving the standard of living in China, it does not matter whether it originates from Marxism or capitalism. With the demise of Marxism, the dependency school has lost its ideological foundation. What remains is their concern with colonialism and foreign dominance. That is a genuine concern. I will address this issue later.

If the dependency school has been ideologically cast in doubt, the modernization school, which some of us interested in communication and development have implicitly followed, has not been able to come up with either a vibrant theoretical framework or a viable practical solution. One and a half decades have passed since Rogers' seminal article on the passing of the conventional paradigm (Rogers, 1976) and Chu's analysis of communication and structural change in China (Chu, 1977). In 1987, the Institute of Culture and Communication of the East-West Center and the Department of Communication at the University of Hawaii jointly sponsored a conference on communication and development, the third of its kind convened in Honolulu. Schramm, Chu, and Joung-Im Kim were coordinators. Many prominent scholars from the United States, Asia, and Europe were in attendance, including Everett Rogers, Steven Chaffee, and others. Schramm participated actively. (This was the last major conference at which he gave the keynote address. Schramm passed away in December 1987.) The discussions were lively and stimulating, reflecting concerns of both the modernization school and the dependency school. The conference ended without a consensus on the theoretical conception or the major research agenda.

IN SEARCH OF A BREAKTHROUGH

This, in short, is more or less where we stand today as far as the study of communication and development is concerned. What does it take to make a major theoretical breakthrough?

If we stand back a little, we can see that the dependency school had some valid points in its criticism of the conventional paradigm. Its diagnosis of the obstacles to development was largely consistent with reality. Unless a country can break up the major constraints in its social structure, through a fundamental social transformation, there can be little hope for effective use of manpower and resources that will be essential for development. And unless the inequitable and one-sided trade relations with the world's major economic powers are corrected, the income generated from domestic production will mostly be taken up by debt-servicing payments to foreign lenders. In this larger perspective, we can see why to scholars in the dependency school it does not seem to matter that much whether a communication campaign is able to promote a particular seed or some nutritious food, especially when a statistically significant finding can mean only a difference of a few percentage points. Their main argument, it seems, is not about the significance of any particular campaign, which few can deny, but is rather about the tendency among some of us to overlook the real issues because we can demonstrate the effectiveness of communication in the implementation of a specific project. Indeed it will be difficult to dispute that argument.

The problem with the dependency school, it seems, is with their proposed solution. In theory, Marx was quite right about the necessity to eliminate exploitation built within a capitalist economic system—the notion of surplus value—and give due reward to workers for their productive labor. Few would argue with that. The problem is in the implementation of the Marxist doctrine. The Communist systems, as practiced in the Soviet Union and China, have proved to be failures. To pin any hope on the Marxist or neo-Marxist approach, without objectively analyzing the colossal inequities and inefficiency of a Communist state, as some in the dependency school seem to suggest would be an exercise of fantasy.

Another problem with the dependency school is that it has built its arguments only on cases of failure, mostly in Latin America, but pays little attention to cases of success in development, as we now see in East Asia, particularly Taiwan and Korea. This is partly because those success stories in Asia were unknown to them in the 1970s. One sometimes wonders whether scholars in the dependency school were not interested in Taiwan and Korea because these two cases might invalidate their arguments about colonialism and foreign dominance as major obstacles to development. As we recall, both Taiwan and Korea were initially heavily dependent on U.S. economic aid. In fact, American troops have been stationed in Korea ever since the Korean War. Yet both Taiwan and Korea have been able to use U.S. aid money effectively. Taiwan's economic development began to take off soon after U.S. economic aid was discontinued in 1963. But U.S. aid during the twelve-year period from 1952 to 1963 was considered to have played a major role in helping Taiwan to recover from the bleak years after the Kuomintang retreated to Taiwan nearly penniless in 1949. Whether foreign dominance is a suffocating factor for development would seem to depend on whether the aid recipient country knows how to turn the situation to its own advantage.

If the modernization school has its own blunders, they are of a different nature. To put it unkindly, the decades of empirical research and sophisticated statistical analyses seem to have dissected trees in great detail but have somehow missed the forest. Partly because of its ancestry in social psychology and partly because of its reliance on quantitative methods, research within what Rogers calls the dominant paradigm has rarely gone beyond the individual mode of analysis, and thus has not been able to shift its attention to problems of social transformation and cultural change as major theoretical concerns of development.

LONGITUDINAL STUDIES

When one steps outside the implementation of specific projects, development has to be conceived as a long term process of change. Yet there are few longitudinal studies of the social and cultural impact of communication. One study conducted in rural Taiwan (Chu and Chi, 1984; Chaffee and Chu, 1992) covered a period of fourteen years, using before-and-after comparison of the same respondents interviewed in 1964 and again in 1978. Significant changes in cultural values, attitudes, and social relations were identified. Life in the villages had become less personal. Social and political influence used to be diverse. They now appeared to be more centrally located in the office of the village head. Family ties remained strong. The traditional Chinese commitment to ancestor worship was as unswerving as ever. Child-rearing practices had become less strict, and there were more favorable attitudes toward women. People became less superstitious. There was an unmistakable increase of political interest among the villagers, which found its vocal expressions years later in local elections and public demonstrations in Taiwan. The role of mass communication as a contributing factor, however, was found to be marginal. The limited contribution of mass communication in rural Taiwan might be artifactual. In 1964 there was no television in any of the villages surveyed. By 1978 nearly all villagers had television sets in their homes. Television viewing, as a major media variable, had very little variation, which made it difficult to demonstrate its impact.

An opportunity arose in 1976 to correct this methodological limitation. The government of Indonesia launched a communication satellite in 1976, partly for sending television signals to rural villages all over the country. Because of the use of ground stations, television could be seen in some areas and not in others. This made it possible for Chu and Schramm to design a quasi-experimental longitudinal research to study the impact of television on social transformation and cultural change in Indonesian villages by conducting before-and-after comparisons of TV viewers with nonviewers. This study, lasting six years from 1976 to 1982, was probably the longest field research in communication and development. It covered all major ethnic and religious groups in Indonesia on a national scale. The fieldwork was extended to remote villages. The findings (Chu, Alfian, and Schramm, 1991) were revealing.

Television programs transmitted by the Palapa satellite had broken the shell of isolation for the rural viewers at a pace few other development programs could hope to achieve, leaping over both time and space. TV viewers in the Indonesian villages learned a great deal about development programs. As many as 64% of the viewers named television as their primary source of news information. The information on television changed the villagers' economic behavior in ways that may have lasting impact. There was an impressive increase in the number of viewers who had learned to market their own produce in town, thereby saving what middlemen might otherwise take off the top of transactions. Television also seemed to have taught the viewers to put their unused resources in savings. When they needed financial assistance, TV viewers were more likely to rely on public institutions, such as credit unions and local banks rather than friends and relatives. Their consumption of items advertised on television, however, also increased dramatically. This finding led to the abolishment of all TV advertising by the Indonesian government.

While television cannot be seen as an initiator, it is definitely aiding the process of social transformation. TV viewers substantially improved their proficiency in the national language, Bahasa

Indonesia, making it more likely for them to participate in national integration programs. They enhanced their social positions in the villages and assumed the roles of opinion leaders more actively. They were becoming more involved in the management of village affairs. They were attending the village meetings more regularly, and participating more actively in the many village organizations sponsored by the government. They were becoming more concerned citizens, and discussed matters of village concerns more than nonviewers. With television, Indonesian villages have begun the process of a major transformation.

HISTORICAL ANALYSES

The Palapa study in Indonesia has confirmed the importance of longitudinal studies as a way of building up our knowledge about the roles of communication in development in a societal perspective. We also need historical analysis at a macro-sociological level to understand the holistic processes of development and identify the roles of communication in these processes. Such historical analysis must go hand-in-hand with project-related research at the micro level as well as longitudinal studies that use individual units of analysis, such as the Palapa study, to make projections about the trends of social transformation. We use Taiwan as a case of success in development to illustrate this type of historical analysis.

In 1949, the government of the Republic of China under Chiang Kai-shek retreated to Taiwan after it had lost the civil war with the Chinese Communists on the China mainland. Chiang brought with him some two million refugees and disorganized troops. At that time, the Taiwanese economy was tottering on the verge of collapse following considerable war damage and four years of neglect and mismanagement after the departure of the Japanese. A Communist takeover appeared imminent and Washington was about to write Chiang off. The Korean War changed the whole situation. The U.S. Seventh Fleet was ordered into the Taiwan Straits to head off a Communist invasion. Meanwhile, U.S. economic aid was resumed in 1952 and proved to be psychologically as well as financially important.

At the same time, Taiwan began to implement a rural land-reform program to redistribute arable land from landlords to tenants. This was a policy advocated by Dr. Sun Yat-sen in the early years of the Republic of China, but was not put into effect until after Chiang's retreat to Taiwan. The rural land reform was an important beginning in Taiwan's economic development. It removed a major structural barrier from the large rural population and stimulated agricultural production. Farmers, now small landowners themselves, kept more of their earnings because the installment payments they made to the government for the land purchase was much less than the rents they used to pay to the landlords. At the same time, the land reform provided incentives for the former landlords, now without large land holdings, to invest the compensation they received from the government in Taiwan's budding industry, thus speeding up a major shift toward industrialization and a cash economy. Mass communication played virtually no role in the decision-making process of the rural land reform. All the media did was to publicize the regulations and explain the implementation in the step-by-step land ownership conversion. The government had such total control of the mass media that the landlords were allowed no opportunity to raise their objections, or to organize to sabotage the land reform, as had happened with rural land-reform programs in some other Asian countries. In a peculiar sense, the success of Taiwan's rural land-reform program depended on the control of mass communication.

The land reform and the conversion of government-owned industries into private enterprises contributed to a slow but steady economic recovery. The next important move came in the mid-1960s. Largely responding to a need for a better-qualified labor force for its young and growing industry, Taiwan extended compulsory education from six to nine years. This step significantly improved the quality of Taiwan's manpower and offered new incentives for many rural youngsters to move to the cities for factory jobs. New opportunities and choices were open to them in a way that never existed before. Interestingly, communication again played virtually no role in the decision-making process. After the decision was announced, the media were used to publicize this policy, which was received with enthusiasm by the schools and parents. Problems of implementation were discussed in the newspapers, but not extensively.

With a higher level of education and a rapid growth of urban population came an increasing demand for mass media Newspapers, radio, and television quickly developed in the late 1960s and early 1970s to fill a fast growing need that few people had foreseen. The physical expansion of the media sharpened the appetite for more information. As a result, the dissemination of information, including new ideas from abroad, expanded and accelerated. Income increased rapidly as Taiwan began to establish export markets, which generated more demand for business news. The people in Taiwan, especially a new middle class of young urban residents, began to develop a new life-style. Their material life improved enormously. Their perceptual horizon broadened. They acquired new aspirations, values, and beliefs. One outcome was an increasing demand for political participation, and this demand has exerted pressure for major changes in the political institutions in the last few years. This broad trend of change is consistent with our research data on cultural change in Taiwanese villages and social transformation in rural Indonesia. The changes in Indonesia were clearly traceable to television, although in Taiwanese villages Chu and Chi were not able to demonstrate a major role of mass communication in the change process due to the way television was introduced. In this historical analysis we see the effects of mass communication in quite a different perspective. It will be extremely difficult to methodologically sort out the effects of mass communication in the complex processes of social transformation because communication is intrinsically tied up with other major forces of change.

A NEW FRAMEWORK

We are now ready to offer a rudimentary conceptual framework for the study of communication and development.

A distinction needs to be made about at least two kinds of communication. For communication studies in relation to specific development projects, we are primarily looking at persuasive communication in the context of local groups. The best summary of recent research findings is Robert Hornik's *Development Communication: Information, Agriculture, and Nutrition in the Third World* (1988). Although Hornik's theoretical foundation is built on information, he is talking about purposive information specifically intended to persuade the recipients to change their behavioral practices and attached attitudes. The communicator starts out with a particular objective, and designs his messages and use of channels to best achieve that objective. A supportive social climate is important, as Schramm used to point out over and again. Even though both the communicator and the recipient enter the communication act on their own initiative, clearly the communicator plays a more active role due to the fact that he is the one who sets the agenda. In this type of research, one can direct one's research attention to such related issues as equity (Roling, Ascroft, and Chege, 1976), effects gaps (Shingi and Mody, 1976), and others. The focal point is on effects of persuasion.

For communication studies in the broader perspective of social transformation, the research agenda is quite different. The research context is not a project, but a society as a whole. We are looking at general information, rather than purposive information. In both the longitudinal studies of communication and cultural change in Taiwan and of the social impact of television in rural Indonesia, the research was not focused on any specific messages, but was directed at the exposure to general information from the mass media. For the communicator of general information, the agenda-setting function is still there, but not as dominant as in the case of project-related communication. The receiver has somewhat more leeway in the selection and interpretation of the information, especially when the media system allows a fair amount of alternatives, as we find in most developing countries not ruled by Communist dictatorship.

Our research agenda would thus be different from one of demonstrating the "effects" of persuasive communication, but is directed at understanding the *dynamic interactions* between the *changing social and economic environment* and the *roles of communication*, both *adaptive* and *initiative*, in that changing environment. This distinction is crucial if we want to make a breakthrough in our studies of communication and development in a societal perspective. It goes beyond the dichotomy of individual modes of analysis and structural modes of analysis. The distinction between individual and structural modes of analysis helps us to break away from the dominant paradigm of the past, and therefore is a major contribution. But it does not identify the core substantive issues which we must address in our research.

In this societal perspective, we begin with the observation that we live in an environment of information. Human beings have lived this way since time immemorial. Today, due to the increasingly complex nature and expanding reach of our economic and political life, our needs for information have vastly increased in both volume and complexity. It is not an exaggeration to say that we live in a global village. The changes in our economic and political life have stimulated the development of new information technologies, and at the same time these changes are sustained by accelerated communication patterns that rely on these new technologies. These dynamic processes of interactions between a changing environment and communication are illustrated by the experiences of Taiwan.

A few hypotheses are suggested by Taiwan's experiences:

1. Economic development can be facilitated by the removal of structural constraints which inhibit the full use of manpower and material resources.

2. A policy decision on reform can be made *without* the aid of communication for mobilizing popular support as long as there is sufficient political will on the part of the government. Ironically, control of media communication can help the implementation of reforms by denying the opposition the means to get organized.

3. Economic development can be further facilitated by improving the capacity of manpower training, in Taiwan's case, by extending public education from six to nine years. Again, communication is not a necessary prelude to this major policy decision, although it proves to be a helpful instrument for its implementation.

4. The combined forces of economic development, especially through industrialization, and the accompanying urbanization as well as improved education generate a growing demand for mass media. Urbanization in this case is different from the concentration of the needy and impoverished in crowded urban ghettos. The latter situation is a breeding ground of social malaise.

5. The expansion of mass media stimulates more demands for information, which inevitably includes new ideas from abroad. This is the pivotal moment when a traditional society begins to undergo a fundamental transformation not only of its economic structure, but also of its ideological and value bases.

6. The emergence of a new middle class begins, with its new life-style, heavy media consumption, and increasing demands for political participation.

7. The mass media of communication, already fast expanding, take on a new role as a forum for expressing political demands in addition to the conventional role of reporting on political developments. Communication plays a key role in aggregating individual interests into collective political input.

8. Major changes begin to take shape in the political institutions as the ruling elites find it necessary to bow to the mounting

pressures from the various sectors in a fast changing society and reluctantly give up its control of power little by little.

The Taiwan case is presented here in a capsule form, without the concrete details that are necessary in order to give a fuller meaning to the processes of interactions between communication and social transformation. Purposive, persuasive communication does not figure prominently in these processes, which involve selective attention to and selective interpretation of general information by the people as they respond to a changing environment. It is important to note that what they respond to is not necessarily the reality of the changing environment itself, but their perception of reality as it is filtered through communication.

Each society is unique in a historical sense. Taiwan is no exception. Taiwan's rural land reform, for example, was successfully carried out by a ruling elite whose members were refugees from mainland China and did not own any land in Taiwan. What we need are more case studies, of both successes and failures, from different geographical regions but following similar historical, macro-sociological perspectives. For these case studies we need to conduct concrete analysis of changes in the economic and political systems, and demonstrate the roles which communication plays in the change processes. This new research agenda entails both individual and structural modes of analysis. The policy input that led to initial rural economic changes in Taiwan was structurally originated. So were the shift from agriculture to industry and the extension of public education. The rapid expansion of mass media was an institutional response to changes of individual media behaviors due to higher income and education. The growing audience sizes further led to changes of media contents, including those of foreign origin. The emergence of a new middle class initially grew out of common individual interests and later became institutionalized through communication. The forced changes in the political institutions are structural in nature, although their impact will be felt by individual members of the society.

These are merely initial ideas that require further refinement. Following this new research agenda, which will necessarily weave together both individual and structural modes of analysis, we can begin to accumulate enough data from historical cases, which will help us to understand more fully the roles of communication in the complex processes of development in a societal perspective. Then we would be in a position to offer a comprehensive theory of communication and development.

REFERENCES

Barnett, A. Doak. 1967. A Note on Communication and Development in Communist China. In Daniel Lerner and Wilbur Schramm (eds.), *Communication and Change in the Developing Countries* 231–34. Honolulu: University Press of Hawaii.

Bolmstrom, Magnus, and Bjorn Hettne. 1984. *Development Theory in Transition: The Dependency Debate and Beyond—Third World Response.* London: Zed.

Chaffee, Steven H., and Godwin C. Chu. 1992. Communication and Cultural Change in China. In Jay G. Blumler, Jack M. McLeod, and Karl Erik Rosengren (eds.), *Comparatively Speaking: Communication and Culture Across Space and Time* 209–37. Newbury Park, Calif. Sage Publications.

Chu, Godwin C. 1976. Group Communication and Development in Mainland China—The Function of Social Pressure. In Wilbur Schramm and Daniel Lerner (eds.), *Communication and Change: The Past Ten Years—and the Next* 119–34. Honolulu: University Press of Hawaii.

————. 1977. *Radical Change through Communication in Mao's China.* Honolulu: University Press of Hawaii.

Chu, Godwin C., and Ginyao Chi. 1984. *Cultural Change in Rural Taiwan.* Taipei, Taiwan: Shangwu Commercial Press.

Chu, Godwin C., Alfian and Wilbur Schramm. 1991. *Social Impact of Satellite Television in Rural Indonesia.* Singapore: Asian Mass Communication Research and Information Centre.

Damle, Y. B. 1956. Communication of Modern Ideas and Knowledge in Indian Villages. *Public Opinion Quarterly* 20:257–70.

Dos Santos, Theotonia. 1971. The Structure of Dependence. In K. T. Kan and Donald C. Hodges (eds.), *Readings in U.S. Imperialism* 225–36. Boston: Extending Horizon.

Dube, S. C. 1967. A Note on Communication in Economic Development. In *Communication and Change in the Developing Countries* 92–97.

Durdin, F. Tillmen. 1976. How Durable is Mao's Policy. In *Communication and Change: The Past Ten Years—and the Next* 134–37.

Foster-Carter, Aiden. 1973. Neo-Marxist Approaches to Development and Underdevelopment. *Journal of Contemporary Asia* 3: 7–33.

Frank, Andre Gunder. 1967. *Capitalism and Underdevelopment in Latin America.* New York: Monthly Review Press.

————. 1969. *Latin America: Underdevelopment or Revolution.* New York: Monthly Review Press.

Hagen, Everett E. 1962. *On the Theory of Social Change.* Homewood, Ill.: Dorsey Press.

Hedebro, Goran. 1982. *Communication and Social Change in Developing Nations: A Critical View.* Ames, Iowa: Iowa State University Press.

Hirabayashi, Gorden K., and Fathalla El Khatib. 1958. Communication and Political Awareness in the Villages of Egypt. *Public Opinion Quarterly* 22:357–63.

Hornik, Robert C. 1988. *Development Communication: Information, Agriculture, and Nutrition in the Third World.* New York: Longman.

Hoselitz, Bert K. 1952. Non-economic Barriers to Economic Development, *Economic Development and Social Change* 1:8–21.

Inayatullah. 1967. Toward a Non-Western Model of Development. In *Communication and Change in the Developing Countries* 98–102.

Keynes, John M. 1936. *The General Theory of Employment, Interest and Money.* New York: Harcourt, Brace & World.

Lerner, Daniel. 1958. *The Passing of the Traditional Society.* Glencoe, Ill.: The Free Press.

Lerner, Daniel, and Wilbur Schramm (eds.). 1967. *Communication and Change in the Developing Countries.* Honolulu: University Press of Hawaii.

McClelland, David. 1961. *The Achieving Society.* New York: Van Nostrand.

Oshima, Harry T. 1976. How Workable is Mao's Strategy. In *Communication and Change: The Past Ten Years—and the Next* 138.

Rogers, Everett M. 1969. *Modernization Among Peasants: The Impact of Communication.* New York: Holt, Rinehart & Winston.

————. 1976. Communication and Development: The Passing of the Dominant Paradigm. In *Communication Research* 3:213–40.

Roling, Niels G., Joseph Ascroft, and Fred Wa Chege. 1976. The Diffusion of Innovations and the Issue of Equity in Rural Development. In Everett M. Rogers (ed.), *Communication and Development: Critical Perspectives* 63–78.

Schramm, Wilbur. 1963. Communication Development and the Development Process. In Lucian W. Pye (ed.), *Communications and Political*

Development 30–57. Princeton, N.J.: Princeton University Press.

————. 1964. *Mass Media and National Development.* Stanford, Calif.: Stanford University Press.

Schramm, Wilbur, Godwin C. Chu, and Frederick T. C. Yu. 1976. China's Experience with Development Communication—How Transferrable Is It? In *Communication and Change: The Past Ten Years—and the Next* 139–48.

Schramm, Wilbur, and Daniel Lerner (eds.) 1976. *Communication and Change: The Past Ten Years—and the Next.* Honolulu: University Press of Hawaii.

Schumpeter, Joseph. 1934. *The Theory of Economic Development: An Enquiry into Profit, Capital, Credit, Interest and the Business Cycle.* Cambridge: Harvard University Press.

Shingi, Prakash M., and Bella Mody. 1976. The Communication Effects Gaps: A Field Experiment on Television and Agricultural Ignorance in India. In Everett M. Rogers (ed.), *Communication and Development: Critical Perspectives* 79–98.

Yu, Frederick T. C. 1967. Campaigns, Communications, and Development in Communist China. In *Communication and Change in the Developing Countries* 195–215.

4

Development Communication: Basic Approaches and Planning Strategies

PREAMBLE

The task of determining which communication approach and planning strategy to adopt in development communication projects is expected to be a deliberate and systematic endeavor. It involves a continuous effort to organize human activity for the efficient use of communication resources and for the realization of communication policies, in the context of a particular social system's development goals, means, and priorities, and subject to its prevailing forms of social, economic, political, and cultural organizations. The execution of development communication programs and projects, therefore, takes as its starting point, both the "felt needs" at the social system level, and the "action needs as identified by development planners.

The operational strategy for meeting these two sets of needs follows four stages of activities (Boyd, 1975). The first, which Boyd

54

called "Diffusion stage" but which we think should be more appropriately called the "Formative Evaluation stage," is identifying and analyzing the innovations sought by the social system and those that development agents want to introduce: who is to do what; who is to benefit; when is it to be done; and with what material and human resources? In the second stage, known as the "Social Process stage," the thrust of activities is toward determining how existing social, cultural, economic, political, and environmental factors, as well as indigenous communication processes would help or hinder the adoption of new practices or structures in the social system. In the third stage, the "Consistency stage" efforts are geared toward identifying existing media facilities and how they relate to one another and to the people. Here, one looks at what combination of existing communication channels—traditional, interpersonal, and mass media—can be used for communication 'feed' both into and from the social system. Finally, after careful examination of these analyses, tailor-made communication programs are drawn up and implemented in phases with real action potential in the social system but also taking into account any available supplementary inputs from the outside.

BASIC APPROACHES

It is only after such careful and critical examination that one can make a realistic decision as to which of the three basic communication approaches (Moemeka, 1989) to communicating development messages within a social system would be most appropriate. These approaches are the Interpersonal, which has two methods—Extension and Community Development and Ideological and Mass Mobilization; the Mass Media, which also has two methods—Centralized and Localized; and the Integrated, which combines all the approaches (and methods) in an appropriate ratio, depending upon the identified felt needs and the sociocultural, economic, and political realities of the social system.

Interpersonal Approach

Extension and Community Development Method. This is the oldest method of using communication to generate development. It is basically oriented to rural community development although it can also apply to suburban and urban development efforts. The main thrust of this method is the communication of useful and practical information on such issues as agriculture, home economics, health, civic responsibility, law and order, sanitation, and so on, through face-to-face and interpersonal (handbills, letters, telephone, etc.) methods of communication.

The utilization of the method is predicated on the assumption that the following basic conditions are present: (a) that the communities or social systems are interested in the new ideas and practices in order to improve their living conditions; (b) that there are necessary and sufficient resources to support the development endeavor, that is, to enable the people to apply available new information toward the development goals; and (c) that, as indicated in the Animation Rurale programs of Senegal, Togo, Ivory Coast, and Benin (Goussault, 1968), there is a crop of educated, intelligent, and public spirited leaders within the community or social system who can motivate the masses to positive development-oriented objectives.

The basic tenets of the method can be summarized as follows:

- that there are no solutions to problems that are imposed on local communities from the outside; that the people must be the principal actors in defining and finding solutions to their problems;
- that the development communicator (social animator) is to be as closely identified with the local community as possible
- that he/she is to be nondirective in his/her approach
- that communication's chief role is to help define the problem, not give the solution
- that community participation and social action is the goal, and therefore feedback from the community is an essential element.

One of the countries in which this method has been used is India. The country held, and rightly too, that the great mass of the illiterate and poor rural population is a highly valuable development resource (Rahim, 1976). The premise followed, therefore, that the individual rural family and the communities can be guided to the path of development if they were given practical knowledge of the social and natural sciences. The government decided that the best way to achieve the projected goals was to decentralize interpersonal communication to the community block level. Each community development block was served by a team of multipurpose village-level workers supported by the subject-matter specialists at the block level and supervised and coordinated by the block development officer. The whole program was planned, guided, and supported by a national-level community development organization (Taylor, et al, 1965). The multipurpose village-level worker is the key communicator in this method; he/she serves as a mediator between the community and the development bureaucracy of the government, and as a facilitator for the community (Dubhashi, 1970).

Ideological and Mass Mobilization Method. This is the second communication method that makes extensive use of interpersonal channels. In this method, the channels are activated not by development agents, but by political party cadres. This is because this method holds that development begins with a radical change in the political orientation of a social system, the ultimate result of which is the formation of new social relations. The main function of development communication therefore is seen as that of promoting and heightening the political consciousness of the people. The primary goal of this method is ensuring the ability of workers and peasants to be self-reliant through the mobilization of internal resources, thereby creating conditions in which they can control their own future. Physical and human development is subsumed under political consciousness, because it is held that political awareness would motivate the people to participate in development activities that would lead to satisfying their needs and aspirations .

The operational structure of this method is virtually the same as that of the Extension and Community Development method, but the structure and direction of message contents are different. While the former deals directly with human and physical development problems, the latter lays emphasis on political awareness as a prelude to any other type of development. While the former is heavily geared toward horizontal and interactive communication, the latter places vertical communication first. Two countries that are best known for the use of the ideological and mass mobilization method are Tanzania and China.

In Tanzania, the ideological messages for rural development in particular and development in general are predicated on the tenets of the Arusha Declaration of the Tanganyika African National Union party, and the essays on African socialism and socialist education by the first president of the country, Julius Nyerere. (After the unification of Tanganyika and Zanzibar, the political party changed its name to Chama cha Mapinduzi.)

Chama cha Mapinduzi is the only political party in Tanzania. It assumes direct responsibility for national development, and therefore for development communication activities. It uses party cadres and government officials to constantly expose the rural and suburban populations to ideologically oriented development messages transmitted through face-to-face communication, village meetings, rural training centers and political meetings. The basic unit used as interaction base is called the cell, consisting of ten households whose main functions are:

- to bring the people's problems and grievances to the party and the government for critical examination and discussions on plans of action directed toward solution in the context of the country's overall development objectives
- to communicate to the people the purposes, plans, and problems of the government and the party
- to mobilize the people in appropriate groups for the implementation of development projects.

Tanzania has since recognized the very pervasive and important impact of new communication technologies, and has linked her ideological and mass mobilization method with the use of radio broadcasting (Greenholm, 1976; Hall, 1973).

In China, development communication messages are predicated on the socialist ideology of the Communist party. The basic unit for interaction and exchange is the commune, comprised of the village-level work teams and the brigades. The communication exchange is carried out along two approved lines of structure, organization, and action: the Mass Line, uses the vertical communication process that regulates the relationship between the top and lower level party officials and the members of the commune (work teams and work brigades); Criticism and Struggle uses the horizontal communication process that regulates ideological education, conflict management, and decision-making at different levels of development planning and execution.

The Mass Media Approach

The mass media have become instruments not only for information but also for education and development. Because of their unique characteristics of speedy delivery of messages and extensive reach (wide-area coverage), they have been found to be particularly useful in the dissemination of development messages to large and dispersed populations, and, when properly used, in immediate follow-up with opportunities for exchange of ideas on the information/messages provided. In the main, mass media approach to the use of communication for development finds expression in two methods: the Centralized Mass Media method and the Localized, or Decentralized, Mass Media method.

Centralized Mass Media Method. This method emphasizes the control of both mass media infrastructure and the direction and flow of mass media messages by a central authority. If we were to construct a continuum with Extension and Community Development method at one end, Centralized Mass Media method would be at the other end. The method relies almost wholly on the mass media for its message flow, virtually ignoring the interpersonal system. Because it uses the mass media for dissemination, its area coverage strength is extensive; and because the content of its messages is usually of a general nature, there is always something of relevance, no matter how small, to different segments of the society. It is based on the assumption (Gunter and Theroux, 1977) that a "good and relevant message" is capable of being accepted by the individual on his/her own, irrespective of the origin of the message, and that the best way to attract and hold a mass audience is to offer open, spontaneous, and continuous vicarious satisfaction as well as education.

This is the method used by most countries in developing societies, especially in Africa. Many scholars argue that developing countries adopt the method because it is the cheapest to finance and easiest to administer. However, research has shown (Heshmat, 1967; Moemeka, 1987) that it is also the least effective in ensuring intelligent understanding and effectiveness of development messages.

Centralized Mass Media method calls for the planning, production, and dissemination of development programs and messages by experts and program officers in the urban headquarters of media organizations with little or no reference to the need for involvement of the receiving audiences. It does not matter which medium is being utilized (whether it is radio, which is the most accessible medium, especially for rural audiences, or the newspaper whose content is almost meaningless to the illiterate, or television—the urban elite medium—whose impact in rural communities is minimal), the procedure is always the same. The programs and messages are planned and executed without the direct participation of the audiences to whom the messages are eventually directed. The result of this noninvolvement of the target audience has been that message contents are always at variance with the felt needs of the people, and therefore have little chance of gaining the acceptance of the people. Not only is there no organization at the reception end, but also, because of the desire to reach the largest number of people, the messages are always of a very general nature, barely fitting any desired solution. Effective development messages demand some sort of organized action at the reception end, and also demand specificity in message content to ensure relevance.

Centralized Mass Media method appears to have derived its operational strategy from the Development Media theory (McQuail, 1983) which requires the mass media to join the government in the task of nation-building and development. While the theory makes no reference to the people—the target audience—it requires control and sanction of the mass media by the government "in the interest of national objectives." This is why centralization of activities is seen by media personnel or organizations that use the method as *imperative*; such control helps to keep a sharp eye on everything that is done or not done, and therefore to avoid provoking the anger of the government.

The method is primarily concerned with what the government wants, and what ideas media personnel have to meet those wants, rather than with the construction of messages that would motivate the people to positive actions through intelligent understanding of their needs and of how to meet those needs. It is therefore no wonder that the result of using this method anywhere, especially in the developing world, has left much to be desired. It generally succeeds in generating *effectedness* of messages, that is, getting the messages to reach the target audiences; but it almost always fails in ensuring *effectiveness* of messages, that is, creating an understanding atmosphere in which the target audiences would accept the demands of the messages and act according to those demands (Moemeka, 1981:85).

Localized (Decentralized) Mass Media Method. Also very mass media oriented, this method draws strength from the Democratic-Participant Media theory (McQuail, 1983). It lays strong emphasis on interaction with the target audiences, and on the establishment of local media channels to provide access for the people. The starting point in this method is the identification of the problems of the people through personal calls, meetings, and discussions with the people by media personnel who are required to enter into the sociocultural contexts of the target audience or audiences. Because of the need for specificity in message content, Localized method calls for the establishment of local media—local radio stations, rural press, television production/viewing centers. Each of these provides direct access and opportunities for target audience participation in the planning, production, and presentation of development messages. The method appears to be an appropriately relevant response to Rogers (1966) warning that:

> Unless a communication strategy includes a two-way flow of messages, makes sure that rural people have access to adequate channels and can express themselves in freedom, and unless the authorities are willing to listen to the messages which come from the country-side (the people) and to learn from them, the 'best' of such strategies will come to naught.

One of the most effective ways of creating opportunities for access and participation for the people is through the provision of local media channels through which their views, opinions and desires can be freely expressed for the attention and action of the authorities. Through local media the people can talk to themselves, talk to the authorities, and participate fully in the construction and dissemination of development messages meant for them. Such interaction creates an atmosphere based on correct interpretation of the needs and aspirations of the people, and an understanding climate in which confidence, credibility, and willingness to make personal and community contributions are at their best.

The Localized, or Decentralized, method is utilized mainly in developed societies. It is what these countries are using in their social change endeavors. The fact that media infrastructure is already decentralized in these highly literate and developed countries makes the Localized method easy to operate. The situation is practically different with regard the developing countries. Because of the cost involved in providing the necessary infrastructure to enable the method to operate successfully, and particularly because of the political implications of the method (creating an open and free communication environment for rural populations, most of whom are illiterate), most of the developing countries have not shown significant interest in the method. In the very few developing countries (Colombia, Brazil, Nigeria) where the method has been used in development activities, evidence of strong commitment on the part of the governments was lacking.

In addition to the external problems associated with the utilization of the method in the developing world, there is an internally-oriented strategy problem. In operation, the method appears to have been used in isolation, that is, without sufficient linkage with existing traditional channels and modes of communication. The result of this has been that it tends to unwittingly alienate many of the people within the social system that it was set up to serve.

Integrated Approach

This approach combines the Interpersonal and Mass Media approaches and links the combination with traditional channels and modes of communication. The approach recognizes that, in spite of their strengths, both the Mass Media and Interpersonal approaches have limitations. Their combination into one is therefore intended to help eliminate their limitations while improving on their strengths.

The mass media have the power to disseminate information and development messages rapidly and throughout a social system. This makes for awareness creation within the population. But they are generally not able to change people's attitudes. The fact that someone knows about efforts being made to ensure positive changes in society does not mean that he/she will automatically change attitude or agree to participate in the change efforts. Without change of attitude, there can hardly be any change in behavior, and without behavioral change, there can be no development or social change. Mere dissemination of information and development messages is, therefore, not sufficient to cause positive personal and societal changes. The communication mode which helps to bring about such changes is the Interpersonal. But, even though it is relatively very effective in inducing attitude change and effective development behavior, it is highly limited in reach. It lacks the rapid and wide-area coverage abilities of the mass media. The thrust of the integrated approach therefore is to utilize the mass media in providing relevant information to the entire population, and through the Interpersonal method, generate exchange of ideas and positive discussions which would lead to intelligent understanding of development objectives and each person's role in achieving those objectives. As research has shown (Rogers, et al, 1977:363) not only are two media better than one medium for effective communication, but also a combination of the mass media and interpersonal communication is better than using either alone.

In its use of the mass media, the integrated approach gravitates more toward the Democratic-Participant Media theory, even though it does not completely ignore the Development Media theory. In other words, the approach incorporates more of the elements of the Localized (Decentralized) Mass Media method than it does those of the Centralized method. While the Centralized method is very appropriate for dealing with development and social change at the national policy level, and helps to crystalize the national objective at the cross-ministerial planning level, the Localized method is more appropriate for putting policies and objectives into practice, especially at the institutional and community levels. To be most effective, however, integration of all the approaches and systems must take into account existing traditional channels and modes of communication which are always a reflection of the sociocultural, economic, and environmental state of the social system. This would appear to find additional support in the categorical statement by Yu (1977:185) that no communication policy or strategy (that intends to succeed) can afford to continue to concentrate on the mass media while ignoring traditional and other channels of popular culture.

PLANNING STRATEGIES

The structure of communication in any society is largely determined by the growth and development of technology and by economic and sociocultural institutions. To the extent that societies or social systems differ in their patterns of economic and sociocultural heritage, their communication patterns also are likely to differ from one another. For example, in traditional societies or rural communities, unlike in developed societies, direct face-to-face interaction is valued as the most reliable and authentic form of communication. In such societies or communities, the purpose of communication is usually to promote community identity and social harmony (communalism) rather than to promote individual well-being (collectivism or individualism); to reinforce stability and order rather than to bring about change and growth. But the ultimate goal of development communication is to cause positive and effective change through the provision of necessary information (backed up with physical inputs) that would create understanding and build up self-confidence and motivation to change.

The planning of development communication must, therefore, take into account the sociocultural context, development environment, and the goals of the social system in which planning takes place. In addition, the system's political ideology, social issues, communication facilities and systems, as well as available resources must all be properly studied before planning the communication strategy that would suit the social system or community. This is not to detract from the fact that there are certain requirements which obtain irrespective of where the strategy is to be implemented and irrespective of the level of technological advancement of the social system. Such universals, which form the bulk of what follows are a necessity for effective development communication.

Unfortunately, communication is usually brought into the planning of development programs only as an afterthought, especially in developing societies. In these countries, emphasis is placed more on publicity. Provisions are usually made for publicizing development plans and objectives, but very little is done to provide opportunities for discussion and feedback. Hence a common complaint among communication researchers and practitioners is that communication policies and plans are all too often in the hands of those who do not know enough about communication to set up or contribute to the communication systems and strategies that would best serve the development needs of their countries (Boyd, 1975).

In the task of development, communication should not be seen only as a tool—a supporting mechanism—or as an independent variable not subject to the impact of changing circumstances. Communication should be seen both as *an independent* and *a dependent variable*. It can and does affect situations, attitudes, and behavior, and its content, context, direction, and flow are also affected by prevailing circumstances. More importantly, communication should be viewed as an integral part of development plans—a part whose major objective is to create systems, modes, and strategies that could provide opportunities for the people to have access to relevant channels, and to make use of these channels and the ensuing communication environment in improving the quality of their lives. The implication here is that in seeking solutions to the problems of communication in development, not only must there be a general and in-depth study of the larger development process and needs of the social system, but also there must be a careful and critical evaluation of the role or roles of communication within the larger system. Such study and evaluation should involve examination of the following:

- the social system's development goals and objectives, particularly with respect to communication
- the consistencies that exist between the infrastructure and the institutions
- the consistencies between project goals and national goals
- the strong and weak points in the linkages among different levels of the development endeavor—project, community, and national
- the state of the existing communication systems
- the appropriateness and adequacy of existing communication systems in achieving identified objectives
- the possible new communication technologies that could be used to make the existing systems more efficient and effective

Information Need

Truthful and realistic answers to these questions can be more easily found through formative research, aimed at providing the information needs of communication planning. This is directed at establishing the condition of existing social, economic, cultural, political, human, and other contexts of the benefitting social system with a view to determining how each and all of them could affect the issues about which communication is to be planned, as well as how they might affect and be affected by communication strategies. The five major activities which UNESCO (1975) suggests would help in identifying the communication needs and resources of a social system would appear to also serve the purposes of helping to identify the information needs of communication planning in any social system.

1. The collection of basic data and systematic analysis of the country upon such bases as population densities, geographic limitations to communication, variety of social structures, ecology and agriculture, industrial capacity, manpower capacity, economic capacity, etc.

Data on such issues as age distribution, minimum wage, social strata, level of education, political climate, religious harmony, literacy, norms and mores, societal aspirations, major occupations, interpersonal and mate relationships, leadership types and styles, hierarchy of authority, decision-making processes, and relationship with surrounding and distant communities or countries, etc., are imperative. Also very important is obtaining correct information on the community's or country's development goals and objectives.

2. The production of an inventory of the present communication resources including modern and traditional media and analysis of the variety of present communication structures. Such inventory should include study of the audience, its communication consumption patterns, etc.

The information data sought here is concerned primarily with the relationship between the people and their existing communication systems. It requires answers to such questions as:

• What traditional communication structures and modes does the social system have and how are they utilized?
• How available and accessible are existing mass media facilities?
• Who uses what medium, when and for what purposes?
• What utilization capacities, receiving sets, literacy, purchasing power, etc.—obtain in the social system?

3. Critical analysis of present communication policies (or lack of it) including such considerations as ownership, structures, decision-making political control, etc.

The concern here is with policy decisions regarding what medium/media to establish, where to locate them and why, staffing, freedom of action for media personnel, availability of financial resources for maintenance and operation, ethics and equity in the distribution of communication content, feedback, openness, and audience participation in the communication process.

4. Critical analysis of communication needs of the social system especially in relation to the existing social and communication structures and the uses to which communication is put.

The demand here is to determine the state of the existing communication systems. And it is intended to find out if existing systems are adequate and appropriate for achieving identified objectives, and whether there is need for new communication technologies that could be used to make the existing systems more efficient and effective. Also required here is ascertaining the policy objective of communication content and how this affects and is affected by the existing social, political, economic, and cultural situations.

5. The analysis of the communication components in all aspects of national development plans and program in order to ascertain the communication requirements of the programs, and be in a better position to reconcile the needs with the means and capacities available.

This activity seeks to determine consistencies that exist between the infrastructure and the institutions, as well as the consistencies between project goals and national goals. Such reconciliations are wont to reveal any weak points in the linkages among different levels of development communication objectives—project, local, and national.

Determining the information needs of development communication planning is but one of the six tasks required to ensure articulate and relevant project plans. The others, generally known as elements of planning, are problem identification, goal clarification, strategy selection, and operational planning, "which are regarded as the 'soul' of development communication planning, and evaluation, which is both the searchlight for ongoing projects and the communication bridge between an executed project plan and future plans" (Moemeka, 1991:17/16).

Problem Identification

The thrust here is not so much pinning down social problems within a social system as it is making a decision as to which of the many social needs or problems of the system should receive priority attention. In any social system, there are various kinds of felt needs of the system and action needs of development agents. All the needs cannot be met at the same time. Common sense dictates that if success is to be achieved, needs must be tackled and problems solved in manageable bits. Therefore, it is important for the development communicator to set agenda for action by sifting through all the needs identified and picking out those considered, in the light of available data and resources, most likely to succeed. Taking on too much would lead to failure. Not only will the effort not succeed, but more importantly, the failure would create aversion to development activities on the part of the people. This is why problem identification also requires the task of operationally defining the problem to be solved and narrowing down its scale to manageable size and in specific and unambiguous terms.

Goal Clarification

Of course, it is not enough to merely identify felt/action needs or social problems. The goal or goals aimed at in attempting to meet the needs or solve the problems must also be clarified. This, in the main, involves making or writing down clear and carefully worded statements of expected outcomes possible with the available and/or expected resources. However, it is important to remember that goals are usually transitional because conditions are always changing. Changes in goal orientation are usually necessitated by changes in prevailing circumstances. Be that as it may, goals have to be set and clarified to make actions towards meeting the goals better focused. When conditions change, set goals should change to meet the new situation. Many a time, efforts at clarifying goals lead to rewording of problem statements and the reordering of priorities.

Strategy Selection

This is selecting from among possible alternatives what is seen as the most appropriate way or ways of meeting the goals set in the plan. Strategies are best selected when the media, physical, and human resources, as well as the attitudinal and behavioral data collected under information needs, are fully taken into account. Sometimes, one strategy, for example, Localized Mass Media, may suffice; at other times, and for some project plans, more than one strategy is required. When more than one or two communication strategies are selected, then it becomes very important to carefully blend them together in such a way as to maximize their strengths and minimize their weaknesses, and to utilize them in positively complementary ways rather than to unwarily allow unnecessary overlap.

It is important to note here that just as there are communication strategies for development and social change, so there are strategies that take their roots from other disciplines. There are, for example, those strategies identified by Zaltman and Duncan (1977) which we have labeled "sociopolitical" strategies. There are four: facilitative, reeducative, persuasive, and power. Their classification is based solely on identified attitudinal and/or behavioral realities of the target group. When the target group acknowledges there is need for a change and is willing to work toward effecting the change but lacks the strength or initiative to take action, facilitative strategy would be most appropriate. When some acts or social situations seen as harmful have become so ingrained into the sociocultural environments of a people that they have begun to see them as inevitable or as necessary parts of living, the reeducative strategy is considered appropriate. When a people have been so disillusioned that they have given up hope of effecting desired change, or when they barely see any need for change, the best strategy to adopt is persuasive, which attempts to create change by reasoning, urging, and inducement. When there is need for social change considered very important to happen within the shortest possible time or when the desired change is one which most of the people within the target group do not even want to consider, then power strategy is generally seen as useful.

Although each of them raises questions of ethics, rights, efficiency, and/or effectiveness, and although they seem very narrow in perspective in comparison to communication strategies which take a holistic view of the environments of the people, the sociopolitical strategies offer some useful basis for planning social change and development. Selected communication strategies would be richer if complemented with carefully selected and relevant sociopolitical strategy.

Operational Planning

This is the planning stage at which actions and schedules of activities are specified in detail, showing what is to be done, where, by whom, and when and what resources are required in what quantity, where, when, and for what activity. Operational planning calls for recording in painstaking detail the sequential order of activities, the hierarchical order of authority or supervision, and specific assignment of responsibilities. It also calls for broad guidelines as to how the assignments are to be carried out with respect to timing, audience, content, context, and direction. Even more importantly, operational planning requires adequate briefing carried out both in written and oral communication. The oral form is particularly recommended because it offers the opportunity for asking questions and providing explanations, both of which are extremely important for correct adherence to guidelines and proper execution of assigned responsibilities.

Evaluation

In development communication projects, evaluation is and should be a continuous task. It is the first action to take (formative research) and the last task to perform (summative research). First, it is used to determine the prevailing communication circumstances within the existing sociocultural, economic and political conditions in a social system in order to have a basis for any meaningful planning, and to know what to plan for and with what resources. Secondly, evaluation is used to guide ongoing communication activities. In this regard, data are gathered and used to examine ongoing projects to see whether or not they are proceeding according to plan; whether they are succeeding or not; and to point up possible strengths and/or weaknesses in organization, implementation, and operation. This helps to identify and nip in the bud any errors or threatening problems before they become too difficult and expensive to solve.

Finally, evaluation provides the data necessary for future plans. The evaluation of the organization, implementation, available resources, and outcomes of completed development communication projects, provides data that could be very useful in the planning of future projects. Such evaluations do reveal both the limits and the strengths of the planning procedures adopted, of the implementation strategy employed, and of the operational guidelines followed, as well as the ease or difficulty with which necessary inputs were forthcoming. They also are likely to reveal the level and quality of audience reaction and involvement.

EPILOGUE

The major role of communication in development is that of "smoothening the path to arrive at development objectives by creating an enhancing atmosphere for the mutual exchange of ideas that would produce a happy balance between physical output or material advancement and human inter-relationships" (Moemeka,

1987:132). This is why development communication is not persuasion-oriented, but interaction-oriented. Selected approaches, strategies, and plans, to be effective, must be the joint decision of development agents, development communicators, and the beneficiaries of the development activity—the people based on available resources,—both human and physical.

As we have pointed out elsewhere (King, 1991), effective development communication is not merely concerned with providing information on development activities. Besides creating opportunity for the people to know about the technical nature of new ideas and how they work and with what effect, development communication plays the more important role of creating an atmosphere for understanding how these new ideas fit into the real social situation in which the people live their lives. Its ultimate goal is to catalyze local development activities, local development planning and implementation, and local communication to smooth the path to development. Communication here should not stop with conventional mass media. If development communication is to succeed, then it must include strong components of social organization and interpersonal as well as traditional modes and media. In addition, those in charge of planning development communication must be those who understand the social structure (those who have entered into the sociocultural contexts of the people) and how change can take place in it—not merely how development messages can be disseminated.

REFERENCES

Boyd, P. D. 1975. Causes and Cures of Communication Neglect in Development Planning. In *Educational Broadcasting International*, March, Vol. 1, No. 3, P. 6.

Dubhashi, P. R. 1970. *Rural Development Administration in India* 67–74. Bombay: Popular Prakashan.

Goussault, Yves. 1968. Rural Animation and Rural Participation in French Speaking Africa. In *International Labour Review 97:* 525–50.

Greenholm, L. 1975. *Radio Study Group Campaigns in the United Republic Tanzania.* Paris: UNESCO.

Gunter, J., and Theroux, J. 1977. Open Broadcast Education Radio: Three Paradigms. In Rogers, et al (eds.), *Radio for Education and Development: Case Studies* Vol. 1. Washington, D.C.: World Bank.

Hall, B. L. 1973. "Mtu ni Afya! Tanzania's Mass Health Education Campaign". *Convergence*, VII(1).

Heshmat, M. Y. 1967. The Role of Radio in Health Education of the Public. In *Medical Annals: District of Columbia* 36(11), Washington, D.C.

McQuail, D. 1983. *Mass Communication Theory: An Introduction*, New York: Sage Publications. 94–96.

Moemeka, A. 1981. *Local Radio: Community Education for Development*, Ahmadu Bello University Press, Zaria, p. 85.

————. 1991. "Communication and Development: Conceptual and Operational Analysis" in King, S.S. (ed.). *Effective Communication: Theory Into Practice*, Kendall/Hunt Publishing Company, Dubuque, Iowa, pp. 17(1)–17(23).

Moemeka, A. A. 1991. Communication and Development: Conceptual and Operational Analysis. In King, S. (ed.), *Effective Communication: Theory into Practice 17(1)–17)23)*. Iowa: Kendall/Hunt Publishing Co.

————. 1989. Perspectives on Development Communication. In *Communicatio Socialis* III: 47–68.

————. 1987. *Rural Radio Broadcasting and Community Health Practices* in Nigeria: A Case-Study of Radio O-Y-O, *Ph.D. Dissertation*, p. 63. State University of New York, Albany.

————. 1985. Communication in National Development: The Use of the Mass Media in Rural Development. In *Informatologia Yugoslavica* 17(1–2): 171–85.

Rahim, S. A. 1976. Communication Approaches to Rural Development. In Schramm and Lerner (eds.), *Communication and Change: The Last Ten Years—And the Next* 152. Honolulu: The University Press of Hawaii.

Rogers, E. M. 1966. The Communication of Innovation: Strategies for Change, Michigan State University, East Lansing, November, *Mimeo.*

Rogers, E. M., et al. 1977. Radio Forums: A Strategy for Rural Development. In *Radio for Education and Development: Case Studies*, vol. II. World Bank, Working Paper No. 266. Washington, D.C.

Rogers, E. M. 1976. Communication and Development: The Passing of the Dominant Paradigm. In Rogers (ed.), *Communication and Develop-*

ment: Critical Perspectives 121–48. Beverly Hills, Calif.: Sage Publications.

————. 1971. *Communication of Innovations: A Cross-Cultural Approach,* New York: Free Press.

Taylor, C., et al. 1965. *India's Roots of Democracy* 169–93. Bombay: Orient Longmans.

UNESCO. 1975. *Report of the Meeting of Experts on Communication Policies and Planning in Asia,* Philippines, Oct. 4–8, pp. 5–10.

Yu, F. T. C. 1977. Communication Planning and Policy for Development: Some Research Notes. In Lerner and Nelson (eds.), *Communication Research: A Half-Century Appraisal* 185. Honolulu: The University Press of Hawaii.

Zaltman, G., and Duncan, R. 1977. Strategies for Change. In Zaltman and Duncan (eds.), *Strategies for Planned Change* 61–166. New York: John Wiley & Sons.

Part II

Part II

SCOTT R. OLSON

5

Television in Social Change
and National Development:
Strategies and Tactics

Bullets are useful to the extent that they hit the target at
which they are aimed, but when they ricochet, bullets can have an
effect different from the one intended. The media magic bullet
conceptualized by the propaganda studies school of communication and based on the simple stimulus-response model (Lasswell.
1927) still serves to guide the aim of social engineers (see Sproule,
1989). Around the world, television is designed with the intention
of promoting national development, social mobilization, and
change, an intention largely based on a presumption that the
effects of television can be controlled the way one controls a tool
(Olson, 1989)—as if a gun aimed at what looks like a pesky fox
could not possibly shoot a dog by mistake. Yet television and other
mass media have been shown to be primarily a reinforcement tool,
not a change agent (Klapper, 1960). Its own role in social change is
a complex and limited one. Television certainly is useful in devel-

opment, but used by itself, or even in a coordinated program, it is difficult to program, predict, and assess. It is indeed a weapon, yet it can be used for development tactically by minorities and individuals as well as strategically by the social engineer, and in that sense used to contradict the developer's intention. The bullet's magic may be out of the shooter's control.

Strategic national development through television can be used by states and by groups within states.[1] States use television to promote development consonant with their interests. Nigeria, for example. uses television to promote a national identity among ethnically, linguistically, and culturally distinct peoples. Ethnic groups that have access to television may use it to subvert the dominant interests of the state, however. The Inupiat ("Eskimos") of Alaska, for example, have used television to help establish a tribal-state in the North Slope Borough, a political unit distinct from the United States. This process, commonly called *devolution*, occurs when an indigenous group which has been absorbed within a larger political construction gains self-determination and regional power, either by having it given to them or by taking it. With the break-up of the Soviet Union, Yugoslavia, and Eastern Europe, overdue academic attention is being turned toward the role of television in this break-down of nation-states (cf. Mickiewicz and Jamison, 1991; Vartanov, 1991; Muratov, 1991; Androunas, 1991). The trend toward devolutionary development is particularly clear in the first world, where there is a greater diversity of television.

Mass media can also be used tactically, in opposition to organized strategies of states and ethnic groups. De Certeau (1984) describes a strategy as an exercise of will and power from a "proper" (i.e., socially sanctioned; "legitimate") institution or enterprise. A tactic, on the other hand, does not rely on proper institutional authority, but rather invades the proprietary space. A shopping mall is an example of a strategy (i.e., a sanctioned use of space designed to encourage shopping—the will of the owners of that space); shoplifting is an example of a tactic (i.e., an unsanctioned use of space against the will of those who own it). Television can be used in this tactical manner against the development strategies of those who control it.

This chapter will discuss the nature of television, then examine its use of strategic development from both statist and nonstatist perspectives. Statist strategies include those designed to fundamentally support the state. Nonstatist strategies include the use of television in devolution. The chapter will also consider the role of television in tactical development, through "guerrilla" and subjectivist use of the medium.

THE TELEVISION MEDIUM

Development via television is not the same as development via other media due to its unique properties. The media primarily used in development are print, radio, and television (film is only rarely used in this way). The use of print is discussed by Nwosu and the use of radio by Moemeka elsewhere in this volume, so their particularities are to be considered here only insofar as they contrast with television. Attributes of television which affect its use in development include that it is iconic, immediate, intimate, "cool," pervasive, expensive, passive/aggressive, and convergent.

To say that television is *iconic* is to describe the particular manner in which it signifies—a manner which gives the illusion of verisimilitude or "realism" (Barker, 1988). Iconic signification means that the sign that is used is analogous to the thing it represents; the word /tree/ is a non-iconic representation of the object it signifies, but the pipe in Matisse's "Ceci n'est pas une pipe" painting is iconic, because it *looks* like a pipe. Because of its illusion of three dimensions and motion, its marriage of sound and image, and to some extent because of its "liveness"—the temporal *immediacy* (Ellis, 1982) of its sign-making (the sense that events are unfolding as they are being seen, whether or not that is the case)[2]—television is the most iconic medium. Also in part because of this immediacy, television is the most *intimate* (Ellis, 1982) of the media. Because world events unfold live in the living room, and because television deals primarily in facial close-ups (an aesthetic consideration due to the size of its screen; cf. Zettl, 1973), it seems as though people on the screen are guests in the home. The size of the set makes the close-ups "life-size," as opposed to a movie where actors are "larger than life." Related to this, television is *"cool"* in McLuhan's (1964) sense, by which McLuhan meant it is low in definition but high in involvement. The viewer is drawn into what is happening, but is cognitively required to create definition. In other words, the development applications of television, if there are any, have more to do with its technological nature as a medium than with whatever message it might consciously try to articulate.

Television is also *pervasive,* which is to say that it is hard to escape. Particularly in the developed world, it is difficult not to be around it, since virtually every private home has at least one set. Sets are increasingly common in public spaces as well: lobbies of hospitals and hotels, department stores, restaurants and bars, night clubs, bus stations, airplanes. This pervasiveness transforms television into an extension of the public nervous system, as predicted by McLuhan (1964). Television is considerably less omnipresent in the developing world, of course, which gives it a considerably different role in development. The reason for the disparity between television pervasion in the developed and developing worlds is cost—television is *expensive.* The equipment needed for the production and distribution of television far exceeds the costs of radio or print media. The aggressive use of less expensive media technologies and distribution systems, such as the relatively decreasing cost of consumer video cameras and playback units, may change this however.

Television is both *passive* and *aggressive* in its engagement of the audience. The popular conception of the television audience is that it is largely passive, "couch potatoes," all eyes and no brain. It is clear that this is true of some of the audience much of the time (Kubey and Csikszentmihalyi, 1990), and the success of many development programs relies at least in part on this perception of a nonanalytic viewership. It is also clear that this is an overly simplistic notion of what constitutes the audience. Since the introduction of structural and literary theories to the study of media, it is evident that much of the audience is very aware of the form and content of the media and the effect that they have on them (Ang, 1985, 1991; Olson, 1987). Fiske and Hartley (1978) have even asserted that television watching is a form of reading, the audience very active, conscious, and engaged, the text polysemic (Fiske, 1986). Audience diversity, not only in demographics but in the manner in which television is watched or "read," has profound implications for media development plans; since it inherently allows a multiplicity of readings, its effects can hardly be uniform.

Finally, due to rapid changes in media technology, television is also *convergent.* This means that what were formerly discrete information technologies—book, computer, telephone, television—are merging into a single technology (Brand, 1987). Already there are book/computers (the Sony DataDiscman), computer/telephones (modems and fax), computer/televisions (Nintendo), and even telephone/computer/televisions (Cameo 2001, a videophone which transmits image telephony through a Macintosh computer); the process is expected to continue, and in fact seems to drive development at the major computer and entertainment companies. While still quite expensive, relative costs in this technology will go down as they always do; in the mean time, the meaning of the technology for the audience is changing, altering its development application. Convergent technology allows user-driven programming, reducing the utility and capability of television as a broadcast medium.

Some adjectives commonly associated with television have more to do with public perception of it than with the realities of the medium, yet these perceptions often (mis)guide the use of television in development. Most can be associated with the magic bullet conceptualization of media. Contrary to common assumptions about it, television does not appear to be predictable, dependable, uniform, monolithic, malevolent, or even insipid. It is some of these at times, but in general, it is inconsistent, making its use as a strategic development tool complex and problematic.

STRATEGIC DEVELOPMENT

In spite of these limitations of the medium, television has been used extensively in strategic development. There are two major types of theories on the role of mass media in this process. One type concerns the use of mass media to serve the interests of the state, or "statist strategies." The second type considers the interests of various groups within the state, or "devolutionary strategies." The two types share assumptions about design and effect of mass media, but differ in their objectives; in a sense they are two manifestations of the same approach.

Statist Strategies

Statist strategies have two schools: the traditional (or dominant or "Communications") school and the critical (sometimes called dependency or *dependencia*) school. The traditional school asserts that media help develop Western tastes in developing peoples, which encourage them to modernize and imbues them with a sense of nationality. Since this school is oriented toward Western-style development, it has come under much criticism; critics charge that it does not respect the legitimacy of a non-Western development path. These critics include, of course, the critical school, which opposes the traditional school, arguing that development along Western lines serves Western interests. The critical school advocates Marxist or self-reliant models of development instead. A thorough examination of each reveals their assumptions and strategies and illuminates the role of television in social change and development.

Traditional School. Traditional theories of development communication saw ethnic use of media as counterproductive to nation-state building. The traditional school's leading advocates were Daniel Lerner and Wilbur Schramm, but Karl Deutsch, Ithiel de Sola Pool, Lucien Pye, G. A. Almond, and others were adherents to its precepts. Lerner and Schramm (1969) were very critical of the "inertia" of traditional cultures, by which they meant the tendency to leave things as they are. Such a disposition was, they felt, contrary to economic development. Their view of legitimacy in politics, then, is very statist. In their view, countries ought to use mass media to foster state-sponsored nationalism on the one hand and should allow free flow of information on the other, linked with what Schramm (1964) called "free and adequate information." This view became the world development paradigm: the 1946 UN Declaration on Freedom of Information, for example, said that "all states should proclaim policies under which the free flow of information within countries and across frontiers, will be protected" (Masmoudi, 1979).

For Lerner, the heart of nationalism is modernization as embraced by any elite who were educated through and sympathetic with Western ideology and who would come to be emulated by their countrymen and women. This elitism necessitated, so the argument went, free enterprise, leading to a transition from non-Western to Western cultural values and structure. The mass media are most important during this transitional stage, when wants and needs are being defined, leading to what Lerner (1969) called the "want: get" ratio. The mass media condition people to want certain things and can also show them how to get these things. Television is particularly adept at manipulating this ratio because of the verisimilitude and omnipresence of its images. For example, not only is the video-iconic image of a beautiful automobile on the internationally distributed American television program *Dallas* a virtual substitute for the thing it signifies, a signifier with an illusion of verisimilitude; in fact, for most of the viewing audience (who will never "really" see the inside of a limousine), this representation becomes the thing it represents. This eclipsing of the signified with the signifier, so easily done on television, is not easily duplicated on radio, in print, or in other media From the perspective of the traditional school, television goes further with its signification. Not only does it denote the signified, but it also connotes the values and behaviors necessary to acquire it. Blake Carrington on *Dynasty*, for example, possesses the sort of material things a developing culture might want, and also illustrates a value system for acquiring such things. Through careful manipulation of television images, a state can engineer a want:get ratio and direct development.

Not only does television engineer wants and needs, but it also causes an individual to look outside of his or her own immediate interests and environment to identify with other individuals. This "empathy" can be seen in such things as the televising of natural disasters on the Cable News Network; because of its intimacy and immediacy, television accentuates the empathy. The ability to see the face of another mitigates one's feelings toward them, a power of television well-illustrated by the growing distaste in the mouths of Americans for the Vietnam war when it became a "living-room war," projected with little abstraction into every home in America. Radio, the dominant medium of the Second World War, could be much more abstract. Television disseminates information about the rest of the world, in a way making it seem familiar, by creating consumer goals that are likely to exceed a people's ability to meet them, and by bringing about a status system which is ripe for nationalists.

Although indigenous movements involve empathy, communications, and literacy, the traditional school does not treat them as legitimate nationalisms because modernity in the Western mode is not their objective. Lerner distinguishes between the rise of nations, which for him is modernity, and nationalism among nationalist movements, which he feels is unmodern and counterproductive. He feels that nationalist movements are "deviations" and "deliberate deformations" of Western nationalism (Smith, 1983). This is because Lerner does not attribute much significance to the spiritual values of a traditional society.

Critical School. Dissatisfaction with this traditional school of development media led to an intellectual reaction headed by Schiller (1971), Smythe, Hettne (1978), Hall, Mattelart, Cardosa. Dos Santos, and others. The goal of this new wave of development communication theory was a rejection of Western-style develop-ment, usually under the rubric of *dependencia* (dependency theo-ry). Politically, the debate surfaced in UNESCO as the New World Information Order (NWIO), and it posited several problems with the traditional model: an economic imbalance between North and South, unequal information resources, a will to control, colonial-ism, and other factors (Masmoudi, 1979).

The critical school disagreed with the traditional school on many points. Chief among them was the appropriate structure of the media. The traditional school had argued that a free media marketplace was the best path to development; the critical school asserted that this served the interests of the West, but not of devel-oping states. It was argued that the "free flow" model of develop-ment communication led to cultural and economic dependency of many countries. Some even question the legitimacy of a free-flow model in the developed world (cf. Akhavan-Majid and Wolf, 1991; Wuliger, 1991). Soviet scholars Androunas and Zassoursky (1979) called "free flow" a synonym for "cold war" in their justification of state sovereignty over mass media. As Gunter (1978) demon-strated, "national sovereignty" became one of the most important issues of NWIO. For many of the socialist and Third World coun-tries in the debate, sovereignty meant the right of states "to con-trol not only the borders of the state but the physical, economic, social, and information environment within these borders" (Gunter, 1978, p. 152). Schiller (1971) described "national self-pro-tection," but he means protection of states, not of nations in the traditional and literal sense of the word. Consequently, the critical school argued that more control should be shifted to national news agencies (Ivacic, 1978).

What is true for dependency between countries, however, may be just as true for dependency inside countries. Androunas and Zassoursky stated that, "the world must collectively recognize that countries are too different culturally and too unequal developmentally to uncategorically accept the 'free flow' of infor-mation . . ." (1979, p. 189). Yet what they describe as cultural dis-parity between states is also true within states, particularly inside such culturally pluralistic states as the former USSR and the USA. If one state can come to culturally dominate the world's media, it is equally possible that one ethnic group, presumably the majority, can come to dominate a state's media. The result is the same: someone's voice is quelled. Masmouli (1979) described democrati-zation of media as one of the aims of the NWIO, and Schiller

(1971) outlined a course for attaining it between states, but little consideration was given to democratization within states. Even self-reliance paradigms equate indigenization with states instead of ethnic groups; Bjom Hettne, for example, said that a "strong state [is] . . . a pre-condition for self-reliance" (1978, p. 36).

Both of these statist approaches make some similar assumptions, but the most fundamental similarity is that social change can be engineered—that whether it serves the interest of the state or the interest of a neocolonizer, television has the power to affect deliberate and premeditated change. This is a profound similarity, demonstrating that traditional and critical schools are in some ways merely different expressions of a similar idea. For both, television retains some properties of a magic bullet: it is a tool which can be manipulated; it has the power to modify perceptions and behaviors; it is thought of primarily as a broadcasting medium. Because these shared assumptions about television do not always accurately describe the reality of the medium, flaws exist in both of the statist approaches. In many (perhaps most) instances, the effects of television are far too unpredictable for it to be an effective tool for social engineering. As Klapper (1960) has shown, television has the power to affect mass perceptions and behaviors only in vary narrow circumstances, as a part of a multi-step flow of influences. Finally, television is not necessarily a broadcasting medium anymore; "narrowcasting," a term used to characterize the state of television in the cable, satellite, and VCR video space which predominates in the West, is a more accurate description. Because of these factors, the traditional and critical schools have failed to describe the real effects of television in much of the world. One example is in the developed world, where some development and change strategies react against television.

Devolutionary Strategies

Traditional models of nationalism asserted that ethnic nationalism would not survive the twentieth century. Karl Deutsch's (1969) model of communication and development, for example, argued that modem mass communications would sweep away ethnicity. Deutsch felt that that would be a positive and inevitable step in modernizing and nation-state building. Deutsch was premature in his analysis, however. In some areas, ethnicity is stronger than ever. According to Smith (1983), ethnic nationalism is resurgent because it is fueled by the success of ethnic movements in Eritrea, Kurdistan, Israel, and other places. For Smith, the new ethnic nationalism differs from early versions in a very important way: "what was lacking in those earlier revivals, was an ideology of national self-determination and a belief in popular national sovereignty" (1983, pp. xxxi-xxxii). Indeed, national integration, such an important concept for liberal and Marxist development theorists, may be declining as a use for mass media. Jayaweera (1986) showed that in many cases the attempt at such integration led to repression and that to repress cultural minorities is immoral; Pavlic (1986) supported self-reliance but saw the need for local and regional horizontal communication. Modern separatist movements have self-determination as a specific goal of their nationalism.

The mass media and indigenous movements do not always get along, however. Many indigenous movements have regarded media in general, and television in particular, as the enemy, because the information they need for the administration of their culture was more readily available prior to the introduction of internationally networked mass media. Inupiat Joseph Senungetuk (1971), for example, felt that modern communication was a threat to indigenous culture because it

> cut off the ancient knowledge of the people . . . the knowledge of themselves, the knowledge of their tribesmen [sic], and the knowledge of their land. It is a strange and forbidding fact, that communication is the greatest need among the people today. We Eskimos, whom historical research has described as "primitive, uncivilized, technologically backward," knew more about one another before European technological influence wrested our land from us, than we do today, when the most modern and sophisticated methods of travel known to man [sic], are available but beyond our reach. (pp. 106-107)

The key to cultural survival is to first keep the people geographically connected to the land, and perceptions and values connected to tradition. This sort of development values spiritual matters more than materialist ones, so inertia becomes a tool, not an impediment.

Television, however, is not always consonant with this goal. If television represents an attempt to standardize culture and perceptions, it is no wonder that devolutionary movements reject it.

Whereas some forms of mass media act as a tie between culture and the land for an indigenous people, television represents a separation from tradition, from the land, from valuable "inertia." As Hornik pointed out, "what to a government broadcast authority is sharing of national language and symbols to foster nation-building, is to its critics the systematic derogation of minority cultures" (1980, p. 16). Many ethnic groups have decided to fight fire with fire, or magic bullet with magic bullet, at least when it is possible for them to do so. Howell (1982) has shown that minority cultures are coming to recognize that in the task of preserving cultural identity, "telecommunication can be an ally rather than an enemy" (p. 53). In using mass media for development, a minority group can assert its own political and economic autonomy, revitalize its culture, and create a nationalism that distinguishes it from the dominant culture. This results in disintegration rather than integration. It is in many cases more successful than integrative campaigns, since it makes use of television's natural tendency to reinforce rather than modify.

Smith (1983) has done foundational work in strategic devolutionary media theory, showing that Western media cannot create new ideas or expectations in a resistant setting; they must have been introduced into a cultural context which was receptive to such ideas. Smith contradicted Lerner by arguing that a people need not necessarily desire Western-style development and that it does not follow that they must necessarily follow the Western path. Lerner built his argument on the assertion that the mass media show a developing people the world, that to see the rest of the world is to want it, and that to want it is to pursue it through Western approaches to ideology, modernization, and nation-building. Smith felt that it is possible for a culture to see the world and not want it, however, and to pursue development through an indigenous ideology and nationalism.

Smith further asserted that Lerner's "transitional state" is more concerned with the role of Western-style commodity consumption than nationalist movements are; for a nationalist, the abstract is more important than the material. Lerner's "transitional man" [sic] seeks food and security, whereas a nationalist seeks "roots and esteem and justice" (Smith, 1983, p. 102). Smith suggested that Lerner was wrong about the mass media, since they can communicate roots and justice as well as consumption and can "constitute as great a barrier to the inculcation of national sentiment and to the appeal of the nationalist movement as it may help to diffuse its ideals" (Smith, 1983, p. 103). For Smith, media are just as likely to subvert loyalty to the nation as they are to encourage it, depending on the context in which they are used. In other words, media can be as much a tool for devolution as for state building. If the key to cultural survival is to first keep the people geographically connected to the land, then mass media can be used to promote literacy and cultural awareness (Nageak, 1984).

Devolution tends to be a phenomenon of the developed world, but development is as much a phenomenon there as anywhere else (Pool, 1977). Weaver, Buddenbaum, and Fair (1985) showed that media diversity and ethnic pluralism are much more successful in states with higher GNPs; Brown (1984) related the growth of regional and local Nordic politics to the growth of local radio. Stavrianos (1976) and Kohr (1978) argued that the world political system is undergoing a transformation, that the Westphalian nation-state system is being deconstructed through various inter- and intra-national forces. This transformation can be seen as another element of postmodernism, the sweeping intellectual and popular reaction against modernism as represented by conventional politics and culture. Postmodernism is one of the most significant cultural events of the century, related to literary theory (Arac, 1986), religion (Cox. 1984), physics (Fischer, 1985), and politics (Stavrianos, 1976), where the Westphalian nation-state system is showing evidence of decline and states are fragmenting into units that Snyder (1982) calls macro- and mini-nations (e.g. the Soviet Union, Eastern Europe). In other words, devolution in many forms may be the wave of the future.

Unfortunately, while other disciplines have explored the political implications of cultural devolution, Communication remains largely statist. Much of the development communication literature confuses nations and states, making it difficult to talk about the role of television in devolution—until recently, the possibility of such a phenomenon was not widely considered. Critical theorists Grachev and Yermoshkin, for example, claimed that "any state is entitled to use the means at its disposal to disseminate information about . . . its way of life, to publicize its dominant social, economic and political ideas" (1984, p. 67); their use of the word "dominant" implied that other nations within the state are not entitled to the same rights.

Media play an important role in strategic devolution, however: they can perpetuate the language (perhaps the most essential ingredient to perpetuate), the mythology, and the traditions of a culture, making an ethnic group identify itself as a nation. Examples of the strategic devolutionary use of mass media are increasing. Print tends to be the medium of choice; radio has also been used by separatist movements (Soley, 1982). Television is only rarely used by indigenous groups seeking autonomy and self-determination. When a state is relatively decentralized and free-market in orientation, the chief impediment to indigenous use of television is access to capital—indigenous movements can seldom afford the expensive equipment and telecasting costs associated with it. When a state is relatively centralized, with a planned market, the chief impediment is access to the public space[3]—access to the radio waves needed for telecast is tightly held by a central, sanctioned authority who has the responsibility to program for the "public need"; indigenous movements find it difficult to infer themselves into this body's conception of what is in the public interest.

An example of an indigenous movement prohibited from extensive use of television due to cost and political centralization are the Samifolken ("Lapps") of Sweden. Because they have limited capital, and because the Swedish broadcasting authority closely guards the airwaves, what little radio and television the Sami have been able to produce has been only as allowed by the state; this includes *Sarmenytt*, a Sami news program, and *Samemagasin*, a magazine program, both broadcast on Sveriges Radio's Lokalradio, the local service of the national radio system. *Samemagasin* is produced in Swedish, not Sami. There is essentially no Sami programming on television. Consequently, the real voice of this movement is in print, such as the *Samefolket, Saminourra, Sápmi*, and *Goaikkanasat* magazines and the *Sami Aiga* and *Rennäringes-Nytt* newspapers (Olson, 1985).

In some instances, when cost is not a problem and there is sufficient political decentralization, devolutionary movements do make use of television. Such is the case with the Alaskan Inupiat, who have been fairly successful with television, in part because they have been very successful in using indigenous land claims to forge a substantial tax base.[4] In addition to indigenous and native-owned newspapers and radio stations, the Alaskan Inupiats own their own cable television station, satellite link, and broadcast quality video studio and field production suites. These and other facilities are used to produce television programming for satellite distribution to remote Inupiat villages. The programs include *Alaska Native Magazine, Amy and the Astros, Right On, Inupiaq*

Literacy Series, Alaskans All, and, in the traditional language, *Ukkaqatigilakuut* (Olson, 1985).

Another example of the strategic devolutionary use of television are the Welsh, who have their own television network on Channel Four, featuring programs such as *Superted,* about a Welsh superhero bear. This has served to keep their language and culture alive (Howell, 1982). Subervi-Velez (1986) pointed out that millions of U.S. Latinos maintain their cultural identification (their nationality) through mass media as well, a reinforcement of their traditional language and culture over their adopted one. What is intertia for one culture is evolution for another. In short, when the political economy allows, television can be a powerful tool for devolution, but more often than not, the political economy rules it out.

What should the devolutionary media strategy for indigenous cultures be? First, it must be an indigenous strategy, one based on linguistic and cultural traditions—to adopt either traditional or critical strategies is to lose the battle for devolution. Much of the NWIO literature describes the "Americanization" of world culture (Grachev, 1984), but the alternative given, as Hettne (1978) has shown, is often equally Western. It is not necessary that an indigenous people fall into a debate where the parameters are entirely Western. The statement issued from the Third General Assembly of the World Council of Indigenous Peoples (1982) stated: "indigenous ideology needs no authorization nor recognition by the forces of colonialism, but stands on its own right . . . it cannot be related to the leftist or rightist ideology of the colonizers" (p. 84). Certainly, the views espoused by the traditional communications school are Western, but then so is the Marx/Lenin-inspired rhetoric of the dependency theorists. Galtung was correct that "liberalism and Marxism are . . . two ways of being Western" (in Hettne, 1978, p. 44).[5] Arac (1986) calls anti-modernism "a distrust of liberal rationalism," and perhaps it is the liberal rationalism of both the traditional school, and the dependency model that leads some indigenous cultures to choose an alternative that is on a completely different political spectrum.

Television has inherent advantages for indigenization that go beyond radio and print, making it a more suitable, possibly less Western devolutionary alternative. One such attribute is that it is inherently anti-realistic and anti-narrative (Polan,1986), suiting it to traditional communication patterns; this is not true of radio, which is extremely linear, or print, which forces an alphabet on a language where none may have existed before. Further, aesthetic modes of perception are central to all cultural rituals (Geertz. 1973), making television an ideal cultural conduit (Thorburn, 1987). It seems appropriate, then, that television could be used extensively in devolutionary strategies. It is possible for an indigenous people to develop their own cultural basis for the conduct of their media systems.

Some factors make it likely that television will be increasingly a fixture of devolutionary strategies. One is the decreasing relative cost of low-end television technologies and the so-called "information revolution," which promotes new technology over more traditional technology and leads to a greater acceptance of media as a mechanism of mini-nationalism. Television consequently becomes as useful a tool in devolutionary development as it is in statist development because (Hornik, 1980) it acts as loudspeaker, catalyst, organizer, and interaction accelerator, all of which apply as much to the minority culture as to the majority culture. Such strategies still do not constitute a magic bullet, however, and can be subverted by audience tactics.

TACTICAL DEVELOPMENT

According to de Certeau (1984), tactics are the "improper" (or "anti-proper") manipulation of events when opportunities occur, a guerrilla act as common in everyday life as in terrorism. Planting a bomb on the London Underground is tactical. but so is using a shopping mall as a hangout rather than as a place to buy things. Watching television can also be tactical, but in two different ways. One is objective tactics, those which are deliberate, conscious, and organized. The other is subjective tactics, which are coincidental, unconscious. and spontaneous. Both can be used for development: on the one hand, toward a social and political goal; on the other, toward a psychological goal.

Objective Tactics

Objective tactical use of television is the premeditated but unsanctioned manipulation of the medium for developmental or counterdevelopmental goals. This sort of tactic has been fairly common on radio, from the commercial pirate radio stations floating off the coast of Europe to the clandestine (and illegal) use of radio by Basque and Catalonian separatists, who tactically infer themselves into a public broadcasting space that does not want them. Because of the cost and security involved, objective tactical use of television is uncommon and unlikely. One rare example of this was the "Captain Video" incident on Home Box Office (HBO) in the 1980s, when a computer "hacker" bounced a simple message off a satellite, interrupting HBO's signal. The message was more commercial than political, urging HBO viewers to complain about an imminent signal scrambling policy which would have required many with satellite dishes who had been getting the signal free to pay for a descrambler, but is nevertheless a perfect example of a television tactic. As television and computers converge, such hacker incidents might become more common.

The notion of what constitutes the "proper" use of space can be loosely defined, however, leading to a broader interpretation of what constitutes a tactical strategy. For example, unconventional financing of a television program or distribution system is one sort of tactic. Local community groups have been known to produce videos which were made available for free overnight rentals at local video outlets. Public access television has generated numerous underground and tactical developmental programs ranging from the silly ("Downtown with Johnny Mason")[6] to the sexually explicit ("The Ugly George Show")[7] to the politically subversive (e.g., Marxist, anarchist, Situationist, or anti-IRS shows)[8] to the culturally bizarre and artistically extreme ("Dan's Apartment").[9] A related phenomenon are those broadcast television shows which home audiences manipulate, asserting themselves. wanted or unwanted, onto the public airwaves. These shows vary from the sweet and funny ("America's Funniest Home Videos" and "America's Funniest People", both patterned after successful Japanese shows) to the alarmist and disturbing ("America's Most Wanted").

Subjective Tactics

Subjective tactics are on the one hand much more prevalent than any of the development strategies discussed here, but on the other hand far more difficult to predict, catalogue, or even describe, since they are so viewer-specific. At the most fundamental level, these tactics involve the (largely) unconscious use of television for personal uses and gratifications (Blumler and Katz, 1974)—such development and social change is selfdirected, one person at a time, and either consonant or contrary to state interests. These uses and gratifications include such needs as to acquire information, to experience love and friendship, to build self-confidence (Katz, Gurevitch, and Hass, 1973); to be amused, to believe in romantic love, and to affirm cultural, ethical, and spiritual values (Berger, 1982). When television is used in these ways, it allows the viewer to develop him or herself, usually to reaffirm self-image, but occasionally, when other factors warrant it (cf. Klapper, 1960), to change.

Of course, using television in these subjective ways may be contrary to the intent of the programmer. Viewers regularly "poach" (de Certeau, 1984) their own meanings from television the way a medieval hunter poached a rabbit in a royal forest, in a sense stealing an improper meaning from a program or commercial (Jenkins, 1988). Thus teenagers may view the "Just Say No" anti-drug campaign as farce, enjoying the public service announcement as a comedy contrary to the intentions of its producers. This is, of course, allowed by the inherent polysemy of television texts (Fiske. 1986). While subjective development tactics are difficult to predict and impossible to program, they are almost certainly the most powerful and direct form of television development, making use of all the unique attributes of the medium—its icons, immediacy, intimacy, "coolness," pervasiveness, passive/aggression, and, eventually, its convergence, since the new media technologies allow more person-directed poaching than existing forms; "everyone becomes a manipulator" (Baudrillard, 1981, p. 182). By allowing a life within the mind, television allows a real if not geographic escape from the state.

At a more complex level, these subjective tactics involve wholesale shifts in human cognition, development driven not by television programmers or the individual, but by the language of television itself. This language, a dense and complex semiotic system of signification and reference, asserts itself beyond sender and receiver intentions. Baudrillard (1983) described this shift as *hyper-reality*, a situation in which the signified to which signifiers refer is so remote that the signifiers in fact only refer to other signifiers. In a sense, the "reality" that television purports to represent becomes inaccessible because its pervasive simulation of life becomes for the audience life itself, as if Matisse's painting of a pipe seemed to be a more "real" pipe than a pipe itself. Hyperreality evolves in four stages: first, signs reflect literal reality; later, this reflection begins to interpret and "pervert" reality; next, the sign hides the absence of the reality it purports to reflect; and finally, it refers only to itself (Baudrillard, 1983). Although this sounds absurd, there is some empirical evidence that those who view television heavily do in fact live in an artificial environment, a "hyperreal" simulation (Meyrowitz, 1985; Kubey and Csikszent-mihalyi, 1990).

How does this affect the television viewer? At one level, it implies that each viewer constructs his or her own reality from the unsignifying signs, what de Certeau (1984) compared to *lignes d'erre*, the incomprehensible subjective meanderings of an autistic person. Baudrillard went further, however, asserting that the developed world has ceded its nervous system to the media: "you no longer watch TV, TV watches you" (1983, p. 53). Control of what television does has nothing to do with strategies or tactics, with governments, artists, guerrillas, or individuals, but with the medium itself, which like the Hal 9000 computer in *2001: A Space Odyssey*, has become a product of human hands with a life of its own. This depressing conundrum, reminiscent of the literary black-hole of deconstruction, means that whatever social change and development occurs through television is a product of neither the intentions of the sender or the receiver, but, in a technologically deterministic sense, of the "intention" of television itself. To the extent that Baudrillard is correct about television, it serves as an indictment of traditional development theory and Western-style development: developing countries may risk losing "reality" itself by using electronic media for social change.

CONCLUSION

The use and effectiveness of television in social change and development depends on the theoretical and ethical orientation of the developer. Traditional and critical strategies attempt to show how television can be used in state-building, on the one hand by forging want-get ratios for Western-style goods and services, on the other by forging counter-dependency or self-reliance. Devolutionary strategies work against state-building using similar techniques, including the preservation of language and culture. Objective tactics seek development through momentary "improper" guerrilla occupations of television space, almost always with devolutionary and deconstructive results. Finally, subjective tactics situate social change in the cognition and psychology of the viewer, who finds him or herself consciously or unconsciously altered by the television consumed.

The effectiveness of television in social change is a direct product of its attributes as a medium, which are often disregarded when social development plans are conceived. Television is not the magic bullet that most developers and the general public still assume it to be. It is more like a grenade, bursting little bits of social change like shrapnel into the cultural fabric, unpatterned and unpredictable, now and then a dud, sometimes exploding in the face of its master. Bullet or grenade, there is no doubt that television is a powerful weapon for national development. The question is how to control it.

NOTES

1. There are other development and social change strategies for which television is used of course, particularly in the developed world where a sense of nationality already exists. These include such development strategies as bringing about linguistic shifts (e.g.. the introduction in the U.S. of the term "Ms." as a title for adult women to replace "Mrs." and "Miss," which was largely engineered through the media); introducing positive role models (e.g., *The Cosby Show*); eliminating antisocial behavior (e.g., the "Just Say No" campaign against drugs, the "Don't be a Butt-head" campaign against smoking, the "Friends Don't Let Friends Drive Drunk" campaign against drinking-and-driving); promoting prosocial behavior (e.g., condom use for prevention of AIDS); or encouraging volunteerism (e.g., public service announcements for charities, such as the "A Mind is A Terrible Thing to Waste" campaign for the United Negro College Fund). Media strategies of these types are essentially reworkings of the theories of national development discussed here. Whether the development is national or social, the use of television in it is basically the same: it serves as a useful tool to generate or reinforce interpersonal communication, but the actual process of change and development occurs at the interpersonal level.

2. Zettl (1973), for example, refers to television's "subjective now," the sense that time as it actually unfolded and time as the audience perceives it are the same.

3. The "space" on radio waves is a part of a public sphere generated and perpetuated by social norms (cf. Habermas, 1989).

4. The Alaska Pipeline runs through Inupiat lands, allowing them to tax the oil which flows through it. On a per capita basis. the North Slope Borough where the Inupiats live is one of the richest counties in the

United States (cf. "Land Selection . . .," 1972). The funds have been largely reinvested in the community: a new high school, a hospital, and the extensive television facilities (Olson, 1985).

5. Grachev and Yermoshkin (1984) go so far as to assert that there are only two opposing sociopolitical systems, ignoring the multitude of other possibilities. This either/or, East/West, Right/Left type of thinking has severely curtailed the origination of truly indigenous media strategies.

6. A program in Hartford, Connecticut which features skits and parodies done in a small studio or with a consumer-model video camera. The effect is homemade *Saturday Night Live,* an exercise in video emulation.

7. Ugly George wanders New York City with a portable camera asking women to disrobe for the camera. Some of them do. Apart from the tastelessness of this premise, the show does portray a form of sexuality uncommon on broadcast television, tactically resisting its norms and conventions.

8. These programs are produced at the national headquarters of the political organization and distributed on videotape to local public access channels. They tend to get more airplay in bigger cities. The developmental implications are obvious; for most of these alternative political movements, this is the only voice on television they have.

9. One viewer at a time would call a number on the screen and give movement instructions to a robot video camera in Dan Kennedy's apartment using a touch tone phone. The image would move through the apartment revealing the kitchen, living room, bathroom, etc. Other viewers would watch these movements as they waited their turn on the phone. The effect is utterly bizarre, calling into question the very assumptions on which television watching is based. It is iconic, in fact, almost purely visual but also extremely immediate and intimate (one is poking around another person's apartment), addictive, and convergent through its use of new technologies (e.g., Laserdisks).

REFERENCES

Akhavan-Majid, R., and Wolf, G. 1991. American mass media and the myth of libertarianism: Toward an "elite power group" theory. *Critical Studies in Mass Communication* 8:139–51.

Androunas, E., and Zassoursky, Y. 1979. Protecting the sovereignty of information. *Journal of Communication* 29:186–91.

Androunas, E. 1991. The struggle for control over Soviet television. *Journal of Communication* 41 (2):185–200.

Ang, I. 1985. *Watching Dallas: Television and the melodramatic imagination.* London: Methuen.

————. 1991. *Desperately seeking the audience.* London: Routledge.

Arac, J. 1986. *Postmodernism and politics.* Minneapolis, Minn.: University of Minnesota Press.

Barker, D. 1988. "It's been real": Forms of television representation. *Critical Studies in Mass Communication* 5:42–56.

Baudrillard, J. 1981. *For a critique of the political economy of the sign.* St. Louis, Mo.: Telos Press.

————. 1983. *Simulations.* New York: Semiotext(e), Inc.

Berger, A. 1982. *Media analysis techniques.* Beverly Hills Calif.: Sage.

Blumler, J., and Katz, E. 1974. *The uses of mass communication.* Beverly Hills, Calif.: Sage.

Brand, S. 1987. *The media lab: Interpreting the future at MIT.* New York: Viking.

Brown, D. 1984. Alternatives for local and regional radio: Three Nordic solutions. *Journal of Communication* 34:***

Certeau, M. 1984. *The practice of everyday life.* Berkeley, Calif.: University of California Press.

Cox, H. 1984. *Religion in the secular city: Toward a postmodern theology.* New York: Touchstone Books.

DeLoria, V., and Lytle, C. 1984. *The nations within: The past and future of American Indian sovereignty.* New York: Pantheon Books.

Deutsch, K. W. 1969. *Nationalism and its alternatives.* New York: ***.

Ellis, J. 1982. *Visible fictions: Cinema, television, video.* London: Routledge.

Fishcher, R. 1985. Deconstructing reality. *Diogenes* 129:47–62.

Fiske, J., and Hartley, J. 1975. *Reading television.* London: Methuen.

Fiske, J. 1986. Television: Polysemy and popularity. *Critical Studies in Mass Communication* 4:391–408.

Geertz, C. 1973. *The interpretation of culture.* New York: Basic Books.

Grachev, A., and Yermoshkin, N. 1984. *A new information order or psychological warfare?* Moscow: Progress Publishers.

Gunter, J. 1978. An introduction to the great debate. *Journal of Communication* 28:142–56.

Habermas, J. 1989. *The structural transformation of the public sphere.* Cambridge: M.I.T. University Press.

Hettne, B. 1978. *Sarec report: Development theory.* Stockholm, Sweden: Swedish Institute for Research Cooperation with Developing Countries.

Hornik, R. 1980. Communication as complement in development. *Journal of Communication* 30:10–24.

Howell, W. 1982. Bilingual broadcasting and the survival of authentic culture in Wales and Ireland. *Journal of Communication* 32:39–54.

"Indigenous Freedom Now Has Become a Working Plan." c. 1978. In World Council of Indigenous Peoples, *Third General Assembly,* Ohcejohka, Finland: Swedish International Development Authority, 10982, p. 84.

Ivacic, P. 1978. The flow of news: Tanjug, the pool, and the national agencies. *Journal of Communication* 28:157–62.

Jayaweera, N. 1986. New technologies and third world cultures. *Cultures* 36:79–80.

Jenkins, H. 1988. *Star Trek* rerun, reread, rewritten: Fan writing and textual poaching. *Critical Studies in Mass Communication* 5:85–107.

Katz, E., Gurevitch, M., and Hass, E. 1973. On the use of mass media for important things. *American Sociological Review* 38:164–81.

Kohr, L. 1978. *The breakdown of nations.* New York: E. P. Dutton.

Klapper, J. 1960. *The effects of mass communication.* Glencoe, Ill. The Free Press.

Kubey, R., and Csikszentmihalyi, M. 1990. *Television and the quality of life: How viewing shapes everyday experience.* Hillsdale, NJ: Lawrence Erlbaum Associates.

"Land selection problems confront Alaskan natives." Dec. 19, 1972. *New York Times.*

Lasswell, H. 1927. Propaganda technique in the world war. New York: Alfred A. Knopf.

Lerner, D., and Schramm, W. 1969. *Communication and change in the developing countries.* Honolulu: East West Center Press.

Masmoudi, M. 1979. The new world information order. *Journal of Communication* 29:172–79.

McLuhan, H. M. 1964. *Understanding media: The extensions of man.* New York: McGraw-Hill.

Mayrowitz, J. 1985. *No sense of place.* New York: Oxford University Press.

Mickiewicz, E., and Jamison, D. 1991. Ethnicity and Soviet television news. *Journal of Communication* 41 (2):150–61.

Muratov, S. 1991. Soviet television and the structure of broadcasting authority. *Journal of Communication* 41 (2):172–84.

Nageak, J. 1984. Interview. Barrow, Alaska.

Olson, S. 1985. Devolution and indigenous mass media: The role of media in Inupiat and Sami nation-state building. Doctoral dissertation. Northwestern University, Evanston, Ill.

————. 1987. Metatelevision: Popular postmodernism. *Critical Studies in Mass Communication* 4:284–300.

————. 1989. Mass media: a bricolage of paradigms. In S. King (ed.), *Human communication as a field of study: Selected contemporary views.* Albany, N.Y.: State University of New York Press.

Pavlic, B. 1986. Redefining the values of development. *Cultures* 36:***

Polan, D. 1986. "Above all else to make you see": Cinema and the ideology of spectacle. In Arac, J. (ed.), *Postmodernism and politics.* Minneapolis, Minn.: University of Minnesota Press.

Pool, I. 1977. Technology and policy in the information age. In D. Lerner and L. Nelson (eds.), *Communication research: A half-century appraisal.* 261–79. Honolulu: University Press of Hawaii.

Schiller, H. 1971. *Mass communications and American empire.* Boston: Beacon Press.

Schramm, W. 1964. *Mass media and development.* Stanford, Calif.: Stanford University Press.

Senungetuk, J. 1971. *Give or take a century.* San Francisco: Indian Historical Press.

Shackle, T. 1984. Interview. Barrow, Alaska, June 20, 1984.

Smith, A. 1981. *The geopolitics of information.* New York: Oxford University Press.

————. 1983. *Theories of nationalism.* New York: Holmes and Meier Publisher.

Snyder, L. 1982. *Global mini-nationalisms.* Westport, Conn.: Greenwood press.

Soley, L. 1982. Radio: Clandestine broadcasting, 1948–1967. *Journal of Communication.* 32:165–80.

Sproule, J. 1989. Progressive propaganda critics and the magic bullet myth. *Critical Studies in Mass Communication* 6:225–46.

Stavrianos, L. 1976. *The promise of the coming dark age.* San Francisco: W. H. Freeman and Company.

Subervi-Velez, F. 1986. The mass media and ethnic assimilation and pluralism. *Communication Research* 13:71–96.

Thorburn, D. 1987. Television as an aesthetic medium. *Critical Studies in Mass Communication* 4:161–73.

Vartanov, A. 1991. Television as spectacle and myth. *Journal of Communication* 41(2):162–71.

Weaver, D., Buddenbaum, J., and Fair, J. 1985. Press freedom, media and development 1950–1979: A study of 134 nations. *Journal of Communication* 35:***

World Council of Indigenous Peoples 1982. Indigenous freedom now has become a working plan. *WCIP Third General Assembly.* Ohcejohka, Finland: Swedish International Development Authority.

Wuliger, G. 1991. The moral universes of libertarian press theory. *Critical Studies in Mass Communication* 8:152–67.

Zettl, H. 1973. *Sight sound motion.* Belmont, Calif.: Wadsworth Publishing.

6

The Newspaper in the Development of Developing Nations

The Newspaper is the Servant
The Leader and the Whipping Boy of the Community
It is a Medium of Information
A Stimulating force behind public betterment
A source of Education and Entertainment
—Goodfellow (1958)

The above statement by a renowned newspaper publisher aptly ties together the theme or focus of this chapter. This is essentially a critical assessment of the role of the newspaper in the development of the developing nations, using some theoretical, research, practical, and professional (experience-based) insights. It also brings to sharp focus and correlates our four key concepts in this chapter—the newspaper, development, development communication/journalism and developing nations.

We shall take the newspaper in this chapter to refer to a general interest publication that contains informative, educative and entertaining news, features, articles,and similar material meant for mass consumption, and which is usually published daily, weekly, or fortnightly or even at irregular intervals. It can also be said to refer to a wide range of publications that include the large metropolitan daily, the Sunday newspaper, and provincial, party, community, and rural newspapers (government or private) that exist in various parts of the developing world.

We understand development (in line with our opening statement) to refer to "a widely participatory process of social change in a society intended to bring about both social and materials advancement (including the betterment) of the greater majority of the people through their gaining greater control over their environment" (Rogers, 1976). Development communication, on the other hand, refers to the application of the art and science of human communication to the speedy transformation of any country and its people through identification and utilization of appropriate expertise in the development process that will assist in increasing participation of intended beneficiaries at the grassroot level (Rosario-Braid, 1979). And, of course, we shall take the newspaper as a potential element in the development communication mix and examine it throughout this chapter as such. Furthermore, we shall understand developing nations, in this chapter, to refer essentially to the less developed countries of Africa, Asia, Latin America, and the Middle East, whose citizens still live below the poverty line and who strive to gain the standards contained in our definition of development above, in various contextual forms.

NEWSPAPER'S FUNCTIONS AND ROLES

In reviewing the standard functions and roles of the newspaper in this chapter, we must draw our readers' attention once again to Goodfellow's description of the traditional and universal functions of the newspaper as a public institution and as a business enterprise. By stressing the newspaper's role in information, education, and public betterment (or development), and even entertainment, he promotes the fact that we cannot reasonably neglect the newspaper as a vital agent of rural and national development.

Emery and his associates (1973) seem to be agreeing with the above observations when they wrote that the major functions of the newspaper everywhere include: to inform, comment editorially on the news, promote business through advertising, support desirable civic projects, fight undesirable social conditions, entertain, counsel, and champion the rights of its readers. Moemeka (1980) seems to have confirmed the application of all these functions of the newspaper when, writing in a development context, he stated that the specific functions of the newspaper include information, interpretation, service, and entertainment while its roles include acting as a watchdog on those in power or government and fueling the engine of business through advertising. Edeani (1990) concurs but reminds us that the dual nature of the newspaper as a business enterprise and as a public institution devoted to the protection and servicing of public interest, makes it most difficult for the newspaper to accomplish all those tasks anywhere, especially in the developing countries. But as Moemeka (1980) contends "On the face of it, there appears to be a conflict here. Actually there should be none. Newspapers which demonstrate alert reporting and courageous editing, gather strength through increased readership. And increased readership means increased sales and more money."

It seems most appropriate, however, for any newspaper publisher or editor in a developing nation to see these expert observations as a recognition that the noted dual nature of any newspaper organization anywhere surely raises some operational problems, especially in the poor economic environments of the developing nations, but that these problems are in no way insurmountable. This posture will indeed help newspaper editors and publishers in the developing countries to understand and accommodate Goodfellow's insightful description of the newspaper above as the "whipping boy" of everyone, including the governments and even the public it is supposed to be protecting or serving as a social institution. This can easily be described as the paradox of newspaper journalism in past and contemporary societies.

This posture will also help us to understand why, in spite of the above problems and many others, in spite of the challenges of the speed and audiovisual punch of the electronic media, the newspaper is still perceived by many experts as being relevant in the developed and developing nations. Part of the reasons for this perception of the newspaper lies in the fact that even though it is slow, the newspaper has a lasting power far beyond that of the spoken word or the visual image, and readers can refer to it again and again. Stories printed in today's columns may be readily examined in the newspaper files decades later (Emery, et al, 1973). Moemeka (1985) in rather forceful language points out that:

> The above characteristics no doubt make the newspaper quite suitable for mass education and mobilization of illiterate and semi-literate populations which are generally slow to learn and are usually in the majority in the developing countries. They also help to make the newspaper a potent medium for mobilization and education in the sub-urban areas of the developing countries where there usually are few literate people like village teachers, priests, retired civil servants and opinion leaders. These categories of ruralites usually buy, read and interpret the newspaper messages or contents to their less-literate friends and relatives, individually or in groups. The characteristics also make the newspaper an appropriate medium for eliciting the sympathy, understanding and moral and financial support of the urban population and government officials for rural development.

Furthermore, this optimistic posture will help us to appreciate the rationale behind the recorded contributions of the newspaper to the historical-political and socioeconomic development of most of the developing countries, as portrayed by the brief historical overview below.

HISTORICAL PERSPECTIVE AND CROSS-COUNTRIES ANALYSES

If recorded history of the newspaper is all we have to go by, we can confidently say that it has been and is likely to remain a vital force in the development of the developing countries. For instance, Daniel Lerner (1958), in his elaborate study of the mass media in fifty transitional societies in the Middle East, pointed out that through the building and sustenance of empathy and the promotion of expectations and literacy, these countries' media had contributed to the growth of these traditional societies. Even though aspects of Lerner's scholarly work have been criticized by some experts (e.g., Rogers, 1976), it still serves as a good indicator of the long-standing importance of the newspaper in the development of the areas covered by his work.

The Press Institute of Bangladesh (1980) offered a good picture of the newspaper's past and recent role in Bangladesh and compared it with those of other Asian countries. It observed that newspapering in Bangladesh has over the years grown into an established industry and a force to be reckoned with in the country's development. But the Institute pointed out that the picture of the newspaper industry is even brighter in neighboring Asian countries. According to its report, compared to other Asian countries, "the number of copies circulated per 1000 population in Bangladesh is only 5 . . . in neighboring India, it is 17, Burma 8, Malaysia 7, Pakistan 18, Singapore 93, Sri Lanka 48 and Thailand 24."

In their incisive interpretation of the historical evolution of the press in Kenya, Abuoga and Mutere (1988) noted that "as the system began to do away with Europeans and their leadership political role, the new African leadership started harnessing the newspaper to provide the atmosphere and channels through which new techniques, life styles, motivations and attitudes of the modernizing sector could be diffused to the backward and traditional sectors." The above book-length historical study of the Kenyan press concluded unequivocally that the newspaper has contributed significantly to that country's socioeconomic and political development.

Present-day Kenyan newspapers are likely to continue making this contribution if they can overcome what NgugiWa-Thiongo (1986) described as the self-imposed censorship, foreign influence, government harassments, and the unsteady growth or "come-and-go" syndrome in newspaper development. It is not easy to determine if they will overcome these problems in the near or even distant future, especially when experts in African communication development have observed that "what happens in Kenya is not an exception; it is the rule in developing societies" (Moemeka, 1988).

Kasoma (1987) traced the history, development, and role of the newspaper in Zambia from 1906 to 1983, starting with that country's first newspaper, the *Livingston Pioneer*, and clearly painted a picture of what he saw as the positive political and other roles of the newspaper in past and contemporary Zambia, in spite of many problems. He offered a critical assessment of these problems, including state ownership and control of the newspaper, which placed a strong limitation on what should have been its much higher contribution to the development process in Zambia.

In the West Africa subregion, starting with Sierra Leone, which is reputed to have established in 1801 the first newspaper in tropical Africa, *the Royal Gazette and Sierra Leone Advertiser,* to the first Ghanaian newspaper, *the Royal Gold Coast Gazette and Commercial Intelligence* (1822), and the first Nigerian newspaper, the *Iwe Irohin* (1859), the earlier newspapers and even the modern ones in these countries have been reported to have contributed in many different ways to their countries' political and socioeconomic development (Hachten, 1971). For example, noting that a total of 51 newspapers was established in Nigeria between 1880 and 1937, and citing facts supplied by Nnamdi Azikiwe (1964), J. S. Coleman (1960), and Kalu Ezera (1960), Nigerian press historian, Fred Omu, concluded that it is "widely acknowledged by writers on Nigeria that the newspaper press has been a significant force in national development." Of course, these newspapers also have had to contend with many of the earlier-reviewed problems facing the press in Africa and other developing countries.

In French-speaking African countries like Morocco, Algeria, Ivory Coast, and Togo, the French colonial policy of assimilation, which viewed its colonies as distant regions of France, did not allow the newspaper and other mass media in these countries to develop as fast as the media in the British African colonies. There were, for a long time, in many of the French-speaking African countries, no indigenous newspapers. The first indigenous newspaper in Ivory Coast, the *Abidjan Matin* of the Breteuil chain of newspapers, was established in 1938. The major reason for this situation was that the few Sorbonne-educated, French-speaking Africans depended heavily on French newspapers like *Le Monde* for news and information about the world and even about their own countries (IPI Report, 1971). This trend changed significantly in more recent years, but has not completely disappeared (Nwosu, 1987). This probably explains, at least partially, the relatively less radical role the French-language African newspapers played in the historical, political and socioeconomic development of their various countries, especially when compared with their British-speaking African counterparts (Hachten, 1971).

Be this as it may, the historical evidence available to us in the literature seems to suggest that the newspaper in most developing countries of the world played relatively enviable roles in arousing political consciousness, and contributed significantly also to raising the awareness necessary for effective social mobilization of the people for rural and national development. It seems necessary, however, to subject these historical insights to further critical analysis, using available theoretical and social scientific research insights or data that will help us to properly draw conclusions on the role of the newspaper in the development of the developing countries.

THEORETICAL AND RESEARCH INSIGHTS

In assessing the role of the newspaper in the development of developing nations, two inescapable and nagging questions are whether or not the newspaper has any effects as an element of the development communication mix in the development of these nations, and if it does, what the nature of such effects are. These questions border on waterttight causal proofs, which many social science theorists and researchers "believe cannot be obtained in complex social situations"(Merril, 1974) such as national development. This is in spite of the existence of sophisticated statistical and computer-based multivariate analytical methods that may be able, in some social situations, to account for various intervening, antecedent, distorter, suppressor, extraneous, or other variables before a causal relationship can be established between an independent variable like the newspaper and a dependent variable like literacy or any other aspect of development.

Yet, these questions have persisted for years and continue to demand answers from social theorists and researchers, answers that we do not seem to be close to yet. But, in the face of the seemingly positive answers, at least, to the first part of the question—that newspapers (and other media) do have some effects on social and national development—we cannot but keep searching. Among the now-popular intuitive positive conclusions about newspaper effects on man, society, politics and socioeconomic development are Napoleon Bonaparte's statement that "three hostile newspapers are more to be feared than a thousand bayonets" (in Dennis, 1978); Will Rogers' confession that "all I know is just what I read in the papers" (in Shaw and McCombs, 1978); V. I. Lenin's pronouncements on the powerful "role of the newspaper in revolutionary politics" (Lenin, 1929); and Joseph Goebbels' unwavering belief in and consistent use of the newspaper and other media as powerful tools of propaganda (Doob, in Katz, et al, 1965).

It is, therefore, interesting to observe that there is more than enough evidence in the research and theoretical literature to show that probably, as a result of the above historical and intuitive positions on the issue, and definitely for many other reasons, the search for the answer as to whether or not the newspaper affects the development of developing nations is quite alive. In fact, the search has generated many useful theoretical and research insights, some of which we will review here. Most of such theoretical constructs and research findings, however, deal with communication or the mass media, of which the newspaper is only a part; all the same, they offer useful insights that will help in our assessment.

Of the many theoretical constructs that exist on this issue, we will adopt McNelly's Pragmatic or Situational Consequence theory of communication impact (1968) and Merril's Cause-Effect Interaction model (1974) for analyzing the role or influence of newspaper communication on development. These seem to be flexible or elastic enough to accommodate most of the critical, theoretical, and research insights on this question. The pragmatic or situational consequence theory maintains that we should realize that there is not yet any adequate theory to predict the impact of communicated messages on different societies in all situations, and so the researcher must seek empirical evidence on the effect of development communication messages in any particular culture, development situation, society or nation in a case-by-case manner. If we apply this in our assessment of the newspaper's effect on development, we can assert that its effect in any development situation can only be ascertained empirically by a researcher observing the total message transmission and noting its impact through observable responses and consequences.

The cause-effect interaction model, similarly, holds that communication and other factors operating simultaneously within a nation bring about growth and progress. They are inseparable— but correlational and relational. The model is inter-sectoral and inter-media in its approach and warns against the danger of single-factor determinism. In assessing the role of the newspaper in development, therefore, other factors involved in the development process of any nation must be taken into account before we can draw scientific conclusions.

The above theoretical constructs will, no doubt, help us to accommodate social theorists and researchers who espouse differing media effects perspectives—the strictly powerful media effect position, the little or no effect, and the modified powerful effect position—on the role of the newspaper in rural or national development as summarized in Nwosu (1986). They also accommodate the learning theories of development communication which emphasize the need for repetition in newspaper and other mass mediated messages, as well as teach us that people need to have their beliefs, habits, attitudes, and opinions reinforced from time to time in development communication situations.

The two working theoretical constructs reviewed above also show that we can learn from and apply the thoughts of Uses and Gratifications theorists in assessing the role of the newspaper in the development of the developing countries. If we do this, we can safely say that for newspapers to succeed as change agents (alone or along with other variables, depending on the development situation), their messages or contents must be geared toward satisfying or gratifying the needs of their target audiences (Blumler and Katz, 1974). The constructs are even flexible enough to accommodate the view of Influence theorists that in most development situations in which the newspaper is used, the influence of the medium on the target audiences is usually indirect, since its messages flow through a web or nexus of individuals or groups before reaching their targets. The personal influence theories which find expression in the two-step, multi-step, and Nth-step flow hypotheses and their other variants have been well described by Katz and Lazarsfeld (1955). In addition, the constructs have direct relevance to the Agenda Setting hypothesis (Shaw and McCombs, 1978) as it affects the role of the newspaper in development. Among other things, this hypothesis reminds us that the importance which target audiences attach to development messages in the newspaper depends largely on the amount of prominence that the newspaper can give to the messages. Through strategic placement (front or back page as opposed to inside pages), illustration photographs, bold or display headings, and other such journalistic techniques, prominence can be given to messages, thus enhancing their chances of achieving effectiveness.

Even more importantly, as working theoretical frameworks, the pragmatic or situational consequence theory and the cause-effect interaction model reviewed above, allow enough room for accommodating most of the research findings on the question of whether or not the newspaper does influence or affect development in the developing countries. And it is interesting to note that most of these research findings tend to support the view that there

is a strong positive correlation between the newspaper and national or rural development, and even individual development. For
example, Lippmann (1922) points out that political officials and
publics depend on "pseudo-events" depicted in the newspaper for
information and decision-making. Lang and Lang (1959) state that
regardless of the course of news treatment decision, media (newspaper) contents convey the state of mind of important others
which could be germane in a development situation. And Wilhoit
(1970) affirmed that the mass media (newspapers) shape perceptions of who are particularly important and/or successful political
officials and publics.

   More specifically, many factor-analytic and other studies
have been carried out with varying conclusions which demonstrate that the newspaper (and other mass media forms) are significantly correlated with development variables. It has been shown
through one such study that "the press has a negative power to tit-
illate, alarm, enrage, amuse, annoy, even to drive a person out of
his community or job," but may not be able to win or stop a war or
revolution, break governments or win an election (Matthew, 1959).
This is a limited effects position toward press influence that fits
snugly into our major theoretical framework, which is totally
against the single-factor deterministic position making the press or
newspaper an all-powerful lone ranger or an independent social
force that does not have to work with other factors to bring about
social or other changes in any person or nation. Other studies
include those by Deutschman and McNelly (1964) and Bostian and
Oliviera (1965).

   There are also many such studies at the national level which
indicate correlational influence. Even though they were not specifically on the newspaper, their findings are about mass media communication of which the newspaper is a significant part. Lerner's
study (1958), which we reviewed earlier, covered 50 countries and
showed that media participation correlates with literacy, urbanization and political participation. A similar UNESCO study (1961),
which covered the developing areas of Latin America, Africa, the
Middle East, and Southeast Asia, also uncovered a strong correlation between mass media factors (including the newspaper) and
economic factors in general development. Carter and Schramm's
study (1959), which covered 100 countries and the one by Farace
(1965), which spanned across 50 countries, both came up with
findings that were similar to the ones reported above. The community level studies include the one by Rao (1969) which compara-

tively studied two Indian villages and found strong correlation between communication and socioeconomic and political development. Frey (1966), in like manner, studied 460 villages in Turkey and reported clear correlation between communication and development.

Note that in line with our theoretical framework, those studies did not prove any causality or did not even attempt to do this. But as Moemeka (1991) rightly observed, "the incidence of correlation is so frequent and the relationships so strong that it does not seem wrong to argue that communication has been both cause and effect in the complex interplay of factors which make for development both national and individual." Compare the above statement with the Cause-Effect Interaction component of our theoretical framework and it should be clear that the current thinking among scholars and other experts on this question seems to be generally at par, or are in a relatively high level of agreement.

Disagreement among experts on this question of media or communication influence on development arises mainly when we consider cross-media or cross-communication-forms comparative studies or analyses. For instance, in his study of the adoption of farming innovations in four western Nigerian villages, Basu (1969) found that the dominant sources of agricultural information among the rural farmers were their friends and communal organizations, not newspapers or other resources. Emenyeonu (1987) also studied 200 rural farmers randomly drawn from eastern Nigeria and found that neither education nor media-use had any significant association with the adoption of agricultural innovation among them; personal communication sources were found to have more influences, as in many other such studies in many developing countries. According to the study only 14% of the respondents chose radio as their primary source of information, 3% chose the newspaper, 8% chose television, while the extension agent—a personal source—attracted 61.3%.

But in their own study of rural farmers' adoption of agricultural innovations in Kwara state of Nigeria, Olowu and Igodan (1989) came up with findings that debunked the above studies. According to them, of the eight agricultural practices analyzed, information about six was sought primarily from radio, while two—marketing and fertilizer information—were sought mostly from seller farmers and extension agents respectively; meaning that farmers generally sought information about most agricultural practices from the mass media. There are in the research literature many other of such studies that give some influence to the mass media, including studies by Sobowale and Sogbamu (1984), Nwosu (1990, 1986), and Soola (1984, 1988), which were done in different but related development contexts.

From this latter set of studies, it can be deduced that the best way to resolve the seeming contradictions among researchers' or expert findings on this question is to differentiate between communication or media influence on the rural dwellers at the awareness-creation or information-acquisition level and the actual innovation-adoption level. This was why Sobowale and Sogbamu (1984) acknowledged the strong influence of friends and relations (personal influence or information sources) in innovation adoption, but insisted that this influence is usually after initial awareness had been created by the mass media information sources. Nwosu's (1990) study said the same thing in different words, when it maintained that, in general terms, mass media influences are mediated by situational, social-relational, and personal factors. Soola's (1984) study also appreciates the primacy of interpersonal communication sources and the value of the traditional sources, but contends that "for a jet-age development, interpersonal communication requires mass media supplement," particularly for awareness-creation and initial information acquisition. Nwachukwu and Akinbode (1989) in their own study maintain that since the number of extension agents in a country is almost always grossly inadequate "the use of the mass media (including newspapers) to complement the efforts of the extension agents (and other personal information sources) becomes imperative."

Our suggestion that we differentiate between the influence of the newspaper and other mass communication media at the awareness-creation or information-acquisition stage and the actual innovation adoption as a way of understanding the nature of their influence in the development process is lent further support by a study carried out in Bendel state of Nigeria by Moemeka (1981). This study analyzed the influence of seven media forms at the awareness or information-acquisition level and the adoption, response, or reaction level, using three development projects— Operation Feed the Nation, Local Government Reforms, and Universal Free Primary Education. The seven media forms were social, forums, town crier, village market, village school (all ora-media or traditional media of communication), and the newspaper, radio, and television (representing the mass media). The findings clearly demonstrated the superiority of the traditional and interpersonal media at the response, reaction, or adoption stage, and the superiority of the mass media (radio and newspaper) at the awareness-creation or information-acquisition stage. According to the study, even though more than 80% of the respondents said they first heard of the development projects on radio, 15% through the traditional media, and 5% from the newspaper, "reactions to the projects and subsequent messages were almost exclusively influenced by discussions and decisions that took place through face-to-face contacts provided by the traditional media."

Based on the above review of theoretical constructs and research findings, it seems safe to say that, as revealed in the earlier historical assessment in the chapter, the newspaper does have political and socioeconomic influence in the development of the developing nations. As we noted above however, these theories and research findings clearly show that this influence of the newspaper (like those of other mass media) is strongest at the information-, awareness-, and knowledge-acquisition levels, but has little or no influence at the reaction, adoption, or behavioral-change level as an independent source of information. It is significant to note, however, that these theories and studies seem to agree generally that the newspaper (like the other mass media) acting together with traditional, interpersonal, group, face-to-face, and other such media can have some positive influence on the development process or the adoption of innovations depending on the nature of interaction of all these communication forms with other societal factors (e.g., political, economic, and technological) that also influence development or innovation adoption.

These and other studies also show that, among the mass media, while the newspaper may trail behind radio as a development agent, it seems to compete favorably with television in different development contexts, mainly because of television's limited availability, accessibility, and cost in most rural settings. However, it still seems most useful in most development projects to adopt the media integrative, combination, or multi-media approach suggested by many development scholars including Rogers (1978), Inayatullah (1967), McAnany (1973, 1978), Beltran (1974), Orewere (1991), Root et al (1980), and Nwosu (1991, 1986), which will allow the newspaper to be integrated into a mesh of mass mediated, traditional, interpersonal and other communication forms for greater efficiency, either at the awareness or adoption levels or both.

THE "WHIPPING BOY" OR PRESS FREEDOM DIMENSION

The newspaper can hardly perform all of the above developmental and other functions if it does not have a conducive environment. And part of this conducive environment is a relatively free operational atmosphere in which newspaper people are seen by the government and other development agents as partners in progress instead of as antagonistic meddlers. This is why it is necessary to consider the press-freedom dimensions of the newspaper's role in the development of the developing nations in the light of Goodfellow's description of the newspaper as the "Whipping Boy" of the community in most countries.

On the surface, it would seem that the simple answer to the press-freedom question is to give newspaper people all the freedom they need to do the good job they are expected to do by contributing to the development process through informing, educating, and mobilizing the masses. Unfortunately, the situation is not as simple as that in any part of the world, developed or developing. In fact, the press-freedom argument has been raging since the invention of the printing press, and to date, no single consensus applicable everywhere has emerged. The now well-known four theories of the press of Siebert and Associates (1963) on the question of press freedom has generated much heat, but no light. Their libertarian, authoritarian, soviet-communist, and social-responsibility concepts or theories have offered very useful bases for the examination of the press-freedom question in various contexts and from various perspectives, but none of the four positions has offered and is likely to ever offer a universal panacea to the press-freedom issue. In fact this was not their aim.

It is perhaps the above situation and other related factors that have led to the emergence of a fifth theory of press freedom, now known as the Development Media theory (McQuail, 1987), which seems to be the most dominant in the developing countries today and is therefore most likely to shape or affect the role of the newspaper in the development of developing nations. According to the theory, the media should support the development effort in line with established policy; freedom of the press is subject to economic and social development needs of society; the media should protect national cultures and languages; the media should strive for the creation of linkages with other developing nations; journalists have freedoms and responsibilities; and the state may intervene or participate in mass media communication to protect the national or group interests, expand media outlets, or protect public morality (McQuail, 1987). In essence, this theory can be described as an amalgam of the above four theories of the press because it situationally and eclectically "picks and chooses roles for the news media according to the nature of government, economy, politics, culture and heritage or historical antecedent" Omwanda, 1991).

All these are no doubt in line with Kwame Nkrumah's (1965) perception of the "Newspaper as a collective organizer, a collective instrument of mobilization and a collective educator—a weapon, first and foremost to overthrow colonialism and imperialism and to assist total African independence and unity." The tenets of the development media theory also agree with the views of the renowned Kenyan journalist and publisher Hilary Ngweno (1968) that the newspaper has the challenge of laying down the foundations upon which future freedoms will thrive. As he put it, "anyone who has lived or traveled widely in Africa, Asia, or Latin America cannot fail to be appalled at the enormous amount of poverty, illiteracy, and disease that are to be found everywhere. Under some of the conditions in which the Asians, Africans and Latin Americans live, it would be sacrilegious to talk about press freedom, for freedom loses meaning when human survival is the only operative principle on which a people live."

The above statements, coming from a former African president and an African journalist, seem to aptly summarize the principles behind the development media theory and the seemingly reciprocal or cooperative mood or spirit that should exist at present between rulers and newsmen in the developing countries, in order that the newspaper can play its proper role in the development of the developing nations. Unfortunately, what the situation should be is not always what the situation is. So, we find that in most developing countries governments and government officials do not adequately reciprocate the willingness of journalists to sacrifice some of their freedoms, at least temporarily, at the altar of rural or national development. This problem often stands in the way of effective usage of the newspaper as a tool of development in the developing countries. The problem must be confronted through proper management of the intra-media controls and disciplinary mechanisms of journalism associations and through joint government-media controls and regulations of organizations such as the Press Council that will ensure adequate freedom for newspaper operators. This will help to avoid the abuse of power by some leaders in the developing countries who choose to trample the human rights of media personnel. It will also help to avoid the abuse of freedom on the part of some unscrupulous newspaper personnel who may want to turn press freedom into press license (Nwosu, 1987, 1991). It definitely calls for a careful balancing of values among the government officials and journalists in these developing countries—a balancing act that will not turn the development media theory into an oppressive and retrogressive media theory.

THE SPECIAL ROLE OF THE COMMUNITY AND RURAL NEWSPAPERS

It seems to be widely accepted after many years of experimentation that the locally based small newspaper rather than the urban big newspaper is more useful for development journalism (Oso and Adebayo, 1990), providing balanced and critical reportage of issues, processes, and events in a community and acting as a catalyst for improving the people's living standards. For one thing, locally based small newspapers not only contribute to the betterment of life in the communities they serve, but also contribute to overall national development by helping to reduce the rural-urban dichotomy and, using the concept of incrementalism, to spread innovative and developmental ideas across communities and nationally. Therein lies the current importance of the rural and community newspaper in the development of developing countries. A community newspaper could be described as one published in a specific locality, whose editorial thrust reflects the interests and needs of that environment and whose circulation range is usually limited to that locality (Igwe, 1991). A rural newspaper, on the other hand, could be described as a community newspaper that operates, circulates, and serves the interests or needs in a particular rural community. A community in this context, refers, of course, to a cluster of villages or communities in a geographical location with distinguishable sociocultural, political, and economic characteristics.

The problem is that, in spite of the increasing acceptance of the rural newspaper in the developing countries of Asia, Africa, and Latin America, many skeptics still cite such factors as poverty and low literacy of the ruralites, logistical problems of circulation, low supply of advertisements, and generally low cost effectiveness as excuses against starting and supporting rural newspapers. While these are weighty problems, we should not see them as insurmountable if we are to benefit from the many advantages of rural newspapers as part of the community press systems. Good newspaper management techniques and adequate government and private-sector support and investments will not only enable us to overcome these problems, but will help us to reap the many benefits of the rural press in helping to educate, mobilize, sensitize, inform, foster communal integration, and fight the social malaise or corrupt practices that stand in the way of development. In fact, one of the reasons adduced against publishing rural newspapers— low literacy—could be used in support of the rural press, considering the fact that one major function of rural newspapers in places where they have been established and properly managed is the promotion of literacy. This explains why it has been described as "the school-master of the common man" (Igwe, 1991). The rural newspaper functions as an agenda setter for the rural communities it serves, and as a symbol of progress. These functions and that of status conferral on prominent ruralites, should not be underestimated in assessing the role of the newspaper in the development process of the developing nations. As one successful rural newspaper editor reported: ruralites "are excited to appear on the pages of a newspaper and reflect their views. The experience is so unique that, in their eyes, you become a kind of a local champion. People hail you on the street and ask you about government programs and expect you to convey their views to government. This kind of thing is more than money." (Dawodu, 1991).

Even though the above statement was made by a Nigerian rural newspaper editor, Asian and Latin American countries seem to be more advanced than African countries in the rural newspaper business. Even in Africa, the disparity among countries that are already putting the rural newspaper to use is quite wide. For example, although Nigeria and Ghana have experimented with rural press, it is Kenya that seems to be taking the lead in this area with the support of UNESCO (Nwosu, 1991; Thompson, 1988). In fact, to deal with some of the problems of the rural newspaper, rural newspaper editors in the developing countries may be guided by some of the findings in a UNESCO-sponsored study of the rural press in Kenya (Mbindyo, 1985). Among the key findings is that "nearly half of the potential audience of rural newspapers do not read them because they are not available," not because of the illiteracy factor. This research report received some support recently from an editor of a rural newspaper in Nigeria—Femi Ogunleye of the Akinale-based *Village News*. He was reported as saying that the barrier of illiteracy in the rural areas cannot completely deter rural people from reading rural community newspapers. According to him, the barrier of illiteracy could easily be overcome by imaginative use of illustrative pictures such as group photographs of the spokesmen—the traditional ruler and elders in Akinale village—because when they see their pictures in print, everybody in the village would buy a copy and get people to read for them (Igwe, 1991). Kabiro (1985) would not only agree with these research and experience-based insights but has expressed his belief in the prospects, survival, and utility of the rural newspaper in the development of the developing countries in these words: "To me a newspaper is a newspaper, whether national, urban or rural. The newspapers in Kenya (and, in fact the whole developing world) therefore should strive to do what other newspapers do to survive." He was referring to the application of sound newspaper management, marketing and editorial principles by these rural newspapers as a panacea to most of their problems. We cannot agree more.

CONCLUSION

Historical and research evidence examined in this chapter indicate that while the newspaper may not be very powerful in changing deep-seated attitudes and behaviors among individuals and groups in developing nations to help bring about rural or national development, it is quite effective in helping to raise awareness and provide the information and education which must be acquired by individuals and groups before development can occur at any level. We can also safely conclude that the newspaper can work along with a nexus of other interpersonal and group communication modes (traditional and modern) in a multi-media scenario to influence people's development-oriented attitudes, actions, and behavior, and thus help to bring about development. We must therefore keep working toward the development of national, state, community or rural newspapers in developing nations in order to keep reaping from their demonstrated ability to contribute to the development of the developing nations. Further research on the role of the newspaper in rural and national development must, however, continue at all levels because there are still many unanswered questions on this issue.

REFERENCES

Abuoga, John, and Mutere, Absolom. 1988. *The History of the Press in Kenya* p. 2. Nairobi: The African Council for Communication Education.

Azikiwe, Nnamdi. 1964. Pioneer Heroes of the Nigerian Press. *West African Pilot*, June 3.

Basu, Aruns 1969. The Relationship of Farmers' Characteristics to the Adoption of Recommended Farm Practices in four villages of Western Nigeria. *Bulletin of Rural Economics and Sociology*, Vol. 1.

Beltran, Luis Ramiro. 1974. Rural Development and Social Communication: Relationships and Strategies. *Communication Strategies for Rural Development*: Proceedings of the Cornell-CIAT International Symposium, March 17–24, New York State College of Agriculture and Life Sciences, New York.

Blumler, Jay, and Katz, Elihu (eds.). 1974. *The Uses of Mass Communication*. Beverly Hills, Calif.: Sage Publications.

Bostian, L. R., and Oliviera, F.C. 1965. Relationship of Literacy and Education to Communication and to Social Conditions on Small Farms in Two Municipios of South Brazil. *Rural Sociological Society*, No. 3.

Carter, R. F., and Schramm, Wilbur. 1959. Scales for Describing National Communication Systems. Stanford: Institute for Communication Research (Mimeograph).

Coleman, J. S. 1960. *Nigeria: Background to Nationalism* 184–86. Berkeley and Los Angeles.

Dawodu, Monzor. 1991. Reported in Udofia, C. (ed. 1991). *African Journalism in Perspective* p. 178. Abak: Itiaba Publishers.

Dennis, Everett E. 1978. *The Mass Media Society* p. 5. Dubuque, Iowa: Wm. C. Brown Company.

Deutschman, P. J. and McNelly, J. T. 1964. Media Use and Socio-Economic Status in a Latin American Capital. *Michigan State University Series No. 3*. East Lansing.

Doob, Leonard W. 1965. Goebbel's Principles of Propaganda. In Katz D., et al, *Public Opinion and Propaganda*. New York: Holt, Reinhart and Winston.

Edeani, David. 1990. The Nigerian Press in a Depressed Economy. In Nwosu, Ikechukwu E. (ed.), *Mass Communication and National Development* 183–87. Aba: Frontier Publishers.

Emenyeonu, B. N. 1987. Communication and Adoption of Agricultural Innovation: Quantifications and Notes Towards a Conceptual Model. *Africa Media Review.* Vol 1, No. 2, p. 166.

Emery, Edwin, et al. 1973. *Introduction to Mass Communications* 173–74.

Ezera, Kalu. 1960. *Constitutional Development in Nigeria* 49–52. Cambridge: Longmans.

Farace, V. R. 1965. Mass Communication, Political Participation and Other National Characteristics: A Factor Analytical Investigation. Lincoln, Neb.

Frey, F. W. 1966. *The Mass Media and Rural Development in Turkey.* MIT Center for International Studies.

Goodfellow, Preston. 1958. Quoted in Mott, George. *New Survey of Journalism* 37. New York: Barnes and Noble.

Hachten, William. 1971. *Muffled Drums: The News Media in Africa* xv. Ames, Iowa: The Iowa State University Press.

Igwe, Dimgba. 1991. The importance of community Newspapers. In Udofia, C. (ed.), *African Journalism in Perspective* 175–84. Abak: Itiaba Publishers.

Inayatullah. 1967. Quoted in Hamdan bin Adnan et al (1985). The Nature of Development. In Clayton, V., and Simmons, J. (eds.), *Development Communication: A Resource Manual for Teaching,* Singapore: AMIC.

International Press Institute. 1971. *IPI Report,* April, p. 2.

Kabiro, Laban. 1985. Economic Viability of the Rural Press in Kenya. In Mutere, A. (ed.), *Workshop on Rural Journalism Report* 23–24. University of Nairobi.

Kasoma, Francis. 1987. *The Press in Zambia.* Lusaka: A Multimedia Publication.

Katz, E., and Lazarsfeld, P. (eds.), 1955. *Personal Influences: The Part Played by the People in the Flow of Mass Communication.* Glencoe, Ill.: The Free Press.

Lang, K., and Lang, G. 1959. The Mass Media and Voting. In Burdwick, E. J., and Brodbeck, A. J. (eds.), *American Voting Behavior.* New York: Free Press.

Lenin, V. I. 1929. *What is to be done?* New York: International Publishers.

Lerner, Daniel. 1958. *The Passing of the Traditional Society.* Glencoe, Ill.: The Free Press.

Lippmann, Walter. 1922. *Public Opinion.* New York: Harcourt Brace.

Matthew, T. S. 1959. *The Sugar Pill* 166. New York: Simon and Schuster.

Mbindyo, Joseph. 1985. A Study of the Rural Press in Kenya. Report of a study carried out on behalf of the UNESCO Regional Office for Communication in Africa, Nairobi, Kenya.

McAnany, Emile G. 1978. *Does Information Really Work. Journal of Communication,* Vol. 28, No. 1 (Winter).

————. 1973. *Radio's Role in Development: Five Strategies of Use.* Academy for Education Development: Washington, DC.

McNelly, John T. 1968. Perspectives of the Role of Mass Communication in the Development process. In David Berlo (ed.), *Mass Communication and the Development of Nations* 1. East Lansing. Michigan State University, International Communications Institute.

McQuail, Denis. 1987. *Mass Communication Theory.* London: Sage Publications.

Merrill, John C. 1974. *The Imperative of Freedom* 53. New York: Hastings House.

Moemeka, Andrew A. 1991. Perspective on Development Communication. *Module on Development Communication* 15–30. African Council on Communication Education. Nairobi.

————. 1988. Mass Media and Rational Domination: A Critical Review of a Dominant Paradigm. *African Media Review,* Vol. 3, No. 2, pp.1–33.

————. 1985. Communication in National Development: the Use of the Mass Media in Rural Development. *Informatologia Yugoslavica* 17 (1–2): 177–85. Zagreb.

————. 1981. *Local Radio: Community Education for Development.* Zaria: Ahmadu Bello University Press.

————. 1980. *Reporters Handbook.* Lagos: Department of Mass Communication Press.

Ngweno, Hilary. 1968. The role of the Press in a Developing Country. Paper presented at the IPI Assembly in Nairobi, Kenya, June 4.

Nkrumah, Kwame. 1965. *The African Journalist.* Dar es Salam: Tanzania Publishing House.

Nwosu, Ikechukwu E. 1991. Mass Media Policies in Africa. In Calix Udofia (ed.), *African Journalism in Perspective* 213. Abak: Itiaba Publishers.

―――. 1991. Planning and Implementing Media Campaigns in Africa. *Module on Development Communication* 45–54. Nairobi: African Council on Communication Education.

―――. 1990. Mass Media and Political Mobilization during Elections: Towards Improved Knowledge and Skills. *Nigerian Journal of Mass Communication*, Vol. 1, No. 1, pp. 30–44.

―――. 1987. An Overview of the Mass Media and the African Society. In Domatob, J. Jika, A., and Nwosu, I. (eds.), *Mass media and the African Society* 1–9. Nairobi: African Council for Communication Education.

―――. 1987. Mass Media Discipline and Control in Contemporary Nigeria: A Contextual Critical Analysis. *Gazette 39*: 17–29.

―――. 1986. Mobilizing People's Support for Development in Africa. *African Media Review*, Vol. 1, No. 1, PP. 46–65.

Olowu, T. A., and Igodan, I. 1989. Farmers' Media Use Pattern in Six Villages of Kwara State, Nigeria. *Rural Development in Nigeria*, Vol. 3, No. 2.

Omu, Fred I. A. 1978. *Press and Politics in Nigeria: 1880–1937*; pp. vii and 26. London: Longman Group Limited.

Omwanda, Lewis. 1990/91. Sources of Authoritarianism in the African News Media. *CAEJC Journal 3*: 24–40.

Orewere, Ben. 1991. Possible Publications of Modern Mass Media for Traditional Communication in a Nigerian Rural Setting. *Africa Media Review*, Vol 5, No. 3, pp. 53–65.

Oso, Lai, and Adebayo, Lanre. 1990. *Communication and Rural Development in Nigeria.* Abeokuta: Millenium Investments.

Press Institute of Bangladesh. 1980. A Study of Circulation, Income and Expenditure of Daily Newspapers in Dacca. *Media Asia*, Vol. 7, No. 2, p. 103.

Rao, L. Y. 1969. *Communication and Development: A Study of Two Indian Villages.* Minneapolis: University of Minnesota Press.

Rogers, E. M. 1978. Re-Invention During the Innovation Process, in Michael Radnor, et al (eds.), *The Diffusion of Innovations: An Assessment*, Evanston, Illinois, Northwestern University, Center for the Interdisciplinary Study of Science and Technology, Report to the National Science Foundation, C(N).

Rogers, Everett M. 1976. *Communication and Development: Critical Perspectives* Beverley Hills, Calif.: Sage Publications.

Root, Gus, et al. 1980. *Communication Planning at the Institutional Level.* Honolulu: East-West Communication Institute.

Rosario-Braid, F. 1979. A User-Oriented Communication Strategy. In Rosario-Braid, F. (ed.), *Communication Strategy for Productivity Improvement.* Tokyo: Asian Productivity Organization.

Shaw, Donald, and McCombs, Maxwell. 1978. *The Emergence of American Political Issues: The Agenda Setting function of the Press.* p. 1. St. Paul: West Publishing Co.

Siebert, F. Peterson, T., and Schramm, W. 1963. *Four Theories of the Press.* Urbana, Ill.: University of Illinois Press.

Sobowale, Idowu, and Sogbamu, M. 1984. Innovation Adoption Among Rural Fishermen in Lagos State, Nigeria. *African Communication Review*, Vol. 1, No. 4.

Soola, Ebenezer. 1988. Agricultural Communication and the African Non-Literate Farmer: The Nigerian Experience. *Africa Media Review*, Vol. 12, No. 3, pp. 75–91.

————. 1984. Communication Policy and National Planning: An Agenda for the 80s. *Rural Development in Nigeria*, Vol. 1, No. 2.

Thompson, Jato. 1988. Nigeria: Mushrooming Media. *New African.* London.

UNESCO. 1961. *Mass Media in Developing Countries.* Paris: UNESCO.

Wa-Thiongo, Ngugi. 1986. Quoted in Andrew Moemeka (1988). Mass media and Rational Domination: A Critical Review of a Dominant Paradigm. *Africa Media Review*, Vol. 3, No. 1, p. 28.

Wilhoit, Cleveland G., and Sup Auh. 1970. Coverage of Public Opinion Polls. *Journalism Quarterly*, Winter.

ANDREW A. MOEMEKA[1]

7

Radio Strategies for Community Development: A Critical Analysis

We take it for granted that the reader is already aware that the concept "community" can be 'correctly' defined in various ways. Basically, it stands for groupings of people, but such groupings are of many types and can be categorized in terms of common interest—the Jesuits, the Quakers, the Critical Theorists; of common ancestry—the Irish, the Eskimos, African Americans; of humanity—society as a whole; or of political or social boundary—a group of people living in the same locality and under the same government. Our concern here is with "community" as defined in the last example, but with particular reference to localities that are development-starved or underprivileged, whether in the developed or in the developing world. The thesis is that such communities need education in order to develop. By education here is meant the creation of an environment in which awareness is at its height, aspirations are rationally raised, and willingness to work hard enough to "progress" becomes the rule rather than the exception

(Moemeka, 1981:9). This is education not for examination and certificates, but for existence and certitude. Education seen in this light finds support in Hickey et al's (1969) definition of community education as:

> A process that concerns itself with everything that affects the well-being of all citizens within a given community (extending its role) from one of the traditional concept of teaching children to one of identifying the needs, problems and wants of the community and then assisting in the development of facilities, programs, staff and leadership towards the end of improving the entire community.

While this type of education can be successfully carried out within communities through face-to-face communication, the pace of success and expansion of activities are generally faster if mass media communication is added. Even though it is held that interpersonal communication generally is considered more effective in inducing attitude and behavior changes, it is also true that two media are better than one in achieving desired objectives (Rogers et al, 1977: 363, Yu, 1977). This is particularly true of the combination of interpersonal and mass media communication. unfortunately, the tendency, especially in the developing world, has been to use one or the other. What follows is a critical explanation of the different ways in which the radio has been used in community education for development.

Since the 1960s, UNESCO has been stressing the importance of radio broadcasting in community education, especially in the rural and/or slum areas of developing societies. The organization's faith in radio is based on that medium's unique characteristics. It is cheap to purchase, and therefore is the one mass medium with which the rural and slum communities are familiar it is versatile in utilization; and anyone—literate or illiterate—can learn from it. After a series of research on the use of the medium in community education, UNESCO (1968) was able to say:

> In the past few years, much attention has been given to the problems of adult education in the rural areas, and to experiments which have proved on several occasions that radio broadcasting, when skilfully used, can be a most effective medium of communication and education in such areas.

The part which radio plays in the transmission of information and culture is generally beyond question. The general impression is that the basic role of the radio (and other mass media) is to survey the environment, collect stories about everyday occurrences, transform them into news and information, and transmit these back to society through dissemination. Underlying the performance of this role is the belief that radio, as well as other media of mass communication, has the power to fully control our behavior. Hence, Sproule (1989) is convinced that the hypodermic needle theory is still largely the underlying basis of the use of mass media communication.

Much as the role of radio in information and news dissemination is seen as a given; its role in the field of education is, on the face of it, not quite evident. It seems paradoxical to talk of educational broadcasting because "education" by its very nature implies exchange of ideas and dialogue or communication, while broadcasting usually involves a monologue—a *talking to* rather than a *talking with*. Broadcasting is addressed to a very widely dispersed and heterogeneous audience whose members are generally unknown (an insignificant part of the audience may sometimes be just barely known). These characteristics of radio, which are very enhancing in the task of information dissemination, are a hindrance in radio's role in education or communication. The implication, therefore, is that in order to make the medium suitable for education and communication, conditions must be created which will enable it to become a channel for dialogue. This means that it must be changed from a mere information-disseminating medium to an educational medium in order to make it an effective instrument in the task of community education, which is the first step toward ensuring community development.

Radio's effectiveness depends, however, not only on its intrinsic qualities but more importantly on how it is used and for what purposes. Any use of radio as an educational medium should be based on the effects that radio is expected to have on the listening audiences, on the level of target-audience participation, on the structure of reception possible, and on the amount of learning and social change that is desired or likely to occur. The success of radio as a medium for education and communication will therefore depend upon adequate clarification and understanding of these preconditions and the assumptions of the various radio utilization strategies, so that a country's needs are fitted to appropriate uses of radio.

RADIO STRATEGIES

These are concrete plans of action in terms of infrastructural and operational arrangements for using radio broadcasting in the task of educating communities for development. These plans generally are about what activities to perform, by whom, with what resources (human and physical), at what time, in which place, at what pace, in what order, and how. They are models for action expected to yield the greatest possible benefit for the community and, subsequently, for the nation.

Five strategies of utilization of radio in rural education and development have been identified (McAnany, 1973). One or the other of these strategies or a combination of them, has been used in different parts of the world, more especially in the developing countries. Their levels of successes or failures have been determined mostly by the presence or absence of the preconditions mentioned above.

Open Broadcasting

Open broadcasting is the strategy in which broadcast messages are directed to an unorganized audience. It is based on the assumption that a "good" and relevant message is capable of being accepted by the individual on his/her own. According to Gunter and Theroux (1977), open broadcast strategy enables more people to have access to information and vicarious education. It is a strategy in which, in addition to programs such as talks, features, and music, a small core of educational programs (usually in local languages) on health, agriculture, family life, sanitation, and child-care, among others, are broadcast. Because of the unorganized nature of the audience, there is always doubt as to whether the people are listening and, if they are, whether they are benefiting from the programs.

In Mexico (Arana, 1971) and the Philippines (Spain, 1971), it was found that even though the radio stations carried information relevant to literacy, civic responsibilities, farming, and health, the surveyed audience knew very little about these issues. They preferred listening to news, drama, and music. In Nigeria (Moemeka, 1972), one of the findings of a survey in rural Lagos of the audience for programs relevant to rural improvement was that more than seventy percent of the listeners were educated young men and women, brought up away from their rural homelands, who saw the programs as "good education in the reverse," that is, for learning later in life what they would have learned as children had they been brought up in their rural villages. They were not part of the audience of rural Lagos for whom the programs were meant. Again, in Lagos (Moemeka, 1988), a federal government-sponsored radio campaign on AIDS prevention barely succeeded in achieving any result beyond confirming widespread knowledge of AIDS as a deadly disease. Very few respondents appreciated the fact that AIDS was incurable; still fewer had taken any preventive measures.

Open broadcast strategy is bedeviled by all the problems that affect the use of radio for the education of the rural population and in community development efforts. First, there is no interaction between producers and consumers before programs are planned, produced, and broadcast. Production is usually based on the vague notion that the people would accept as relevant the studio-decided content of the program. Second, these programs are conceived in the studio, with very little or no consultation with specialist agencies, and virtually no coordination between them and the communication specialists. The result always is that such programs are generally based on perceived or assumed knowledge both of the subject matter and of the sociocultural and environmental conditions of the audience. Third, and perhaps most importantly, is the fact that there is no guidance at the reception end. It is in the open broadcast strategy that a shot-in-the-dark approach to programming is most pronounced. This approach leaves the target audience forgotten while programs are being planned; remembered just before the programs go on the air; and forgotten again as soon as the programs have been broadcast. When this shortcoming is added to the lack of consultation and coordination between broadcasters and education and development agencies, and the lack of interaction between producers and the consumers of the programs, it becomes difficult not to conclude that the best one can expect from the strategy is chance success. This, of course, is not an expectation on which a true rural community emancipation program should be predicated.

Instructional Radio

Instructional radio is the second strategy for using radio broadcasting for social change and development. Instructional radio is directed at an organized learning group, with someone able to supervise and direct as well as elicit feedback. This is the strategy used in Tanzania (Greenholm, 1975; Dodds, 1972) to teach practical skills and cooperative and civic responsibility to rural communities. It is known as Radio Study Group in that country. In Nigeria, it is known as Schools Broadcast. Using the strategy requires much more than mere broadcasting. It requires a structure for organizing listening and learning practices, provision of support materials, presence of monitors or teachers, and some kind of assessment. A very important aspect of the strategy is that reception infrastructure is an integral part of its process.

Instructional radio operates on the principle of cooperation and guided listening. There is usually cooperation between broadcasters and educationists. For example, most educational programs in Nigeria are written by teachers in the field. Because of the demand for guided listening, some captive audience is assured, and if the programs are sufficiently appealing and relevant to audience situations, one can expect favorable reaction—both attitudinal and behavioral. Where audience reactions are recorded (as was the case in the Tanzanian projects), such reactions may well serve as signposts to guide future programming.

The extent to which this strategy can be used on a wide scale is doubtful, because of its strong demands on factors like finance, transport, and personnel. Tanzania has been able to operate the strategy fairly successfully because, first, it is a relatively compact country, and secondly, and perhaps more importantly, the government places a very high priority on rural community education. Nigeria's experience in using this strategy (for formal education) has not been encouraging. For example, in a study of the use of the strategy in Lagos (Dare et al, 1973), it was found that an overwhelming majority of teachers (92%) do not use the broadcasts; 53% of students do not listen to them; and of those who do listen, less than 30% classified the broadcasts as "helpful." If the situation is bad in Lagos schools, then it cannot be any better in schools in rural areas which have the additional disadvantages of shortage of radio sets and distortions of radio signals caused by distance. And if the effect of the strategy can be so minimal in formal education, it is doubtful that it can be any greater in nonformal learning situations. Because instructional radio has mainly been used (except in Tanzania) for formal education, there appears to be a tacit understanding that it is not very appropriate for the nonformal, "soft-hammer-blow" type of education required for community development.

Rural Radio Forum

The rural radio forum is the strategy for using radio with discussion and decision for rural groups. It involves the presentation of regular weekly fifteen- to thirty-minute radio programs of a mixed nature to rural audiences formed into listening groups. Such programs usually contain news, answers to listeners' questions, family advice, a talk, discussions, etc. The groups listen and discuss under the guidance of a group leader, and make decisions on the points of discussion. The strategy makes extensive use of audience reaction, where available, for subsequent programs. Because of this, there is usually a temptation for broadcasters to work on their own without cooperation with other change agents in the rural communities. However, the sense of involvement which this strategy engenders in the rural communities as a result of its demand for some action-decision by the group is a great asset in development effort .

The forum strategy has a number of advantages. First, the follow-up of a radio message with localized discussion and decision ensures positive commitment to agreed-upon decisions and subsequently to social change. "The combination of a message carried to many groups by a mass medium like radio, then localized by discussion in small groups and guided to a group decision conforms closely to existing theories of communication and social change" (McAnany, 1973:10). Secondly, membership in the group helps to expose the participants to information important to the rural communities, and this turns such individuals into opinion leaders whose views would tend to be respected in the community. This is one aspect of the radiation effect of rural radio (Moemeka, 1987), that is, the effect of rural radio on nonparticipants as a result of the impact of forum participants—an effect which leads to changes in attitudes, behaviors, and practices. Thirdly, forums do send back reports and messages, thus providing the vital feedback which is often missing in mass media activities. And finally, the forum strategy is based on the conviction that rural community development must essentially be the duty of the rural people themselves and should not be dropped on them from above. The built-in localized discussions and decisions ensure that the people are put in a position in which they can be the subject and object of their own development.

The forum strategy also has weaknesses. There are certain obstacles in the way of successful use of this strategy. First, there is strong need for a network of supervisors, so that forums can be in contact with project leadership and do not have to depend entirely on written reports for asking questions and getting help. Unfortunately, this desired situation does not always obtain; supervisors or change agents—the most important factors in adoption of innovations (Rogers et al, 1970)—are always in short supply. Secondly, production centers are usually far away from most of the village groups, and so cannot always benefit from contact with forums to get the feedback which is a vital factor in program content improvement.

Summing up his observations of the Indian Radio Rural Forum, Schramm (1967) said: "Forums may have been made up of people in villages who were least likely to need them (that is, the local elite); programs needed more localness (decentralizing the programming activities); adequate materials to follow up on innovations were often lacking to villagers; more involvement by the development officers with the field experience was called for (network of supervisors to keep personal contact)." These missing links have greatly affected the successful utilization of rural radio forums. In other words, this strategy will be successful if all rural people, not just the local elite, are involved; if radio stations are near enough to the communities and program contents are relevant and fully localized; if adequate and prompt actions are taken to provide materials to implement new projects and follow up on implemented innovations; and if there are sufficient development agents around to supply the intimacy and encouragement of personal contact.

Radio Schools

Radio schools is the most widespread strategy for using radio for rural community education in Latin America. It originated in Sutatenza, Colombia, and it has now permeated the life of the rural population of that country. The "schools" are small, organized (mainly illiterate adults), listening/learning groups meeting in houses or in churches under a guide. The basic aim of this strategy is to offer fundamental, integral education which goes beyond mere reading, writing, and cognitive skills and tries to change the passive and dependent attitude of the people, creating a deepening of their sense of dignity and self-worth, and turning them into "new men and women."

An organization mostly associated with this strategy is Colombia's Accion Cultural Popular (ACPO)—a private organization which at present has the most powerful radio transmitter in that country. ACPO also has stations all over the country, including some one-kilowatt transmitter stations in some areas. Although radio is the most important medium used, it is, by no means, the only one. The radio schools approach is basically multi-media, employing at least radio and printed booklets almost everywhere, but also frequently adding newspapers, charts, booklets for reading, film strips, and actual teaching/learning methods. The schools are based on the principle of homophily, so that group members do not only know one another, but largely have identical perceptions of the world and their own environment. Field organization usually exists in the form of a supervisor who tries to coordinate activities, distribute materials, and visit groups from time to time in order to encourage them.

Like the forum strategy, radio schools has its own strengths and weaknesses. As typified by ACPO, this strategy has been successful in arousing the rural people to action. This is precisely because its orientation and identity is with the rural population and its problems. The schools foster greater knowledge of the real needs of rural areas by having a significant number of rural leaders in the organization of its activities, ensuring real contact of policymakers with the rural people and with their problems, and enabling functional feedback to flow from the audiences. Secondly, the radio schools are basically listening/learning groups. This means that the advantages of group listening and of local monitors and supervisors also accrue to this strategy. The solidarity of the group encourages perseverance in pursuing group goals, while visits from supervisors create a sense of identity. Perhaps the one peculiar aspect of this strategy as operated by ACPO is the fact that the activities are a continuing process—a factor which makes radio and the schools part of the everyday life of the people.

There are certain weaknesses, however. ACPO'S efforts are almost entirely directed to literacy and basic education, in spite of the professed "integral education" ideal of the strategy. This leaves out almost completely the political, social, and physical developmental aspects of rural problems. Because of this cautious stand on the part of the radio schools to engage in mobilizing the people toward community action, merely because it is political, there is no collaboration between them and rural change programs of a more developmental nature. This is "action in isolation," which does not foster concerted efforts toward total development.

Radio and Animation

Radio and animation, also known as the radio participating group, is a strategy which aims at promoting among local communities a trained cadre of decision leaders. It is used to train leaders whose role is to promote, in a nondirective way, a dialogue in which community members participate in defining their development problems, putting them in a larger social context and working out ways of mobilizing their people to take a common action to overcome these problems. The strategy places emphasis on radio *defining*, but not *suggesting*, solutions to the people's problems. Programs are made from recorded views and responses about a definite problem presented by some members of the listening public. The participating groups then listen to these responses and views and discuss the problem further, thus creating avenues for further responses from the public, and subsequently eliciting some decisions.

The assumption of this strategy can be put into five statements:

- there are no solutions to problems that are imposed on local communities from the outside; local communities must first arrive at the problem definition and then its solution on their own.
- the social animator is to be as closely identified with the local community as possible.
- he/she is to be nondirective in his/her approach.
- information's chief role in this approach is to help define the problem and not give the solutions.
- community participation and social action is the goal, and therefore feedback from the community is an essential means.

The strategy which developed from the French government's action toward rural development in its former West African territories has been used in Senegal, Benin, Togo, and Niger. It started in Niger in 1963. The primary objective of the radio broadcasts and discussions here, as in the other countries, was to foster awareness of national development plans in terms of local problems, and not to provide information on a problem defined by the experts from the outside. In Senegal, the strategy was directed at inculcating new farming methods, diversifying agriculture and improving the administration and management of cooperatives. The Senegalese project known as Radio Educative Rurale was a cooperative venture between the Ministry of Information and Tourism, which is in charge of broadcasting, and all other ministries that have any responsibility for the rural population. Of particular importance in the Senegalese attempt was that feedback was an essential ingredient of the broadcasts. The opinions, actions, and expectations of the people formed the content of the programs.

The animation strategy, in spite of its enhancing strengths, also has its weaknesses. First, to place the burden of taking initiative on the local people assumes that local control and local leadership will be forthcoming. This, however, has not easily happened in the many places where the strategy has been used. Many communities are slow to get themselves organized, and many more are not able to organize at all. There is, therefore, the temptation to try to organize them from the outside, if any positive action is to be taken. Secondly, the idea behind this strategy's local-participation principle is that people will feel that they are the ones developing themselves. But localizing development effort is not controlling that effort. There is the danger that the people may be manipulated in their sense of participating in the development of their community, and merely be given the opportunity to criticize and complain as a safety valve to forestall rural unrest, while no real policy changes may result from the local participation. The fact that this strategy has not produced significant results in the African countries where it has been used confirms this fear.

A final problem facing radio and animation strategy, just as other strategies, is the conflict between mass message and local peculiarities. Localities in the rural areas are not completely homogeneous; each local area has specific problems which can be solved better when viewed with its social, economic, and political environments in context. It is therefore not possible to satisfy every locality from a central point. This is the problem of relevance and appropriateness which local radio systems can help to ameliorate.

THE APPROPRIATE STRATEGY

All five strategies discussed above have been tried with some measure of success in different parts of the world. In Nigeria, two strategies—the open broadcast and the instructional radio—are used. The former is used for rural information and education, and the latter for formal education. The Nigerian languages section of broadcasting organizations in the country use the open broadcast strategy for their nonformal education activities. But the strategy is not succeeding because it is too disorganized for any purposeful and mass education of the rural population. Programs are planned and produced in the broadcasting houses with little or no consultation with other development agencies, and without research to find out the best way to get to the heart of the problems of rural communities. There is no interaction between the people and the broadcasting houses because these broadcasting houses are generally too far away from the people and their communities. At the reception end, there is no direction as to how to make good use of the programs being broadcast—no structure providing a conducive atmosphere for discussions and group decision-taking. The community spirit of the Nigerian rural inhabitants is not brought into play, despite the fact that it is realized all over the country that individual action, especially where long entrenched values and behaviors are concerned, is very hard to come by in the rural areas. The result is that few rural people listen to these programs, and even these do so without any intention of accepting the message content.

Instructional radio, the other strategy used in Nigeria, is too formalized and structured along the line of the teaching/learning process to be of much use in rural community education. The rural adult does not want to be a receptacle for the knowledge of "strangers" who have failed to recognize his/her own type of knowledge. He/she needs to be taken into confidence before he/she can grant his/her attention. Furthermore, if instructional radio, that is, Schools Broadcast in Nigeria, has not proved appreciably effective in formal education, it would amount to wishful thinking to believe that it can succeed in the persuasive context in which rural community education should be carried out.

The other three strategies—rural radio forum,radio schools, and radio and animation—would appear to approach what one may propose as the ideal strategy. But each, as now utilized, has some unnecessary self-imposed limitations. The rural radio forum strategy concentrates almost entirely on the identification of, and discussions and decisions on, local problems. As a result, it tends to attract those who least need arousal and development consciousness, that is, the local elite. Change agents are known to be mostly associated with such local elite, leaving out those for whom rural education is imperative for purposes of personal and community development, that is, the uninformed and the apathetic. It is true that rural forums can help in rural transformation, but unless the marginal rural people are brought in to play actively positive roles, the transformation will benefit only the few who are already better off than the majority.

The radio schools strategy focuses primarily on illiterate rural adults, and almost all effort is directed to literacy and basic education, in spite of the professed aim of providing fundamental, integral education. To do only this is to tackle only one aspect of the problems of rural development. Even though the marginal illiterate is the most affected by rural underdevelopment, others within the rural social milieu are also affected. In addition, education to create a "new human being" that does not lead to actions of a physical developmental nature is not likely to bring about change. It is noteworthy that ACPO, the main user of this strategy, has come to realize this fact and now has programs designed to stimulate action toward self- and community help.

The radio and animation strategy places an almost exclusive emphasis on local initiative in identifying problems and finding solutions to them. This approach assumed a strong latent capacity within the rural population which only needs to be tickled in order to go into action. But it is only in very self-conscious communities that this capacity and willingness obtain. Most others have to be motivated from outside, and continuously reinforced if any improvements are to occur. The emphasis on voluntarism may mean that many communities will, if not given direction, remain where they are. Such communities need more than sermonizing on local initiative.

THE IDEAL STRATEGY

The ideal strategy, one may venture to suggest, should be one which combines the involvement (consequent upon local group discussions and decisions) of the rural radio forum, the literacy/basic education of the radio schools, and the local initiative of the radio and animation approaches. This is because rural community education and development spans the whole range of the specific areas treated in isolation by each of these strategies. The people have to be motivated to identify their problems; they have to be led to discuss these problems and to take action decisions on them; and they have to be taught the techniques of reading and writing. All these are necessary to "create the new human being" without whom community development would be impossible. This strategy, which we have called "Local Radio Strategy" (Moemeka, 1981) should aim at improving the lot of the rural people in their totality—make them literate, widen their horizons, raise their aspirations realistically, point to their problems, create in them the willingness to find solutions to these problems and imbue them with a sense of dignity and self-worth.

The point about literacy is particularly important. Radio alone cannot completely handle the task of changing the rural man/woman into a development resource, and rural communities into substantially productive components of the nation. To ensure some good measure of success, and a long-term effect, there must be some accompanying written materials to drive home the points made on radio and to refer back to from time to time. The use of such study follow-up materials would require the employment of interpreters, unless the people have acquired the ability to read and write intelligibly enough to comprehend written communication. However, literacy should not be the prerequisite for rural community education and development. It should, instead, be the outcome of increased awareness and the thirst for more knowledge that are bound to follow effective rural educational campaigns.

This ideal strategy—the local radio strategy—combines the qualities of the rural radio forum, the radio schools, and the radio and animation strategies. It utilizes their inherent and operational advantages and strengthens its position by eliminating their detected deficiencies. Two of the most conspicuous deficiencies are the spatial gap between production centers and the consuming rural audiences, and the general nature of program contents which treats only marginally issues of concern to many areas. If, therefore, the new strategy is to have a better chance of success, there is a strong need for proximity of radio stations to the rural audiences, and for localization of program materials. This is saying, in effect, that the new strategy should be based on a local radio broadcasting system, and this means decentralization of broadcasting infrastructure and delegation of powers concerned with programming and content materials to the local station working in close collaboration with the rural community.

Waniewicz (1972) suggested four different models of coordination and cooperation in using radio for education and development. All four models emphasize the need for research (entering the sociocultural context of the people), a broad-based advisory council, and a utilization service department in addition to a programs department. Moemeka (1981: 93), using elements from these models, proposed a structure of Local Radio Strategy for Community Development which calls for, among other things, local radio advisory councils with representatives from government departments and voluntary agencies that have responsibility to the community, and representatives of the community and of the broadcasting organization. The council is meant to guide the station in its work, ensuring that program content and the contexts under which the programs are presented are relevant to the community's needs and expectations.

As research has shown (Katz, Blumler and Gurevitch, 1974), the relevance of mass media content to listener's needs and aspirations is a determining factor in media message effectiveness. To achieve this relevance, not only must media personnel enter into the sociocultural contexts of the people but media infrastructure must also be near enough to enable the people to actively participate in media activities (Moemeka, 1981). A further important factor in achieving relevance in content is working with other agencies involved in the attempt to improve the living conditions of the people. Community education and development involve the work of many agencies, e.g. health, social welfare, education, local government and various voluntary organizations. A coordinated approach toward relevantly educating the community for development requires concrete collaboration among all these agencies and between them and broadcasting.

To be meaningful to rural communities, such collaboration must obtain within the communities to enable the people to be part of the process. Local radio strategy appears to be the most appropriate route to reaching these goals. As Schramm (1964) rightly points out, local media are of great importance in social and economic development not only because they are in a better position to know and serve the particular needs of local areas, but also because they make it easier for more people to have access to the media and therefore to take part in public (community) affairs. The greater the number of people that actively participate, the broader the base of community decision-making, and the greater the chances of individual commitment to the community's collective decisions. It is this individual commitment to community objective which gives expression to the aims of community education as summarized by Faure et al (1972) as:

The complete fulfilment of man in all the richness of his personality, the variety of his forms of expression and his various commitment as an individual, as a member of a family and of a community, citizen and producer, inventor of techniques and creative dreamer.

NOTE

1. This is an updated version of an original (shorter) article first published in *Media Development*, Vol. XXX, March, 1983.

REFERENCES

Arana, E. 1971. Informe sobre la influencia que la radio ejerce en una comunidad indigena. Xoxcotle, Morelos; Friedrich Ebert Foundation Seminar on Rural Radio, Mexico. (Memeo).

Dare, O., et al. 1973. Consumption of Schools Broadcast in Secondary Schools in Lagos. Sessional Project Essay, Department of Mass Communication, University of Lagos.

Dodds, T. 1972. *Multi-Media Approach to Rural Education: Case Studies.* Insternational Extension College, Broadsheet on Distance Learning, No. 1. London.

Faure, E., et al 1972. Learning to be: The World of Education Today and Tomorrow, UNESCO: Paris.

Greenholm, L. 1975. *Radio Study Group Campaigns in the United Republic of Tanzania.* Paris: UNESCO.

Gunter, J., and Theroux, J. 1977. Open Broadcast Education Radio: Three Paradigms. In Rogers et al (eds.), *Radio for Education and Development: Case Studies* Vol. 1. Washington, D.C.: World Bank.

Hickey, H., et al. 1969. *The Role of the School in Community Education.* p. 36. Midland, Mich. See also C. LeTarte and J. Minzey. 1975. *Community Education: From Program to Process*, p. 17. Midland, Mich.

Katz, E., Blumer, J., and Gurevitch, M. 1974. Uses of Mass Communication by the Individual. in W. P. Davidson and F. Yu (ed.), *Mass communication Research: Major Issues and Future Directions.* New York: Praeger.

McAnany, E. 1973. *Radio's Role in Development: Five Strategies of Use.* Information Center for Instructional Technology, Washington, D.C.

Moemeka, A. A. 1988. The AIDS Epidemic: The Impact of Mass Communicated Prevention Messages. A Paper presented at the Federal Ministry of Information Seminar on AIDS Prevention, Institute of International Affairs, Lagos.

————. 1987. *Rural Radio Broadcasting and Community Health Practices: A Case-Study of Radio O-Y-O in Nigeria.* Ph.D. Dissertation, State University of New York, Albany.

————. 1981. *Local Radio: Community Education for Development.* Ahmadu Bello University Press.

————. 1972. Nigerian Broadcasting Corporation's Igbo Languages Program: Audience, Preferences, Involvement and Benefits in Lagos. Unpublished B.A. degree Essay. University of Lagos.

Rogers, E. M., et al. 1977. Radio Forums: A Strategy for Rural Development. In *Radio for Education and Development: Case Studies*, Vol. II. World Bank, Working Paper No. 266. Washington, D.C.

Schramm, W. 1967. Ten Years of the Radio Forum in India. In *New Education Media in Action: Case Studies for Planners*, Vol. 1 Paris: UNESCO.

————. 1964. *Mass Media in National Development: The Role of Information in Developing Countries.* Stanford University Press.

Spain, P. 1971. Survey of Radio Listenership in the Davao Province of Mindanao, the Philippines. Unpublished Report. Stanford University.

Sproule, J. 1989. Progressive propaganda critics and the magic bullet myth. *Critical Studies in Mass Communication* 6: 225–46.

UNESCO. 1968. *Reports and Papers in Mass Communication*, No. 51, p. 3. Paris.

Waniewicz, I. 1972. *Broadcasting for Adult Education: A Guide-book to Worldwide Experience.* Paris: UNESCO.

Yu, F. T. C. 1977. Communication Planning and Policy for Development: Some Research Notes. In Lerner and Nelson (eds.), *Communication Research: A Half-Century Appraisal* Honolulu: The University Press of Hawaii. 185.

Part III

DONALD P. CUSHMAN
SARAH S. KING

8

High-Speed Management, Organizational Communication, Multinational Corporations, and Host-Country Development

If economic development is understood as a sustainable increase in the material, educational, and physical well-being of a nation and its citizens (World Bank, 1991), then all nations and their people have a vested interest in economic development. However, despite the remarkable gains in political freedom and technological development witnessed over the past ten years, over one billion people, or one-fifth of the world's population, live in nations where the average annual income is declining and live on less than one dollar per day. Conversely, another one billion people live in nations in which the average annual income has doubled or tripled in the past ten years, giving them access to a sustainable increase in material, educational, and physical well-being (World Bank, 1991).

In those nations where significant economic development has taken place, the engine driving rapid economic development has been a new alliance between national governments and private sector multinational organizations, and their participation in trade within global competitive markets, which have led to the effective allocation of a nation's economic and natural resources. At the center of this new allocation process is the privatization of a nation's agricultural, manufacturing, and service industries; the transfer of advanced technology by multinational corporations from one country to another; and the creation by national governments of a favorable economic climate for entering into world trade, thus allowing the competitive market to allocate a nation's economic and natural resources.

Concurrently, at the center of this allocation process is the creation of private-sector organizations which, through high-speed management and new effective organizational communication processes generate continuous organizational improvement programs which in turn stimulate and sustain economic development. It is in this creation and maintenance of world class private-sector organizations within the agricultural, manufacturing, and service sectors of the world economy that effective allocation of a nation's economic and natural resources occurs in such a manner as to create sustainable economic development (Cushman and King, 1992).

It will be the purpose of this paper to explore (1) the critical forces in the global economic environment which create the opportunity for economic development, (2) three separate models for capitalizing on these economic opportunities, (3) the unique role high-speed management and the effective use of organizational communication play in developing continuous organizational improvement programs, and (4) some examples of their use in sustaining organizational and national economic development.

THE CRITICAL FORCES FAVORING RAPID
ECONOMIC DEVELOPMENT

According to the *World Development Report.*

Economic history shows that it is possible for countries to develop rapidly and indeed for many countries the pace of change has accelerated. It shows at the same time that many countries have developed very slowly, if at all. The key to development, clearly, is to understand why the range of experience has been so wide (World Bank, 1991:12).

Three economic forces have become apparent in the accelerated process of economic development over the past fifty years. In this development process we have witnessed a dramatic shrinkage in the time required for substantial change to take place in a nation's quality of life—from sixty years for Great Britain in the 1780s to ten years for many nations in the 1980s (World Bank, 1991:13). Three factors have accelerated this economic change process.

First, over the past forty years, the *growth* in world trade has increased three times as fast as the growth in the world's gross domestic product. International exports and imports were about one-fifth the world GNP in 1962, one-fourth in 1972, and one-third in 1982, and are projected to approach one-half the world GNP in 1992 (*Wall Street Journal*, Sept. 21, 1990). Thus rapid economic growth is tied directly to a nation's effective participation in this growth in world trade (World Bank, 1991:21).

Second, over the past forty years, a single model of governmental economic policy has emerged for all nations who wish to participate in this increase in world trade (*Economist, Jan. 4, 1992:15*). The generalization of such a model does not imply that all governments or all economies are alike; it merely suggests broad central tendencies in the economic policies of most nations as they begin to participate in the global economy. This model includes seven general features—(1) control of inflation through fiscal austerity and monetary restrictions; (2) reduction of labor costs as a percentage of product cost; (3) increased productivity and profitability through the effective use of information and communication technology; (4) restructuring of industrial and service sector by disinvesting from low profit areas and investing in high growth, high profit areas; (5) privatization and deregulation of some aspects of the economy by withdrawing from state ownership and control in favor of open market forces; (6) relative control over the pricing of raw materials and energy assuring the stability of pricing systems and exchange flows; and (7) opening up gradually to world markets and increased internationalization of economies (Castells, 1986; Macrae, 1991).

As Castells (1986:300) argues:

Such a model is not necessarily linked to a particular political party or administration, or even to a country, even though the

Reagan or Thatcher governments seem to be the closest examples of the fulfillment of these policies. But very similar policies have developed in most West European countries, in those governed by Socialists, and even in Communist-led regions (in Italy) or Communist-participating governments (France, for a certain period). At the same time, in most Third World countries, austerity policies, inspired or dictated by the International Monetary Fund and other world financial institutions, have also developed along the same lines, establishing not without contradictions and conflicts (Walton, 1985) a new economic logic that is not only capitalistic but a very specific kind of capitalism.

Third, technological progress, more than any other single factor, has fueled this economic advance in trade. Innovation has provided great strides in the growth of organizations. In the global marketplace organizations, irrespective of their country of origin, have tended to converge with respect to worker performance and product quality, user friendliness, and serviceability. Failure to achieve world class production standards normally leads to economic decline from a lack of competitiveness (World Bank 1991:13).

The great catalyst for the diffusion of world class technology and organizational performance standards (world class benchmarking) has been the multinational organization. Toyota, GE, and ABB each have branches of their organization in over 250 countries throughout the world. In each of those units, workers from different cultures adjust their cultural traditions in order to hold jobs which require that they modify their traditional values in ways that allow them to reach world class performance levels or else suffer the economic consequences involved. In economic development the adjustment of technology to cultural biases or the use of appropriate technology has given way to the adjustment of local culture to world class technology and performance standards or world class benchmarking (Pollack, 1992:1A).

THE EMERGENCE OF THREE SEPARATE MODELS FOR CAPITALIZING ON THESE ECONOMIC OPPORTUNITIES

Within the emerging global economy, comparative advantage is shifting toward those regions of the world with (1) a large core market, (2) a strong scientific and technological workforce, and (3) a private and public economic sector which can attract the capital necessary to provide the infrastructure needed for increased growth and development. Three such economic trading blocks or zones have begun to emerge, each with its own unique model for economic development. The first is the American Free Trade Zone consisting of the United States, Canada, and soon Mexico forming a free trade zone and core market of some 280 million people with a combined GDP of 6.2 trillion dollars. The second is the European Economic Community made up of Great Britain, Ireland, Spain, Portugal, France, Italy, Greece, Germany, Luxembourg, Belgium, Denmark, and the Netherlands forming a free trade zone and core market of some 360 million people with a combined GDP of 5.5 trillion dollars. The third is the Asian Development Corridor made up of Japan, Singapore, Thailand, Indonesia, Malaysia, and the Philippines, a trade zone and core market of 250 million people with a combined GDP of 4.2 trillion dollars.

Each of these core markets has developed its own unique model of the appropriate relationship between government, private sector organizations, and the competitive marketplace aimed at ensuring rapid economic development for its own nations and home-based multinational organizations. In the American Free Trade Zone the government encourages all-out open competition in most economic areas, with the government regulating enterprise size in order to maintain competition, and employing select trade barriers to prevent dumping and the diffusion of technology critical to national defense. The paradigm multinational corporation is GE, a conglomerate aimed at being number 1 or 2 in market shares in each of its product areas. In the European Economic Community the national government provides subsidies and gives tax breaks to critical private sector organizations, forces the combination of multinational organizations by industries, and limits non-EEC members participation in the core market by quotas, government purchasing patterns, and regulations preventing dumping, inspection, and contract entry. The paradigm multinational organizations are Air Bus and the Bull cartels which control the airline and computer industries in the EEC. In the Asian Development Corridor the Minister of International Trade and Industry in Japan makes available over 16 billion dollars in funds for infrastructure development for countries in the region, which allows MITI to assist its government in coordinating economic development among the nations involved. MITI also provides technical assistance, loans, and tailored trade agreements between Japan and these nations. The paradigm multinational corporation in the region is the Japanese kieretsu (large industrial grouping) like Mitsubishi (Rapoport, 1991).

What has been the effect of the emergence of these core markets on the allocation of economic and natural resources for national development through world trade? How do these core markets influence the international division of labor? Who develops? Who does not and why?

First, the group of countries located in core markets, with large scientific and technological bases and a private sector with the ability to attract capital includes the United States, Canada, Mexico, Japan, Thailand, Indonesia Malaysia, and the European Economic Community. These countries will experience relatively steady economic growth with a rebirth of production facilities within their boundaries. Further advances in information technology and an increased diffusion of existing technology will substantially increase the quality of life of their citizens.

Second, the group of countries consisting of Australia and the nonmembers of the EEC located in Western Europe have small populations, modest scientific and technical bases, and modest capital accumulation potential. The fortunes of these countries will be tied closely to the core market areas they service. Their growth will be erratic as they benefit from upswings in the core markets, but suffer unduly from downswings. Such swings will significantly slow the rate of diffusion of information technology and the corresponding increase in the quality of life they offer.

Third, the group of countries including the newly industrialized nations of South Korea, Taiwan, Hong Kong, and Singapore have medium sized population bases which collectively could become a new core market, a modest and increasing scientific and technological base, and governments which are capable of significant capital accumulation. These nations will become more and more tied to the core markets they service with some production shifting offshore, automation at home, and a growing need to invest heavily in upgrading their labor force.

Fourth, the group of countries including Brazil, India, Russia, China, and Eastern Europe will find the attempts at economic development a mixed blessing as they seek to dramatically upgrade the motivation and quality of their workforce, while experiencing a growing demand by their citizens for investment capital and for capital goods, with insufficient resources to provide for both economic growth and consumer demand. Each of these areas has the potential to become a core market, if it can maintain political stability, control inflation, and achieve consistent economic growth. All have a growing scientific and technological base. However, Brazil, China, and most of Eastern Europe are huge debtor nations, and Russia, China, and Eastern Europe have only begun the process of moving from a central-planning to a market economy. Effective leadership and the patience of their people will be the key to their emergence as full participants in the world economy.

Fifth, the major oil producing countries—Iran, Iraq, Saudi Arabia, Venezuela, and Nigeria—have access to sufficient capital accumulation to begin modernization, but lack the scientific and technological base and population base to become a core market. In addition, internal and external political forces are at work creating instability in the form of religious wars in Iran and Iraq, weak political institutions and ethnic cleavages in Nigeria, and weak economies due to large national debts in Venezuela and Nigeria. This suggests that rapid economic development will bypass the general population, but may intersect certain economic sectors, mainly the military and political elite.

Finally, most of the remaining Third World countries will be bypassed and denied access to the emerging global economy. Some countries such as Sri Lanka, Mozambique, Nicaragua, and Peru will try to maintain their national integrity by meeting the needs of their countries with domestic production and thus avoid the global economic imperatives.

THE UNIQUE ROLE OF HIGH-SPEED MANAGEMENT AND EFFECTIVE ORGANIZATIONAL COMMUNICATION IN ORGANIZATIONAL CONTINUOUS IMPROVEMENT PROGRAMS

While each of these core markets and their respective models of organizational and regional development have their own unique characteristics, they all have in common (1) a need to participate effectively in each of the world's core markets, and (2) a need to develop high-speed management and effective organizational communication processes in the form of continuous improvement programs in order to sustain national and organizational economic growth and development.

The Rise of High-Speed Management

According to Cushman and King (1992:1):

> Being a successful business executive in the 1990s will be very difficult and require a new management orientation. Rapidly changing technologies, the globalization of economic forces, unexpected competition, and quick market saturation are creating an increasingly complex and volatile business climate. As environmental turbulence increases, the rate of organizational change necessary for survival also increases. To compete successfully in such an environment requires that executives employ new management assumptions and practices which emphasize organizational innovation, flexibility, efficiency, and speed of response.

Rapid environmental change creates organizational problems but also creates organizational opportunities. An organization's management system, its integration, coordination, and control system must have certain specifiable characteristics in order to respond to the opportunities created by successive, rapid, environmental change. A management system which capitalizes on environmental change must be innovative, adaptive, flexible, efficient, and rapid in response—a high-speed management system.

Innovative management refers not only to product development, but innovation in corporate structure, manpower utilization, outsourcing, inventory control, manufacturing, marketing, servicing, and competitive positioning.

Adaptive management refers to an organization's appropriate adjustment to change in employee values, customer tastes, investor interests, government regulations, the availability of global economic resources, and the strategic positioning of competitors.

Flexible management refers to the capacity of an organization to expand, contract, shift direction on products and competitive strategy, and to assimilate acquisitions, joint ventures, coalitions, and to excise unproductive or underproductive units.

Efficient management refers to maintaining the industry lead in world class products, productivity, investors' equity, return on investment, employee satisfaction, customer support, product quality, and serviceability.

Rapid response management refers to gaining and maintaining the industry standard in speed of response to environmental change.

Due to a shrinking product life cycle, today's new-generation companies compete by decreasing the time required to bring a product to market. Such companies remain innovative, adaptive, flexible, efficient, and rapid in response by concentrating on reducing if not eliminating delays and using this response advantage to obtain increased market shares. The organizational benefits which flow from a high-speed management system can be breathtaking.

First, order-of-magnitude changes occur in response time. General Electric reduced from three weeks to three days the amount of time required to deliver a custom-made circuit breaker. Motorola used to turn out electronic pagers three weeks after the factory order arrived, now the process takes two hours.

Second, order-of-magnitude changes occur in profits. McKinsey & Company management consulting group demonstrated that high-tech products that come to market six months late earn thirty-three percent less profit over five years, while coming out with a product on time but fifty percent over budget cuts profits only four percent. More significantly, IBM obtained a six-month lead over all competitors in the mass production of four megabyte computer storage chips. This occurred in an industry where the average product life cycle for storage chips is 18 months (Vescy, 1991:25).

Third, order-of-magnitude changes occur in productivity, product quality, and market shares. Hewlett Packard, General Electric, and AT&T report (Dumaine, 1989) improved productivity, product quality, and market shares from implementing rapid response systems. A recent survey of fifty major U.S. corporations by Kaiser and Associates, a large consulting firm, found that all listed time-based management strategies at the top of their priority list. Why? Because speed of response tends to improve productivity, profits, product quality, and market shares (Dumaine, 1989:54).

The focus of this new corporate perspective and thus the goal of high-speed management is the use of the new information technologies and human communication process to rapidly develop, test, and produce a steady flow of low-cost, high-quality, easily serviced, high-value products which meet the customers' needs, and of quickly getting these products to market before one's competition, in an effort to achieve market penetration and large profits.

A management system with high-speed characteristics can, in the final analysis, be developed, implemented, and maintained only by the appropriate use of information technologies within a unique communication environment which adjusts people to technologies and technologies to people through the use of effective communication processes in developing and maintaining continuous organizational improvement programs.

The Effective Use of Communication to Develop Organizational Continuous Improvement Programs

While it is clear from our previous analysis that a successful global competitor carefully monitors changes in global economic forces and then quickly reorients an organization's operations in ways which create competitive advantage, it is far from clear what the philosophical rationale is for guiding the communication activities involved in these organizational adaptation processes. Fortunately, several well-developed studies have explored this problem in detail, with convergent results (Rockert and Schort, 1989; Venkatraman and Prescott, 1990; Cvar, 1986; Smith et al 1989).

The Center for Information Systems Research at the MIT Sloan School of Management in 1989 summarized these convergent studies when it stated that an organization's ability to continuously improve its effectiveness in managing organizational interdependencies was the critical element in successfully responding to the competitive forces of the 1990s (Rockert and Schort, 1989). Effectiveness in managing organizational interdependencies refers to an organization's ability to achieve *coalignment* among its internal and external resources in a manner which is equal to or greater than existing world class benchmarks for responding to environmental change.

Coalignment is a unique form of organizational interdependence in which each of a firm's subunits clearly articulate its needs, concerns, and potential contributions to the organization's functioning in such a manner that management can forge an appropriate value-added configuration and linkage between units. An appropriate value-added configuration and linkage between units is one which integrates, coordinates, and controls each unit's needs, concerns, and contributions so that the outcome is mutually satisfying to the units involved and optimizing in value-added activities to the organizational functioning as a whole.

World class benchmarking refers to the standards one holds in setting goals for improvement. These benchmarks or goals to be met in improving an organization's innovation, adaptation, flexibility, efficiency, and rapid response to environmental change must be set at world class levels. They must reflect the highest standards of the best companies in the world. Only then will improvement in an organization's coalignment process provide for the value-added gains necessary for sustainable competitive advantage.

Our analysis of the philosophical rationale for the primary function of communication within an organizational context suggests that communication serves to continuously improve organizational effectiveness in managing a firm's co-alignments between its internal and external resources benchmarked against world class standards in responding to environmental change. Co-alignment is a unique communication relationship in which each of a firm's stakeholders clearly articulates its needs, concerns, and contributions in such a manner that management can forge an appropriate value-added configuration and linkage between stakeholders that is mutually satisfying and optimizing to the value-added activities of the organization when benchmarked against world class standards, thus creating sustainable economic growth and development.

While such a philosophical rationale seems clear and responsive to a volatile economic environment, what theoretic principles are available to guide this continuously improving communication process of organizational co-alignment and world class benchmarking? Four dynamic communication processes, each with its own theoretic rationale, currently form the basis for such a continuous improvement of organizational co-alignment processes based on world class benchmarking. These are: (1) negotiation linking, (2) a New England town meeting, (3) a cross-functional teamwork, and (4) a best practices case-study program.

A Negotiated Linking Program. A unit or function is created within an organization whose purpose is to continuously scan the globe to locate resources in the form of customers, partners, technologies and/or consultants capable of enhancing an organization's competitiveness. Such resources may include land, labor, capital, market entry, distribution channels, technology, training, etc. This unit then:

- interacts with the unit holding the potential resource in order to locate its interests, concerns, and contributions to co-alignment.
- develops the form of co-alignment preferred by both units, such as acquisition, joint venture, alliance, partnership coalition, collaboration, licensing technology leasing, transfer, and/or training.
- determines the world class benchmarking targets in market shares, productivity, quality, flexibility, and/or rapid response time to be met before co-alignment can take place.

The organizational negotiated-linking program then formulates the co-alignment agreement aimed at mobilizing external resources for organizational usage.

New England Town Meeting. A unit or function is created within the organization to implement a worker continuous-improvement program within a New England town-meeting format. Its goal is to improve an organization's productivity, quality, flexibility, adaptability, and/or response time. It is an attempt to eliminate nonessential, nonproductive, or "bad" work and replace it with "good work." These New England style town meetings last from one to three days. They begin with the division head calling together 20-100 workers, suppliers, and/or customers.

The meeting then proceeds in the following manner:

- the division head opens the meeting with a presentation of key market issues, the organization's vision in responding to these issues, how the organization and its competitors are responding to this vision, and specific organizational needs for increased productivity, quality, flexibility, adaptability, and rapid response time. The division head leaves at this point in the meeting.
- teamwork facilitators take over and generate a list of bad work to be eliminated and good work to be undertaken in responding to the various areas of concern.
- the group is then divided into teams of five to ten members to analyze, discuss, and debate potential areas for improvement.
- each team then provides a cost/benefit analysis and action plan for the solutions recommended.
- the division head then returns and listens to a cost/benefit analysis and action plan from each group.

The division head acts on all high-yield ideas by selecting a team champion, training the team champion in project management, empowering a team to implement the change, and setting performance targets, measurement criteria, a time frame, and feedback procedures. The worker-improvement team then implements the action plan.

A Cross-Functional Teamwork Program. A unit or function is created to set up cross-functional teams whose goals are to map and then improve cross-functional organizational processes. Many of the most significant improvements in organizational performance have come from mapping important cross-functional organizational processes and then asking those involved in the process to simplify and/or improve the functioning of that process. This approach has been very profitable for organizations since many of these processes have developed and expanded over time without anyone examining the entire process and exploring its improvement.

Here cross-functional teams are set up and assigned the task of mapping the decision, implementation, and review levels of important organizational processes. The cross-functional team is then asked to evaluate and make improvements in the process mappings. This is accomplished in four steps:

• developing a clear understanding of the process goal.
• identifying the necessary and sufficient critical success factors for achieving that goal.
• mapping and improving the essential subprocesses to meet these critical success factors.
• rank ordering each subprocess and evaluating its productivity, quality, flexibility, and adaptability, and how to make improvements.

The unit and/or function then implements the change process and fine tunes its subprocesses.

A Best Practices Case-Study Program. A unit or function is created to scan the globe for world class competitors and to study how various parts of these organizations succeeded in setting world class benchmarking standards in regard to productivity, quality, flexibility, adaptability, and response time. This unit usually:

• locates such organizations and makes a site visit.
• develops a case study of the processes involved.

• trains personnel at its own organization in ways to adapt these innovations to its organization.

This unit then sets up monitoring and feedback procedures and implements the change

These then are our four dynamic communication processes, each with its own theoretic rationale for developing organizational continuous improvement programs.

SOME EXAMPLES OF ORGANIZATIONAL AND NATIONAL DEVELOPMENT THROUGH CONTINUOUS IMPROVEMENT PROGRAMS

Continuous improvement programs aimed at improving organizational co-alignment through negotiated linking, cross-functional teamwork, New England town meetings, and case studies in world class benchmarking are necessary elements in establishing a world class organizational information and communication capability. Continuous improvement programs are essential information and communication processes in high-speed management which have rapidly diffused to small and large organizations in the private and public sectors of the world economy. Let us therefore examine the practical bases of continuous improvement programs by exploring the four dynamic communication processes functioning first in a small local organization, the Danville, Illinois Bumper Works, and second in a large multinational organization, the General Electric Corporation.

The Danville, Illinois Bumper Works. In 1978, Shahid Khan, a naturalized U.S. citizen from Pakistan, borrowed $50,000 from the Small Business Loan Corporation and took $16,000 of his own savings to establish the 100-person Bumper Works in Danville, Illinois. This company designed and manufactured truck bumpers. Between 1980 and 1985, Khan approached the Toyota Motors Corporation on several occasions attempting to become a supplier of bumpers for their trucks but without much success.

In 1987, Toyota Motors called together a group of 100 potential suppliers and released their design, quality, quantity, and price-range specifications for the product. The officials at Toyota Motors also indicated that they expected increased quality and a reduction in price each year from the supplier. By late 1988, only Khan's Bumper Works company could produce a product that met

Toyota Motors exacting requirements. In 1989, Toyota Motors sent a manufacturing team to Danville to negotiate the contract and co-alignment agreement between the two firms. The negotiations failed because the Bumper Works could not produce twenty different sized bumpers and ship them in a single day. If they could not do this, it would slow down the production of all Toyota trucks, increasing their price dramatically (White, 1991:7A).

Khan called a New England town meeting of workers from his own and Toyota Motors Japanese factories to explore how this problem might be solved within Toyota's design, quality, quantity, and price requirements. It was decided that the Bumper Works would have to switch the factory from a mass-production to a batch-production line and that a massive stamping machine in which it took ninety minutes to change each cutting die would have to be modified so as to make such changes in twenty minutes (White, 1991:7A).

Next, the workers at both the Bumper Works and Toyota Motors set up cross-functional teams to make a process map of current production procedures. They studied, simplified, and restructured the process to allow for batch production. The large stamping machine was studied for modifications that would speed up die changes. All this was done with considerable help from Toyota Motors, which had solved these same problem, but in a different way, in Japan (White, 1991:7A).

Then, the Bumper Works remodeled assembly line was ready to begin production. For six months, employees with stopwatches and cost sheets observed the restructured process and benchmarked its operations against the world class standards of the Toyota plant in Japan—but still could not meet Toyota's quality, quantity, and speed-of-delivery specifications. They videotaped the process, studied it, modified it, and sent it to Japan for review. In July 1990, Toyota Motors sent a team over to help retrain the workers. They returned again in December of 1990 to fine tune the process, meeting Toyota Motors' contract requirements.

The new production line increased productivity 60 percent over the previous year, decreased defects 80 percent, cut delivery time by 850 percent, and cut waste materials cost by 50 percent. A manual and videotape of the manufacturing process were prepared for training, the first of their kind at Bumper Works, and continuous improvement teams were formed to meet contract requirements for increased quality and decreased costs for each subsequent year.

Now that representatives of each unit involved in the value chain linking the Bumper Works and Toyota Motors had communicated their interests, concerns, and contributions to the co-alignment process, each firm's management was able to forge a linking process that was satisfactory to the units involved and optimizing to the value-added activities of each organization in order to create a sustainable competitive advantage. Khan, the owner of Bumper Works, profited from this experience and proceeded to build a new plant to employ 200 workers in Indiana to supply truck bumpers for a new Isuzu Motors plant located there (White, 1991:7A).

The Toyota Motors Corporation of Japan served as a catalyst for the transfer of technology, training, world class product standards, and global access to all three core markets for a small American corporation. Each day numerous multinational corporations throughout the world stimulate this type of economic development in tens of thousands of large and small businesses within most nations throughout the world. In so doing, these organizations become productive world class competitors, upgrading their host nation's economic development.

The General Electric Corporation. In 1990, General Electric had $58.4 billion in sales and $4.3 billion in profits and had 298,000 employees worldwide. As Stewart (1991:41) indicates:

> Few corporations are bigger; none more complex. GE makes 65 cent light bulbs, 400,000 pound locomotives, and billion dollar power plants. It manages more credit cards than American Express and owns more commercial aircraft than American Airlines. Of the seven billion pounds of hamburger Americans tote home each year, 36 percent keep fresh in GE refrigerators, and after dinner, one out of every five couch potatoes tunes in GE's network NBC.

This is the organization that CEO Jack Welch, Jr. wants to be lean, agile, and aggressive—to run like a small business. His corporate goal is to make GE the most competitive corporation in the world by having each of its thirteen businesses ranked number one or two in world market shares, while increasing sales 15 percent, profits 10 percent, and productivity 5 percent per year, and decreasing costs by 5 percent per year. It goes without saying that Jack Welch, Jr. is a strong advocate of continuous improvement programs. Let us explore GE's continuous improvement program.

Since 1981 GE has divested itself of $5.9 billion in low growth businesses and acquired $11.1 billion in high growth businesses in order to maintain its number one or two world market shares in each of thirteen businesses. It is a difficult task for an environmental scanning unit to locate such a large number of potential acquisitions capable of performing at the level required by GE and then to negotiate the linking agreement so that the acquisition is quickly brought up to speed. For example, Philips Corporation of Holland purchased Westinghouse's lighting business, Electrolux of Sweden purchased White consolidated major appliance division, and Brown and Bovevi of Switzerland and ASEA of Sweden merged their power systems division. Each of these acquisitions and mergers threatened GE's first- or second-place market-share ranking in the lighting, major appliances, and power systems industries. In each case GE scanned the globe for potential linking arrangements that could restore their market dominance and which could meet their world class growth, productivity, product-quality, and rapid-response targets. Acquisitions were located, linking arrangements negotiated, and co-alignment processes put in place so that market shares and performance targets could be met. Over ten years, such acquisitions amounted to $11.1 billion.

In order to become the most competitive corporation in the world, Jack Welch realized that his business leaders had to find a better fit between their organization's needs and their employees' capabilities. To reorient this fit, GE in 1987 established a New England town meeting program called "Workout." The purpose of Workout town meetings, according to Welch, were:

> To see a team work together to face its problems and candidly discuss issues which negatively affect their work by giving each employee the power to define and shape his job, to give it meaning so he can feel responsible for it, get value from it, and have it be an enriching experience instead of a draining, numbing nuisance. In the end, each employee will have worked to create more customers, more job security, and more job satisfaction. That's our ultimate goal for the 1990s at GE (Workout, Dec. 1989:1).

By the end of 1991, over 50,000 GE employees participated in three-day Workout town meetings with remarkable results. In GE's plastics division alone, over thirty workout teams were empowered to make changes. One team saved GE plastics $2 million by modifying one production process, another enhanced productivity four fold, while a third reduced product delivery time 400 percent (Workout, Sept. 1991, 2). Another business, NBC, used Workout to halt the use of report forms that totaled more than two million pieces of paper a year (Stewart, 1991:44); GE Credit Services used workout to tie its cash registers directly to a mainframe, cutting the time for opening a new account from thirty minutes to ninety seconds. Similar results were reported from Workout projects in GE's other businesses, demonstrating a remarkable company-wide reorientation of co-alignment processes between worker capabilities and organizational needs.

While this internal transformation of GE's value chain was taking place, Jack Welch also realized that some other global organizations were achieving greater productivity, quality control, flexibility, adaptability and rapid response time than GE, even with the workout program in place. In the summer of 1988, GE began its "Best Practices Program," aimed at locating those organizations which had outperformed GE in a given area, developing a case study of how they did it, and then employing these case studies as world class benchmarks for improving GE's performance.

GE scanned the globe and located twenty-four corporations which had in some area outperformed GE. They then screened out direct competitors and companies that would not be credible to GE employees. Welch then invited each corporation to come to GE to learn about its best practices and in return to allow GE people to come to their companies and study their best practices. About one-half of the companies agreed. They included AMP, Chapparral Steel, Ford, Hewlett Packard, Xerox, and three Japanese companies. GE sent out observers to develop case studies and ask questions. These best-practices case studies were turned into a course at Crotonville, GE's leadership training center; it is offered to a new class of managers from each of GE's thirteen businesses each month (Stewart, 1991:44–45).

Finally, as GE's top management team reviewed the projects that had been successful from both their Workout and Best Practices programs they noticed a difference in the types of project which saved up to a million dollars and those which saved 100 million. The latter always involved changes in organizational processes which spanned the entire value chain. They cut across departments and involved linking with suppliers and customers. All emphasized managing processes, not functions. This led GE to establish its cross-functional teamwork program aimed at mapping and then improving key organizational processes. Such process maps frequently allowed employees for the first time to see and understand organizational processes from beginning to end. They also demonstrated the need for a new type of manager, a process manager who could co-align an organization's total assets. It allowed employees to spot bottlenecks, time binds, and inventory shortages and overflows.

After implementing the cross-functional teamwork program, GE appliances cut its sixteen-week manufacturing cycle in half, while increasing product availability six percent and decreasing inventory costs twenty percent. The program cost less than $3 million to implement and by mid-1991 had returned profits 100 times that (Stewart, 1991:48). Product mapping programs have also provided an empirical basis for changing how GE measures its management and workers' performance. GE now employs world class cross-functional process benchmarking standards to evaluate its various business performances and to award its bonuses and merit awards for process improvements.

Continuous improvement programs like those we have observed at the Bumper Works and General Electric are using negotiated linking, New England town meetings, cross-functional teamwork, and case studies of world class benchmarking to revolutionize how the practical basis for communication effects the co-alignment or organizational processes to obtain sustainable economic growth and development.

New, competitive, large multinational and small local corporations have developed through continuous improvement programs in a number of countries, including Taiwan, Hong Kong, Mexico, Thailand, and Brazil. Such organizations begin by being good or average local market competitors and develop over time through continuous improvement programs into world class competitors stimulating economic development at home and abroad.

SOME EXAMPLES OF MULTINATIONALS STIMULATING NATIONAL ECONOMIC DEVELOPMENT

Central to national and organizational development has been the rise of multinational corporations which through their positioning of organizational units throughout the world and their linking with indigenous suppliers in these countries transfer technology, training, and investment to those countries. The products made by such organizations in turn contribute to world trade generating work and income in the host nation.

High-speed management and effective organizational communication in the form of continuous organizational improvement programs have fueled the economic development of nations and multinational organizations throughout the world. Three examples of this national and organizational economic development process are to be found in Singapore, Mexico, and Denmark. Let us examine each in turn.

Singapore is one of the newly industrialized nations of Southeast Asia which owes its economic development to heavy foreign investment by multinational corporations. Between 1960 and 1980, Singapore's GDP grew at about nine percent per year. The citizens of Singapore experienced a tripling of their average income over this twenty year period of time. Foreign multinational organizations by 1992 accounted for sixty percent of manufacturing workers and seventy-two percent of capital expenditures (Wilkinson, 1986). According to Sanger (1991:6):

> Having relied on cheap labor and some of the world's most finely honed economic incentives to shape itself into an island of other nation's multi-national corporations, Singapore is now struggling to become an economic power in its own right. . . . They are spreading Singapore's management techniques throughout Asia funding venture start-ups in everything from chip making to bio-technology, and prowling the world for good ideas to bring home.

Singapore has progressed from a low-income economy to a middle-income economy and is attempting now to develop its own multinational corporations and move to a high-income economy (World Bank, 1991:4).

Mexico is one of Latin America's oil-rich nations and is attempting to rapidly accelerate its economic growth through a vigorous program aimed at privatization of state-owned industries, upgrading its technical education programs in engineering, computer science, and management, and luring multinational corporations to Mexico (Sanderson and Hayes, 1990; Perry, 1992). In the past five years, inflation has gone from 200 percent to twenty percent per year, economic growth has held at roughly 4.3 percent and foreign capital investment has increased by $80 billion (Main, 1991). At the same time, foreign investors open 5,000 *maguiladere* assembly plants, creating over 25,000 jobs along Mexico's border with the U.S. (Fallows, 1991:48). Mexico's annual debt has shrunk from sixteen percent of GDP to six percent (Nash, 1991). Sanderson and Hayes (1990:40) report:

Today Mexico graduates more engineers per capita than does the U.S. Throughout Mexico one finds well trained engineers, computer scientists and managers many of whom have studied in the U.S. Nor is the stereotype of languid work habits valid any longer as a visit to any well run Mexican company will confirm.

Finally, as Baker and Lee (1991:47) observe, many manufacturing jobs are returning from Asia to Mexico.

Denmark has a highly developed economy which ten years ago was near collapse. Forman (1991:14A) reports:

Denmark, which once seemed headed for economic oblivion, is bouncing back. Less than a decade ago, inflation here raced into double digits, devaluations came like clockwork and the economy was near collapse under heavy welfare spending. Now, Denmark has a strong economy, the developed world's lowest inflation rate, a widening trade surplus and a shrinking foreign debt.

This economic turnaround has come about by Denmark becoming a key supplier for multinational organizations located in the-European Economic Community. It has developed its own multinationals and has become a center for biotechnology, computers, and auto parts. Exports have grown twelve percent annually since 1990, while manufacturing costs fell twenty percent below those in Germany.

Singapore, Mexico, and Denmark are but a sampling of the many nations around the world that have had multinational corporations serve as catalysts to national economic development. Access to the world's core markets, technology transfer, training, and world class products are but a few of the resources multinational corporations have provided these nation states. However, it is through high-speed management and effective organizational communication in the form of continuous organizational improvement programs that such organizations gain and maintain world class competitive standards.

CONCLUSION

All models of economic development, including this one, have limits. Some limits to economic growth based upon open competition and free trade throughout the world are beginning to appear within this model.

First, core market access is being limited by increasingly restrictive rules favoring the national development of nations within the core market at the expense of those nations outside the core market. This is aimed at preventing the flow of highly skilled jobs out of the core market, penalizing the wage advantage of nations outside, and halting the threats from superior competitors. These limitations to access distort the competitive allocation of economic and natural resources in favor of the political allocation of these same resources.

Second, the demand for capital, technology, and training outside the core markets are greater than the available resources. This in turn is leading to economic decline and political instability in the nations which cannot meet the demand. In the long run, these shortages may be equalized, but in the short run, military and political dictatorships may be the response to economic unrest.

Third, open competition within the core markets favors large rich nations and encourages the economic domination of the core markets by these super economic powers. This in turn leads to an economic dependency on the powers by others that may not be resolvable.

However in spite of these potential limits to economic development, several advantages of the current use of this model have also emerged.

First, the competitive core market allocation of economic and natural resources has minimized political power and spread economic development more evenly throughout nations and the world. This in turn has minimized the political distortion of power in favor of the military, larger nations, and initially well-developed regions of the world.

Second, the multinational diffusion of technology, training, market access, and skills has lead to the rapid development of formerly backward and resource-poor nations. This in turn has created world class opportunities for all willing to pursue them and has served to minimize the importance of national boundaries and ethnic diversity by placing all participants in a common development system.

Third, high-speed management and effective communication in the form of continuous organizational improvement programs have fueled rapid economic change and local creativity in the direction of the development of world class products and economic development rather than political alliances and military hardware development. This in turn encourages the development of a nation's infrastructure and human productivity—especially education, a strong work ethic, significant national savings, and economic interdependence among people.

NOTES

1. Portions of this chapter are taken from D. P. Cushman and S. S. King, High-Speed Management: A Revolution in Organizational Communication in the 1990's. In S. Deetz (ed.). *Communication Yearbook 16*, 1993.

2. The Role of Mass Media in World Community. In Won Yung Kang (ed.), *Proceedinqs of the World Academic Conference of the Seoul Olympiad 88*, Korean Olympic Committees, Seoul, Korea, 1989, pp. 326–49. Reprinted in *Informatologia Yugoslavica* 20, pp. 131–51, 1988.

REFERENCES

Baker, S., and Lee, D. July 1, 1991. Assembly Lines Start Migrating From Asia to Mexico, *Business Week* 43.

Castells, M. 1986. High-Technology, World Development and the Structured Transformation: The Trends and Debate. *Alternatives* 11:297–342.

Cvar, M. 1986. Case Studies in Global Competition Patterns of Success and Failure. In M. Porter (ed.), *Competition in Global Industry*, 483–517. Boston: Harvard Business School Press.

Dumaine, B. Feb. 13, 1989. How Managers Can Succeed Through Speed. *Fortune* 119:54–59.

Economist. Economic Growth: Explaining the Mystery. Jan. 4, 1992: 15–17.

Fallows, J. Nov. 7, 1991. The Romance with Mexico. *The New York Review* 46–52.

Forman, C. Nov. 3, 1991. Denmark' s Miracle Is Gaining Believers. *Wall Street Journal*, 14A.

Macrae, N. Dec. 21, 1991. A Future History of Privatization, 1992–2022. *The Economist*: 15–18 .

Main, J. April 8, 1991. How Latin America is Opening Up. *Fortune* 84–88.

Nash, N. Nov. 13, 1991. A Breath of Fresh Economic Air Brings Change to Latin America. *New York Times* 1A.

Perry, N. Feb. 10, 1992. What's Powering Mexico's Success. *Fortune* 109–15.

Pollack, A. Feb. 1, 1992. Technology Without Borders Raising Big Questions for the U.S. *New York Times* lA.

Rapoport, C. July 15, 1991. Why Japan Keeps On Winning. *Fortune* 76–85.

Rockart, J., and Schort, J. Winter, 1989. IT in the 1990's: Managing Organizational Interdependencies. *Sloan Management Review* 30:7–17.

Sanderson, S., and Hayes, R. Sept.–Oct. 1990. Mexico—Opening Ahead of Eastern Europe. *Harvard Business Review*, 32–41.

Sanger, D. Oct. 13, 1991. In Singapore, a Search for a Second Act. *New York Times* 3, 6, 7.

Smith, K. G., Grimm, C. M., Chen, M. J., and Gannon, M. J. 1989. Predictors of Response Time to Competitive Strategic Action: Preliminary Theory and Evidence. *Journal of Business Research* 19:245–58.

Stewart, T. August 12, 1991. GE Keeps Those Ideas Coming. *Fortune* 41–49.

Venkatraman, N., and Prescott, J. 1990. Environment-Strategy Coalignment: An Empirical Test of its Performance Implications. *Strategic Management Journal* 11:1–23.

Wall Street Journal. The Global Giants. Sept. 21, 1990:R27.

Walton, J. 1985. The IMF Riot, Paper delivered at the I.S.A. Conference on the Urban Impact of the New International Division of Labor, Hong Kong.

White, J. Sept. 9, 1991. Japanese Auto Makers Help U.S. Suppliers Become More Efficient. *The Wall Street Journal* 1A, 7A.

Wilkinson, B. 1986. Human Resources in Singapore's Second Industrial Revolution. *Industrial Relations Journal*, Vol. 7 No. 2: 99–114.

Workout, (Dec. 1989 and Sept. 1991). Special Edition of *GE Silicones News*.

World Bank 1991. *World Development Report* 1–300.

Vescy, J. C. 1991. The New Competitors: They Think in Terms of Speed-to-Market. *Academy of Management*, Vol. 5, No. 2: 23–33.

CORNELIUS B. PRATT

9

Public Relations, Industrial Peace, and Economic Development

ABSTRACT

This paper outlines the limitations of models for Third-World development and presents public-relations strategies for attaining industrial peace and development in the developing nations. Because of the continuing need for industry-driven economic development, rather than an emphasis on only government-generated economic growth, in the Third World, two major contributory roles of public relations (a subsystem of organizations) to development are presented. They are institutional-sociopolitical stability and institutional-sociostructural integration.

Kruckeberg and Starck's (1988) reconstructed theory of public relations and the theory of corporate social responsibility provide the theoretical underpinnings for the role of public relations in the management process for industrial peace and economic development.

At the turn of this century, it will be more than forty years since a number of major Third-World nations became independent from colonial governments. Since the initial event in 1947 in India and in 1957 in the then Gold Coast, no fewer than forty other developing nations of the more than 120 countries of the Third World had earned that status. But earning political independence is just one of the hurdles that developing nations strive to overcome. Other hurdles are even more daunting. Asia and Africa have the notoriety of having two of the world's most economically disadvantaged nations: Bangladesh and Mozambique, respectively. Their extensive economic problems have earned the two countries the nonfacetious status of Fourth-World nations. Therefore, establishing economic and social infrastructures and workable political systems has been a major element in the development agendas of most Third-World nations.

This chapter introduces two concepts, which, to date, have received minimal attention in the literature on communications for development: public relations for industrial peace and economic development. This chapter, therefore, presents public relations perspectives on the extant models of communications for Third-World development. Its rationale is that practitioners of public relations have skills that are useful in implementing development programs that go beyond message distribution and communication effects; nurturing a sense of community is crucial to sustained development.

Clarification of Concepts

The focus of our discussion suggests the clarification of three concepts: public relations, industrial peace, and economic development.

Public Relations. What is public relations? What do people *in* public relations do? To answer these questions, one may use the following dialogue that illustrates precisely what public relations is not:

Q. I understand you are a sales representative for one of the largest manufacturing companies in the area. What do you specifically do?
A. I am involved primarily in sales and marketing.
Q. You mean you market your company's products by canvassing door to door? Or, just how?

A. Yes, largely so. I also work on building and expanding our clientele.
Q. And, how much success do you have?
A. Considerable.
Q. To what do you attribute that?
A. I like people. I put forward a good impression, use a lot of humor, do the best I can to establish rapport with I prospective clients. In short, I use good public relations!

This dialogue, albeit with some illustration of what public relations really accomplishes, provides the dominant use and the traditional misconception of the term public relations:

That it is a sales function. Such a misconception is a legacy of the evolutionary characteristic of public relations, a characteristic that subjects the practice to a broad, nominalist interpretation of the activities of the practitioner: Public relations *is* what a public-relations practitioner does.

A receptionist at the information desk at a government ministry responds to questions from visitors; a sales clerk at a department store assists a patron in her or his shopping; a union representative fields questions from the mass media about planned mandatory retirement for and layoffs of employees; a publicist makes a new toy the toddler's dream. All these people are in contact with various publics. But are they *in* public relations? It is clear from the dialogue that the sales representative makes frequent contact with clients, as do the receptionist, the sales clerk, the union representative, and the publicist.

Public relations involves much more than what our sales clerk or sales representative does in his or her contact with the public. Ideally, public relations is a nonmarketing function. Its practitioners build strategic relationships within organizations and with their publics. They relate to organizational and public sensitivities in a continuous, systematic way to build continuous relationships that are rooted in a practitioner's understanding of an organization's environments, boundary-spanning units, and transformational processes. The continuation of relationships is a major focus of public-relations programs. The long-range objectives are to bring about an understanding among all parties and to encourage responsive, mutually satisfactory actions from all.

Even though this description is simple, public-relations practitioners and scholars have had difficulties formulating a widely accepted definition of the practice in the past half century. Its meanings and definitions are so diverse that, in October 1975, research funded by the Foundation for Public Relations Research in the United States was begun in an attempt to develop an acceptable definition of pubic relations. Four hundred seventy-two definitions from the public-relations literature were analyzed, and a definition constructed and sent to 80 top public-relations practitioners in the United States for their comments (Harlow, 1988). Follow-up analyses produced descriptive and working definitions with three major thrusts: (1) as a distinctive management function, (2) as mutual lines of communication, and (3) as an early warning system to help anticipate organizational needs. These thrusts spell out the relevance of public relations to both industrial peace and economic development. And they also provide the crux of the potential contributions of public relations to industrial peace and development in the Third World.

More recently, in 1986, the Public Relations Society of America, the world's largest organization of practitioners, set up a special committee to examine precisely the activities that constitute public relations (Public Relations, 1987). That committee reviewed more than 30 definitions of public relations and reported that no definition covered the diverse activities of its practitioners.

While it is not the purpose of this chapter to engage in a debate or an excursus on what public relations is or is not, it adopts the position that public relations is an organizational activity that aligns the public interest with that of an organization, for the benefit of both. Thus, to what extent are the activities of an organization consistent with those of the larger society that it serves? How responsive are an organization's actions to the development interests of its host nations? Answers to these questions will be discussed within the context of two additional concepts: industrial peace and economic development.

Industrial Peace. Industrial peace, as used in this chapter, means the visible, demonstrated existence of harmony (or the visible, demonstrated absence or near-absence of conflicts in relations) and the presence of compatible values between an organization and its publics. Conflict here means a relationship in which participants hold incompatible and mutually exclusive values (Dahrendorf, 1959; Galtung, 1965).

From a practical standpoint, development agencies establish peace when their communications staffs, acting as boundary personnel, undertake activities that establish and promote understanding between such agencies and their publics, on the one hand, and among the agencies publics, on the other. Industrial peace (and conflicts) also occur in other forms: among employees, between investors and host countries, and among organizations. To the extent that the goal of the communication is to foster meaningful relationships among all stakeholder publics, a common ground for industrial communications could be established and industrial peace attained.

Economic Development. In general terms, development in a national context is the provision of the living standards that a people aspire to have. It is the kind of situation that enables a society to attain living conditions consistent with its values that can provide a greater control of its environment. Consequently, development agendas tend to vary from one society or nation to another. It is the variation in such agendas that makes the comparison of development levels troublesome to some development economists. Some indices of development are not subject to quantitative analyses; hence, comparative analysis tends to be fraught with inaccuracies. This means, for example, that the heritage and culture of a people cannot be compared with those of another group because such a group may hold qualities, practices, and norms that may be unique to that group. Further, the indices used by the World Bank to measure a country's economic development—for example, gross national development—ignore the often pervasive nonpecuniary, difficult-to-measure sectors of developing economies. Nonetheless, the Bank categorizes countries as either developed or developing, based on indices such as gross national product, life expectancy, and the accessibility of educational opportunities to a country's citizens.

Third-World development programs have been influenced by a number of development theories and models, which Narula and Pearce (1986) categorized into four types: modernization, interdependency and dependency, basic needs, and communications.

The modernization paradigm was proposed in generally similar forms by Lerner (1958), Rogers (1962, 1976), and Inkeles and Smith (1974). It is in two forms: the dominant paradigm of the earlier phase and its revised version, the new paradigm (Narula and Pearce, 1986). The dominant paradigm, on the one hand, equates underdevelopment with poverty and the lack of division of labor, specialization, differentiation, and of material goods. Thus, because a number of industrialized nations have substantial evidence of the presence of these indices, the only way for the developing nations to move into developed status is for them to acquire Western attributes of development.

On the other hand, the dominant paradigm holds that, because Third-World value systems are not conducive to development, modernization can only occur if changes occur in such value systems. While the dominant paradigm was essentially unidimensional in its approach, the new paradigm was relatively multidimensional, examining other factors such as labor-intensive technology and social systems that are also keys to development.

Melkote (1991) notes that because development theories are rooted in Western civilization, their communication approaches have major limitations. For example, development approaches need not focus on economic growth and industrialization, but on "meeting specific needs of particular poverty groups; fulfilling such basic needs of people as health care, nutrition, sanitation and shelter; . . . and self-determination, self-reliance and cultural autonomy . . ." (p. 176). Sonaike (1988) makes a similar assertion:

> . . . the dominant paradigm failed primarily because it created glaring infelicities between social groups in the less developed countries. The wealth of nations became concentrated in the hands of minute minorities while the huge majorities, mostly but not exclusively in the rural areas, languished in poverty. (p. 96)

In recognition of these failures of the dominant paradigm, "the new paradigm has a less restrictive purview, encompassing labor-intensive technology, decentralization in planning, both domestic and international economic factors, and the characteristics of the local social structures" (Narula and Pearce, 1986, p. 33). The paradigm recognizes the importance of traditional values, but calls for their blending with modern values.

The second approach to development is the interdependency/dependency model (Narula and Pearce, 1986), a critique of the dominant paradigm's focus on the domestic environment as presenting a stumbling block to development. The interdependency model holds that "the international sociopolitical system decisively determines the course of development within each nation" (Narula and Pearce, 1986, p. 45). The third category, the basic needs model, is a commitment to meet the basic needs of the poor through decentralization and integration. Decentralization is crucial for local autonomy in planning development programs and for communicating with the poor. Integrated development planning requires the restructuring and provision of the infrastructure that is important for attaining community-determined development goals.

Finally, the communication perspective orients development strategists and practitioners to interactions with their environment and with other publics. Melkote describes the need for such interactions through the use of "another development" in which communication models "allow for knowledge-sharing on a co-equal basis rather than by a top-down transmission of information and persuasion" (p 270). Melkote (1991) explains the importance to development of such an approach:

> Communication on a co-equal basis is ethically correct and practically more relevant and useful. By promising a more democratic forum for communication it supports the *Right to Communicate*, a basic human right recognized by the United Nations charter affording access to communication channels to all people at the national, local, and individual levels. Practically, it is important too. By allowing a symmetrical exchange of ideas between senders and receivers, it provides access to the storehouse of useful information and ideas of people at the grassroots. (p. 252)

These four emerging views of development provide the context for using public-relations strategies for economic growth in the developing nations. This context recognizes the value to Third-World development of existing models of "participatory" and "another" development, and suggests that public-relations tools be applied to them. The rationale is that communication strategies must maximize their outreach to the audience and their impact on development goals.

THEORETICAL FRAMEWORK

The communication strategies suggested in this chapter are based on two theories: Kruckeberg and Starck s (1988) reconstructed theory of public relations and the theory of the social responsibility of organizations.

Kruckeberg and Starck's (1988) Reconstructed Theory

The reconstructed theory of public relations argues that, because the current practice of public relations does not tackle the problems of restoration and maintenance of community, modified public relations strategies need be used. Thus,

> . . . an appropriate approach to community relations should be an active and direct attempt to restore and maintain a sense of community. Only through such a conceptual approach does the practice of community relations deal directly with the problems shared by the organization and its geographic public (Kruckeberg and Starck, 1988, pp. 82–83).

This theory is exemplified by "another development" or "participatory" approach that places emphasis on community involvement.

The practitioner contributes to a sense of community, which, in turn, contributes to industrial peace. To do so, practitioners have available to them some of the following tools: opinion surveys, publicity, promotion, public affairs, merchandising, marketing, advertising, press agentry, issues management, and lobbying.

The Social Responsibility Theory for Development

One of Peterson, Schramm, and Siebert's (1971) seminal four-point typology is social responsibility, which views the press as obligated to fulfill certain essential functions, for example, the right to know. It is within this framework that information staffers—most of whom got their start in the press—conduct their day-to-day work. Ethical public relations must be responsive to the public interest. In the Third World, that responsibility is almost always translated as being responsive to a nation s development needs.

Third-World public-relations practitioners are perhaps best suited to contribute to the development programs of their environments. The very nature of public relations encourages the form of "alternative development" and "communication perspective" proposed by Melkote (1991) and by Narula and Pearce (1986) as crucial to Third-World development in the 1980s and beyond.

Ideal public relations is a two-way symmetrical process, which means that the interests of the development agency are balanced in favor of both the agency and the receivers of the agency's messages. In such a process, message dissemination is not the driving force of such relationships. Rather, the agency and its receiver publics have mutually beneficial relationships that enhance information delivery, acceptance, and understanding.

Practitioners can also contribute to the decision-making vis-à-vis the development process, using communication strategies to translate government programs to the poor, the needy. With the obvious limitations of the dominant paradigms, and renewed interests in alternative paradigms of development, it behooves Third-World practitioners of public relations, most of whom are government staffers, to contribute to the development process through applying public-relations strategies targeted at the public interest. In doing so, practitioners will necessarily be applying to their function the ideals of the social responsibility of the public-relations process. The point here is that the social responsibility of Third-World public relations underscores the alternative/communication paradigms of development.

To whom *is* the public-relations practice responsible in the Third World? To whom *should* it be responsible?

Third-World public relations, for the most part, is a communications, not a management, function (Mohamed, 1984; Pratt, 1985). This focus on communication makes it more of a conduit for communicating "programmed" development news than for nurturing development-oriented norms among audiences. Its responsibility is largely to the limited interests of the government. This means that it is a "programmed communication function rather than a nonprogrammed managerial function. Third-World governments are eager to establish information offices staffed with officers that are more likely to provide the much-needed government publicity. Publicity, not public relations, is the emphasis of communication programs. It is the reference point for evaluating effective public relations, Third-World-style. In essence, much of the function is reduced to the status of that described earlier in the hypothetical dialogue. Public relations, whose goal is to communicate the wishes of the powers-that-be, is consistent with the asymmetrical, two-way communication model of the function; that is, it is driven largely by the self-interests of the development agency and not by those of the consumer publics.

Third-World nations, in searching for ways to achieve national development, therefore, demonstrate their interpretation of social responsibility in terms of mandated, unified national-development roles. The Third-World practitioner is considered socially responsible only when she or he makes a direct contribution to national development. Governments assume responsibility for national development plans and expect loyalty and compliance from communication practitioners.

Development programs in the Third World that are driven by a symmetrical, two-way, public-relations model, strive to attain a symmetry of interests between those of the agency and its publics. Such ideal public relations places national development interests at least at par with, if not above, those of the development agency. Ideally, public relations should be responsible to the public interest. It should encourage corporations and development agencies to exercise a social responsibility that contributes to the growth of the economy and to the attainment of social goals in the Third World. Program development and implementation must be driven by strategies anchored within a framework of development theories and evaluation research that is sensitive to the development status of the environment. Such a framework would also require that the practitioner draw upon her or his skills in continually evaluating public attitudes with the intent of ascertaining their relationships to organizational peace and institutional contributions to development.

Further, public relations should be reflective of the sociopolitical environment in which it is practiced. Because practitioners develop programs that can influence their publics in a variety of ways, they are expected to act in ways that demonstrate the organizations responsibility to its publics. Practitioners in the Third World should be responsible primarily to their publics, among whom is management.

Third-World industrial public relations, very much in its infancy, has, theoretically, the same goal as that in the developed West: fomenting symmetrical, mutually beneficial relationships with stakeholders. The corporate communications departments of a number of multinational corporations (MNCs) in the developing world also handle relations with host countries. Such departments role vis-à-vis industrial peace is necessitated by a number of challenges MNCs face. Such challenges are the extent to which the operations of MNCs from the developed world are perceived by their host countries—particularly those in the Third World—as susceptible to external sociopolitical interests; as inconsistent with domestic interests; as perpetuating economic *dependencia* on foreign economies; as threatening to the physical and cultural environments; and as exploitative rather than developmental (Akinsanya, 1984; Barnet and Müller, 1974; Biersteker, 1978;

Schiller, 1989; Turner, 1973; United Nations, 1974). Public-relations practitioners are best suited to address these conflict-generating situations for a major reason: they can counsel managements of MNCs on how to deal effectively with the industrial conflicts. By extension, the public-relations inputs can better prepare organizations to establish, support, and maintain active relationships with their communities.

PUBLIC RELATIONS FOR INDUSTRIAL PEACE AND DEVELOPMENT

Since the early 1960s, there have been well-meaning arguments on the extent to which the mass media in the Third World can indeed contribute to the region's development. In essence, there has been a concern about what Stevenson (1988) described as "the failed efforts to use mass media as the magic multiplier of development efforts" (p. 173). This concern has generated interest in alternative strategies for Third-World development. As stated earlier, while it is not the purpose of this chapter to identify *all* the alternative strategies to Third-World development, it focuses on two areas in which one form of communication—public relations—can,within the context of a reconstructed theory and social responsibility theory, contribute to industrial peace and economic growth.

I

The first is institutional-sociopolitical stability. A number of Third-World governments have been politically unstable. Yet, political stability is a precursor to economic growth and industrial peace. In sub-Saharan Africa, for example, following a wave of independence from colonial administrations in the 1960s, a rash of unstable governments sought to subject their citizens occasionally to inhumane policies by designing lip-service policies on economic and social well-being. A number of African, Asian, and Latin American governments, run by the military, suspended their countries' constitutions and invoked emergency powers. Individual freedoms and human rights, fragile at best, even during civilian administrations, were further curtailed. Some of the media were nationalized and their criticisms of government further curtailed. Newsprint became a tool for governments control of the media. Further, as Faringer (1991) describes it in the African context, the

... philosophy of development journalism seems to be based on several elements—among them the tendency toward requiring "positive reporting" from the press, which can be explained by many African countries' authoritarian political systems as well as the urgent need for the Third World to work toward national consolidation and development, regardless of ideology. (p. 127)

McGowan (1986) observes that "military-led coups d'etat represent the typical fashion in which regimes are changed, and rule by the military is as widespread as that by civilians" (p. 539).

Morrison and Stevenson (1971) define political instability "as a condition in political systems in which the institutionalized patterns of authority break down, and the expected compliance to political authorities is replaced by political violence" (p. 348). In their factor-analytic study of instability in 32 African nations, the authors operationalized three forms of instability: elite, in which there is a violent removal of incumbent political authority; communal, in which there is a radical restructuring of the authority relationships between communal groups or between the national government and communal groups; and mass, in which a revolution or intensive violence results in a radical change in the structure of the political system. Factors that account for any of these types of instability in the Third-World context include cultural heterogeneity, low regime legitimacy, lack of coercive power, economic backwardness, and structural simplicity (Ake, 1973).

These perspectives are useful to our purposes in that, on the overall political scene, much of the Third World has, since attaining political independence, had frequent, violent nonconstitutional changes in its administrations. And, as observed by Hakes (1973), "The ease with which these extraconstitutional changes of power were accomplished seemed to indlcate that the outgoing regimes had generated less popular support than was previously assumed . . ." (p. 7). The succeeding military governments also had difficulties maintaining regime stability, and, as the experiences of the Third World indicate, the "attentive publics," who are crucial in influencing such a stability, have not been given their due attention by their governments.

Consequently, the region's civilian and military administrations have developed policies to achieve institutional and sociopolitical stability and national development and to encourage public participation in development programs.

In Nigeria, for example, civilians have, since June 1967, been invited to serve in top decision-making capacities in Nigeria's civilian-military dyarchy in order to broaden the base of support for the military and to help in its decision-making process. The local governments have been restructured to improve grass-roots participation, and consultations with civilians on key issues have become commonplace.

Nonetheless, these well-intentioned actions face two major problems: public skepticism and the lack of popular support. The government's policies, because they are decreed rather than constitutionally enacted, are perceived occasionally as coercive. Dissenting opinions are not readily welcomed. And the current military government further limits the extent to which information can be distributed. The responsibility of military public relations for clarifying the whys and wherefores of the policies and actions of the nation's largest beat—the government—is given short shrift, and attempts by private-sector public relations to fill the void are constrained by the current military government's squeeze on the information marketplace.

Admittedly, Third-World governments' public-relations officers attempt to relate with publics and to explain to them the governments' rapidly changing, sometimes inconsistent, policies and actions. But public relations role in the developing nations vis-à-vis institutional-sociopolitical stability is primarily supportive, rather than primarily evaluative.

The public-relations practitioner, therefore, in functioning under a "developmental/authoritarian" media system, as the communication systems of the Third World are commonly described, supports institutional policies, criticizing and evaluating, within occasionally rigid limits, their validity and the wisdom of their enactment. As Jose (1975) put it in specific reference to the press in Africa, but, no doubt, applicable to public-relations activities in the Third World:

> . . . many African journalists still believe that a good press is one that is in a constant state of war with the government; that a "progressive" journalist is one who writes anti-government articles every day and a leading journalist is one who is in and out of prison for sedition. My own strong view is that the African press cannot use the strategy and weapons we used against colonial governments against our own govern-

ment whether elected or in army uniform. It would be self-destructive. (p. 259)

This view is consistent with Hachten's (1987) developmental concept of the media, which are established to fulfill significant nation-building roles for their societies. In the absence of a broad democratic base, government and corporate practitioners fill the void, acting, within limits, as a conduit for institutional-sociopolitical stability and for public understanding and acceptance of institutional policies.

Reconstructing a theory of public relations to provide a community-relations framework for development is "among the most important and among the most typical in the application of public relations skills" (Kruckeberg and Starck, 1988, p. 23). In the Third-World context, that theory suggests that the public-relations practitioner communicate community-oriented development news, using both traditional and modern mass media to provide information on the peoples' civic responsibilities in making national development a continuing reality. Such a framework is premised on relating with the publics through the use of communication programs and research tools; the application of specific public-relations techniques and principles in supporting development programs and objectives constitutes the use of public relations for development. In so doing, the practitioner becomes socially responsible; that is, she or he becomes involved in some development activities not directly related, at least in the short run, to the well-being of her or his institution.

II

The second development role for public relations is institutional-sociostructural integration. Etzioni (1965) describes a politically integrated community as one that has "(a). . . an effective control over the use of the means of violence. . . (b) a center of decision-making that is able to affect significantly the allocations of resources and rewards throughout the community; (c) . . . the dominant focus of political identification for the large majority of politically aware citizens" (p. 4). Integration in the new Third-World nations seeks to prevent the occurrence or recurrence of ethnic conflict, societal fragmentation, intensive violence, and instability. All these have been some of the key issues of Asian, Latin American, and sub-Saharan African countries' development programs, particularly those of Ethiopia, Nigeria, Rwanda, Burundi, Sudan, Bolivia, and Nicaragua, in which the scars of civil wars are still prominent.

One element in the Third-World model for communication and development proposed by Haule (1984) is the promotion of cooperation among nations. At the country level, this translates into the promotion of harmony and good will among disparate cultural groups. Because public relations has traditionally encouraged relationships among various publics, it has an inherent potential to foster national integration, based on programs that can establish understanding among various groups. For this reason, each of the thirty state governments in Nigeria was quick to establish a public relations-type unit: the ministry of information, charged with the responsibility for bringing the government and its publics closer. Beyond this, ministries of information and culture, or similar agencies, are a permanent feature of the organizational structure of Third-World governments.

Mutinies in Kenya and Tanzania and coups d'etat in a number of developing nations have primarily resulted from the military's perceived breakdown in official responsibility and accountability to the people and from a perceived lack of long-range programs that demonstrate an awareness of the citizens' concerns. Sometimes, however, segments of the military are motivated by their own desires to maximize their own gains.

On May 27, 1967, the military administration of Nigeria's Yakubu Gowon described the creation of twelve states from four geographic regions as the only possible basis for stability and equality. This was the government's response to the pervasive ethnic-group politics and rivalries and minority-group strife. In response to public demands seven additional states were created in 1976 and some were renamed to reduce the vestiges of ethnic antagonism. Today, the number stands at thirty, created largely in response to potential group conflicts.

In Nicaragua, information staffers in the former left-leaning government of Daniel Ortega, prior to 1990, used political communication to project government programs targeted at development and to project an image of the Sandinistas as the peoples champions. The staffers also used (1) murals across the country to express political ideologies, (2) the telecast program "Face the People" to bring the government and the people closer to each other, (3) military events that had development undertones, and (4) health-promotion programs to reduce the incidence of polio and smallpox.

Public relations for sociostructural integration can also contribute to programs whose goal is to influence public attitudes in that direction. Because public relations is a planned, systematic, continuous process, not a sporadic or haphazardly contrived one, persuasive communication tools at the disposal of the practitioner can be used to initiate programs targeted at attitudes, which otherwise might be detrimental to integration. The practitioner, as a communicator with direct access to the public, can distribute information to the public and assist institutions to formulate policies and implement programs whose goal is to influence beliefs and attitudes that have implications for development. Thus, the practitioner's in-depth knowledge of the publics' sentiments, feelings, needs, and wants enables her or him to identify problems and to develop public-communication campaigns geared toward influencing those attitudes in favor of social integration.

It is indeed appropriate that, given the increasing interdependence of regional and national economies, and the historical dependence of those of the developing nations on Western economies, the role of multinational corporations (MNCs) in Third-World development be also discussed. For one thing, the involvement of MNCs in Third-World development provides additional challenges for public relations in the adoption of pro-development attitudes. Five reasons suggest that the role of such MNCs in Third-World development programs is likely to increase toward the end of the present century.

First, the results of a 1989 survey of 433 chief executive officers (CEOs) in the United States, Canada, Japan, Europe and the Pacific Rim nations indicate that about fifty percent of the CEOs think that expanding abroad is crucial to the success of their organizations and that such expansion is a very important part of their plan to increase revenue and profit in the next five years (Anders, 1989; Surveying the CEOs, 1989). A similar survey of foreign business investors indicated that, with the bulk of the world's population in the less-developed nations, they are both rapidly growing markets for finished products and sources of supply of competitive products to world markets (Weigel, 1988).

Second, MNCs will find Third-World governments more pragmatic and less ideological in the 1990s than they were in the 1970s (Chaudhuri, 1988). In fact, this possibility is underscored by the results of a recent cross-national study which indicated that a high level of foreign investment from multiple countries is associated with less conflict in the less-developed countries and with more conflict in more developed countries (Rothgeb, 1990).

Third, the business environment will be much more favorable than it was in the last decade because of the region's renewed interest in private foreign investment (Chaudhuri, 1988). This new environment has encouraged Singapore, Malaysia, Kenya and Brazil to top the list of middle-income developing countries where foreign direct investments play a relatively large role in obtaining benefits from capital, technology and management provided by foreign investors (Weigel, 1988).

Fourth, even though the Third World does not have the international power it exercised in the mid-1970s, it is an important actor in a number of arenas. Because it has several important resources, it will become a central political and economic focus in the international system (Holm, 1990).

Finally, studies reveal that both transnational corporations and the developing nations were worse off as a result of industrial and social conflicts that characterized their relationships in the 1970 (Chaudhuri, 1988). With the rapid increase in international trade and investment, there is a reduced possibility for national control of economies (Holm, 1990). This strengthens industrial interests in joint ventures, which, while not an easy task, can have major impacts on corporate profits in domestic and global markets (O'Reilly, 1988). This point is iterated by management consultant Drucker (1980):

> The world economy in this century has become interdependent. There is no country today large enough . . . to be an autonomous unit of economic activity or of economic policy. . . The world economy has rapidly become "transnational" rather than international. The dependence on raw materials from all parts of the globe is only one symptom; the rapid development of production sharing is another. (p. 165)

To maximize corporate and, in turn, national benefits from MNCs' activities in the developing nations, it is important that corporate communication practitioners contribute to management's decision-making process. Averting industrial strife is not just desirable for the MNC, it can spell the difference between good and bad business, as was indicated in the fallout from Union Carbide's Bhopal, India, disaster in December 1984. For MNCs' public-relations practitioners to live up to their social responsibilities in development, Corbett (1984) suggests that they act as watchdogs of corporations to make sure that they (1) work with local government or groups to support areas of broad social concern, (2) make charitable contributions, (3) create community events that promote organizational identification, (4) seek opportunities to work with like-minded groups or agencies, (5) foster a climate or readiness to help, and (6) encourage the development of local vendors and suppliers. These strategies have the potential to encourage an organization to live up to its social responsibility by addressing participatory needs, thereby enhancing the public credibility of governments and organizations. By applying community-relations strategies to promoting industrial peace, public relations can contribute to the development of the Third World.

CONCLUSION

This chapter discusses the potentials for the use of public relations in attaining industrial peace and development in the developing nations. Two major areas in which the public-relations practitioner can be most useful are in developing and implementing programs whose goals are to achieve institutional-sociopolitical stability and institutional-sociostructural integration. Nations that are not politically stable or are not sociostructurally integrated will have monumental difficulties in establishing the necessary infrastructure and good will for sustained development. Practitioner-driven program development and implementation must be based on strategies anchored within a framework of development theories and evaluation research that is sensitive to the development status of the environment. The present development scenarios in most of the Third World, while cognizant of the failures of the dominant development paradigms of the 1960s and 1970s, need further demonstrate community-based programs that apply public relations skills and strategies to establish, maintain, and enhance development benefits for both the agency and the community.

REFERENCES

Ake, C. 1973. Explaining political instability in new states. *The Journal of Modern African Studies*, 11:347–59.

Akinsanya, A. A. 1984. *Multinationals in a changing environment: A study of business-government relations in the Third World.* New York: Praeger.

Anders, G. 1989, September 22. Going global: Vision vs. reality. *The Wall Street Journal Reports: World Business,* p. R20.

Barnet, R. J., and Müller, R. E. (1974). *Global reach: The power of the multinational corporations.* New York: Simon and Schuster.

Biersteker, T. J. 1978. *Distortion or development? Contending perspectives on the multinational corporation.* Cambridge, Mass: The MIT Press.

Chaudhuri, A. 1988. Multinational corporations in less-developed countries: What is in store? *The Columbia Journal of World World Business* 23:57–63.

Corbett, W. J. 1984. *The corporate conscience and national development: The role of public relations.* Paper presented at the symposium on Communication and Development, International Public Relations Association, Trinidad, West Indies.

Dahrendorf, R. 1959. *Class and class conflict in industrial society.* Stanford, CA: Stanford University Press.

Drucker, P. F. 1980. *Managing in turbulent times.* New York: Harper & Row.

Etzioni, A. 1965. *Political unification.* New York: Holt, Rinehart and Winston).

Faringer, G. L. 1991. *Press freedom in Africa.* New York: Praeger.

Galtung, J. 1965. Institutionalized conflict resolution: A theoretical paradigm, *Journal of Peace Research* 2(4):348–97.

Hachten, W. A. 1987. *The world news prism: Changing media, clashing idealogies.* Ames, Iowa: Iowa State University Press.

Hakes, J. E. 1973. *Weak parliaments and military coups in Africa: A study in regime instability.* Beverly Hills, Calif.: Sage Publications.

Harlow, R. F. 1988. Building a public relations definition. In R. E. Hiebert (ed.), *Precision public relations* (pp. 7–16). New York: Longman.

Haule, J. J. 1984. Old paradigm and new order in the African context: Toward an appropriate model of communication and national development. Gazette: *International Journal for Mass Communication Studies* 33:3–15.

Holm, H-H. 1990. The end of the Third World? *Journal of Peace Research* 27(1): 1–7.

Inkeles, A., and Smith, D. H. 1974. *Becoming modern: Individual change in six developing nations.* Cambridge, Mass: Harvard University Press.

Jose, B. 1975. Press freedom in Africa, *African Affairs*, 74 (296): 255–62.

Kruckeberg, D., and Starck, K. 1988. *Public relations and community: A reconstructed theory.* New York: Praeger.

Lerner, D. 1958. *The passing of traditional society: Modernizing the Middle East.* New York: Free Press.

McGowan, P. 1986. Sixty coups in thirty years—Further evidence regarding African military coups d'etat. *The Journal of Modern African Studies* 24(3):539–46.

Melkote, S. R. 1991. *Communication for development in the Third World: theory and practice.* New Delhi: Sage Publications.

Mohamed, R. 1984. Public relations in Lebanon: No task for the timid. *Communication World,* January, 35–38.

Morrison, D. G., and Stevenson, H. M. 1971. Political instability in independent black Africa: More dimensions of conflict behavior within nations. *The Journal of Conflict Resolution,* 15(3):347–68.

Narula, U., and Pearce, W. B. 1986. *Development as communication: A perspectivee on India.* Carbondale, Ill: Southern Illinois University Press.

O'Reilly, A. J. F. 1988. Establishing successful joint ventures in developing nations: A CEO's perspective. *The Columbia Journal of World Business* 23(1):65–71.

Peterson, T., Schramm, W., and Siebert, F. S. 1971. *Four theories of the press.* Urbana, Ill: University of Illinois Press.

Pratt, C. 1985. Public relations in the Third World: The African context. *Public Relations Journal* 41(2): February, 11–12, 15–16.

Public Relations Society of America. 1987. Report of special committee on terminology. *International Public Relations Review* 11(2):6–11.

Rogers, E. M. 1976. *Communication and development: Critical perspectives.* Beverly Hills, Calif.: Sage Publications.

Rogers, E. M. 1962. *Diffusion of innovations.* New York: Free Press.

Rothgeb, J. M. 1990. Investment dependence and political conflict in Third World countries. *Journal of Peace Research*, 27(3):255–72.

Schiller, H. I. 1989. *Culture, Inc.: The corporate takeover of public expression.* New York: Oxford University Press.

Sonaike, S. A. 1988. Communication and Third World development: A dead end? *Gazette: International Journal for Mass Communication Studies*, 41(2):85–108.

Stevenson, R. L. 1988. *Communication, development, and the Third World: The global politics of information.* New York: Longman.

Surveying the CEOs. 1989, September 22. *The Wall Street Journal Reports: World Business*, p. R21.

Turner, L. 1973. *Multinational companies and the Third World.* New York: Hill and Wang.

United Nations Department of Economic and Social Affairs. 1974. *Multinational corporations in world development.* New York: Praeger.

Weigel, D. R. 1988. Investment in LDCs: The debate continues. *The Columbia Journal of World Business* 23(1):5–9.

Part IV

THOMAS L. McPHAIL
BRENDA M. McPHAIL

10

Television and Development Communication: A Canadian Case Study

The history of Canadian television has been a history of countering the influence of television from the United States. In large part, since ninety percent of the Canadian population is located within 100 miles of the U.S. border, even as early as the 1950s, U.S. television was available over the air in many Canadian homes. Major Canadian cities, such as Halifax, Montreal, Toronto, or Vancouver could easily receive U.S. broadcast signals, including both radio and television stations. For example, Buffalo, N.Y., stations were received in Toronto, Ontario, and Spokane, Washington, stations were received in Vancouver, British Columbia. The U.S. media exposure was fueled by the introduction of cable in Canada. Cable systems in Canada developed rapidly during the 1960s. The prime motivation was to bring U.S. channels into distant areas where over-the-air television signals were weak or nonexistent. Further motivation for cable was to bring clearer color television pictures with the introduction of color TV around the same time. At one point, Canada was the most cabled nation in the world, and, it was not to bring their national public broadcaster, the Canadian Broadcasting Corporation (CBC), or the major private broadcaster, CTV, into Canadian living rooms. Rather the prime motive for cable in Canada was to bring U.S. networks such as ABC/CBS/NBC into Canadian homes. Indeed, some Canadians were not satisfied with cable. Many bought their own satellite dishes in order to pull in such services as CNN or ESPN prior to their availability on cable (McPhail and Downey, 1984).

The Toronto-based *Globe and Mail* deals with both the anxiety and paradox when it states, "In order to protect Canadian television, it seems, we have to allow into this country huge new amounts of U.S. television. This appears to be the current (and surprisingly unanimous) thinking of Canadian producers, broadcasters, cable operators, and the CRTC" ("Descrambling the Logic," 1991).

The Canadian media situation is an important area of study in terms of development communication for three major reasons.

First, since the introduction of radio in the 1920s down to more current concerns over trans-border data flows involving electronic information, Canada has enunciated various public policies, undertaken various royal commissions, established certain laws, and passed broadcasting legislation to promote indigenous media and, thereby, counter the impact or influence of foreign, mostly U.S., media.

Second, much of early and ongoing concern deals specifically with U.S. media, beginning with attempts in the 1920s by NBC Radio to purchase stations in Canada to current concern over the vast number of satellite dishes which are used almost solely to pick up U.S. stations in Canadian homes and businesses.

Third, Canada, as an industrialized nation, has been attempting for decades to counter media influence from another industrialized nation, namely, the United States. Now, other nations, or groups of nations, particularly the European Community, are examining quite closely the Canadian Content regulations (details later) and other measures which have attempted to counterbalance the pervasive influence of U.S. media in Canada, where Canada's media are frequently referred to in a derogatory fashion as "Hollywood North." (McPhail, 1987).

What is presented in this chapter is background history relating to the origins of concern, and various public policy initiatives aimed at promoting a positive sense of Canadian identity in the communication sector. But it is important to note at the outset that there has not developed in Canada a consensus as to what, indeed, represents Canadian identity. For example, the Quebec viewpoint is frequently diametrically opposed to other viewpoints concerning aspects of national identity.[1] In addition, certain legislative and regulatory actions have, in essence, backfired, and promoted a greater influx of U.S. networks' or first-run U.S. feature films rather than the opposite, intended effect of decreasing U.S. media and Hollywood's influence in Canada.

DEVELOPMENT COMMUNICATION

Development communication is a theoretical model which postulates that various communication undertakings (including both hardware and software) are encouraged for the utilization and support of broader social, economic, cultural, and political goals. These latter goals are of a general public policy nature, and they are the overall umbrella under which development communication initiatives are pursued. For example, development communication would encourage the introduction of computer systems in terms of these systems allowing the enhanced functioning of government agencies, educational institutions, social agencies, etc. Or, development communication would permit the support of an indigenous feature film industry in order to create a domestic film industry and employment opportunities, along with promoting a pro-social orientation concerning a country's history, politics, social environment, values, etc. In essence, development communication does not view communication as a neutral. Beneficial types of development communication are clearly of a positive, prosocial nature, but others, encompassing technological determinism, may be dysfunctional or disruptive in terms of indigenous cultural values and norms.

Development communication attempts to evaluate and select various communication options including both media and messages, in order to promote a domestic, positive communication agenda. Foreign programming or equipment is, in turn, viewed in terms of the extent to which it contributes to the larger strategy and goals of the domestically inspired development communication system. As a result, certain activities, for example, the importation of violent feature films or the importation of direct-broadcast satellites may either undermine or, in some cases, totally negate indigenous programming or the domestic communication agenda in certain cases.

Development communication as a theoretical construct is difficult to adequately position. For example, even though development in itself is a macro-concept, it is not applied in the abstract; namely, development communication on a nation-by-nation basis has to be seen within the context of the broader national public policy objectives of each nation-state. In turn, this requires an analysis of the national public policy objectives across several areas. This could be considered a super-macro construct. Development communication does not work on its own, it works against a broader set of objectives established by national governments. Some of the national governments are democratically elected, and when political parties change, so also do the national government policies; thus, the framework for the development of communication also shifts. Other nations are led by military or authoritarian regimes which are also subject to radical change, such as coups, change in military leadership, etc. This also reverberates in a downward fashion, ultimately, on the internal development communication objectives. But the point is the same: developmental communication is a theoretical construct subordinate to national public policy objectives, which form national public policies across all sectors. The importance of development communication is by virtue of the fact that what comes under its mandate is the mass media, and the mass media have a substantial role in conveying national and cultural goals. When the mass media contain a substantial amount of foreign and nonindigenous programming, this has the capacity to alter or in some cases challenge media messages that are produced by indigenous groups or leaders.

The following reflects some of the various components which have to be addressed in terms of development communication:

The difficulties for the adoption of a viable development communication policy has to take into account that there is a horizontal and a vertical level which require simultaneous approach. The horizontal level consists of diversified institutions such as governmental developments, semi-governmental agencies (Rural Extension Service, etc), independent development organizations, and private media, which are all active in communication in one way or the other. The co-ordination of these institutions, e.g. the problem of assigning them to communicative tasks they are able to perform best becomes thus a major item of a meaningful development communication policy. The vertical level is defined by the need for a mutual information flow between the population base and the decision-making bodies. On this level even more institutions are involved because of the local and supra-local administrations which, of course, are active in handing out directives and in feeding back reports to the government. Co-ordination of development communication becomes a more difficult task on this level because with the exception of the governmental extensions no institution is really prepared until now to pick up the information from the grass-roots levels and feed them back meaningfully to the administration. (Habermann, 1978, p. 173)

Jan Servaes, in his article, "Rethinking Development Communication: One World, Multiple Cultures," makes the following valid point:

In other words, each society must attempt to delineate its own strategy to development, based on its own ecology and culture. Therefore, it should not attempt to blindly imitate program and strategies of other countries with a totally different historical and cultural background. (Servaes, 1990, p. 38).

Servaes also marked the important point and distinction that it is not only programming or software that has the potential for being destructive of development communication objectives, but that the technology itself, in a McLuhanesque sense, may also present anti-development problems. Servaes puts it this way:

When one has to import foreign technology, which is not available inside the country, a major criterion can be whether this technology can contribute to autonomous development. Since communication policy-makers have often concentrated on the procurement of hardware only, careful analysis and projection ought to be made regarding the secondary impact of communication technology, in terms of the distribution of political, economic and cultural benefits. The danger of technology transfer is precisely that technological models are adapted to the social structures of the technology exporters, and thus primarily are a product of an institutional structure designed for the maximization of profit and advantage (even though some social needs are not met or some regions are not serviced) rather than for the maximization of the national development effects of the technology. (Servaes, 1990, p. 42).

Canada is an excellent case study in point concerning the above. For example, much of worldwide advanced satellite technology research was conducted in Canadian laboratories. Canada has had a long series of major experiments in designing advanced technology satellites, but very little, if any, planning or money went into software or indigenous impact studies. Rather, technological determinism for over two decades was allowed to run rampant and now Canada finds itself with an inordinate number of satellite dishes scattered across the country for the main purpose of picking up foreign, mostly American, satellite signals. Little Canadian input or programming is being beamed into these various homes, community centers, or remote villages.[2]

But this current satellite-inspired communication problem is but an extension of early communication concerns. Some of the significant issues and milestones are discussed next.

CANADIAN TELEVISION HISTORICAL BACKGROUND

In order to appreciate current issues and legislation as they pertain to development communication in Canada, it is important to note some of the early events which precipitated a nationalistic orientation for the role of broadcasting.

Wireless telegraphy was the first subject of communication legislation passed by the government of Canada in 1905. Responsibility for enforcing the legislation rested with the Department of Marine & Fisheries until 1932. This department received control because of the ship-to-shore nature of much of the early wireless communication transmissions. But, at the same time, private radio stations were appearing. For example, the first private radio station was established in Montreal in 1919 and licensed to the Marconi Company. But even in these early years, for those who did have radio, as much as eighty percent of the programming was of American origin (Prang, 1965).

During the 1920s, there was an attempt by the NBC radio company to purchase radio stations in Alberta, Canada. This and other matters precipitated the first Royal Commission on Broadcasting, which was established in December 1928 and headed by Sir John Aird. This royal commission concluded that radio was an important cultural medium, and that national sovereignty issues were at stake because of the strong influence of U.S. radio programs being aired on Canadian stations. An important recommendation was the creation of a public radio network to receive a federal subsidy and to promote directly Canadian issues and interests. The end result was the creation of the Canadian Broadcasting Corporation (CBC).

Mark Starowicz, one of Canada's leading producers, stated quite succinctly the cultural dependence concern in his article, "Slow Dissolve: How Canada will Lose Its Broadcasting Sovereignty":

The Canadian Radio Broadcasting Act of 1932 is the constitution of this country's cultural sovereignty, the declaration that the population north of the 49th parallel had decided it would have its own culture, and evolve its own agenda, cover its own news, produce its own radio plays, radio comedies, that its children would be raised hearing programs which reflected our sensibilities, our values. That one Act of parliament had a more profound effect on playwriting than all the theatres of the Dominion would, more on orchestral and popular music than all the conservatories and entertainment halls in this country. The economic ripple of declaring a sovereign cultural market reached generations of writers, singers and musicians who, like Grey's Elegy Turned Around, might never have been. There is little doubt as to the objective which we, as a nation, set for ourselves in 1932.

Prime Minister Bennett, when introducing the Broadcasting Act into the Commons, did so with these words:

"This country must be assured of complete Canadian control of broadcasting from Canadian sources, free from foreign interference or influence."

He was unequivocal about the method as well:

"No other scheme than that of public ownership can ensure to the people of this country, without regard to class or place, equal enjoyment of the benefits and pleasure of broadcasting. . . . I cannot think that any government would be warranted in leaving the air to private exploitation and not reserving it for the use of the people." (Starowicz, 1984)

The above illustrates the central concern from a communication development prospective of the Canadian government in dealing with its broadcasting undertakings.

Following World War II, another royal commission was created with a broad cultural mandate which also included the task of developing strategy for the introduction of television in Canada. The Massey Commission, as it was known, reported in June 1951, and described broadcasting as "one of the great forces in our country in promoting Canadian unity and Canadian cultural life" (Canada, 1951:295).

In 1952, the CBC began operating television stations in both Montreal and Toronto. Shortly thereafter, a station was established in the nation's capital, Ottawa. By 1955, there were six CBC stations across Canada providing television for a limited number of daytime hours, but as the number of hours of programming increased, even in these early years, the percentage of Canadian indigenous programming decreased. Even during these early years, approximately fifty percent of the shows on the public CBC network were U.S. in origin. This fact was the primary incentive for the establishment of a third royal commission in 1955, headed by Robert Fowler.

This report which reviewed many aspects of Canadian television is important for three reasons: It pointed out that the private television broadcasting stations in Canada showed even greater proportion of American programming than the publicly funded CBC. It called for a national regulator, which would be responsible for both public and private undertakings in Canada. As an early recognition strategy, the report advanced the central proposition: "As a nation, we cannot accept these powerful and pervasive media, the natural and complete flow of another nation's culture without danger to our national identity . . . assuming, as we must that their broadcasting system is satisfactory and suitable for Americans, there is no basis in thinking it is desirable for Canadians" (Canada, 1957, p. 9).

As a result of the Fowler royal commission, a new broadcasting act was passed in 1958. It established a Board of Broadcast Governors. This board has some similarities with the Federal Communications Commission in the United States, and it was replaced 10 years later by the Canadian Radio/Television Commission (CRTC), which is still the national regulator of both broadcasting and telecommunication undertakings in Canada.

The mandate of the Board of Broadcast Governors was to ensure an efficient and orderly national broadcasting system, including both radio and television, public and private, which was essentially Canadian in both character and content.

The Board of Broadcast Governors, because of its concern with private television broadcasters showing a preponderance of American programming, particularly in prime time, put forward an idea concerning Canadian content quotas. These would require broadcasters, both public and private, to quantitatively demonstrate that after April 1962, at least fifty-five percent of their programming was Canadian.

It became evident during the 1960s that the CBC was viewed as the major television broadcaster which should attend most closely to promoting Canadian productions. The private television sector reluctantly agreed to regulatory aims in this general area, but with considerably less zeal than the CBC.

A new broadcasting act was passed by parliament in 1968 and remained in place until 1991. It dealt with all aspects of the Canadian broadcasting system, but has a distinctly nationalistic flavor in one section. Two items of particular note are:

Section 3B: The Canadian Broadcasting system should be effectively owned and controlled by Canadians, so as to safeguard, enrich and strengthen the cultural, political, social and economic fabric of Canada.

Section G:IV: Contribute to the development of National Unity and provide for a continuing expression of Canadian identity. (Canada, 1968, pp. 3–4).

Although the intent of the 1968 act is consistent with development communication philosophy, it was essentially blind-sided by the introduction of cable television systems in Canada. Cable produced an onslaught of more U.S. channels into Canadian living rooms. The situation was exacerbated by the private television broadcaster in Canada, in order to capture a large audience for their advertisers, being inclined to purchase U.S. sitcoms, etc. for their prime time schedule. As a result, both technology and economics were creating a deleterious impact on the Canadian production industry. With every new channel or every new cable system in Canada, the net result was the further Americanization of Canadian viewers. These problems were recognized by several federal government studies and reflected very clearly in a January,

1983, CRTC set of new regulations. The following policy statement recognizes clearly the sad state of affairs, because of the preponderance of U.S. programming and the necessity of maintaining
a strong Canadian presence on Canadian television:

> Canadian television programming must attract, engage and
> entertain. It must also inform, educate and enrich our cultur-
> al experience. For if Canadians do not use what is one of the
> world's must extensive and sophisticated communication
> system to speak to themselves—if it serves only for the
> importation of foreign programs—there is a real and legiti-
> mate concern that the country will ultimately lose the means
> of expressing its identity. Developing a strong Canadian pro-
> gram production capability is no longer a matter of desirabili-
> ty but of necessity. (CRTC, 1983, p. 3).

Despite the tightening up of the Canadian Content Regulations for television, things did not improve for the Canadian television production industry. As a result, in May, 1985, a new task
force was established to make recommendations on both a cultural
strategy and an industrial strategy to positively promote the evolution of the Canadian broadcasting system. It was co-chaired by
Gerald Caplan, a noted Canadian socialist media critic, and Florian
Sauvageau, an internationally respected communication scholar
from Laval University in Quebec City.

The Task Force on Broadcasting Policy received 253 submis-
sions and held public hearings across Canada. Many critics pointed
to the inadequacies of the Canadian situation, but also there were
a number of individuals who discussed the complexity and difficulty of enacting appropriate legislation to see the broadcasting
system through to the turn of the century.

In their final report which details the crisis in Canadian
broadcasting, the authors refer to the problems in the Canadian
broadcasting system as follows:

> The problems are clear enough: inadequate Canadian pro-
> gramming; inadequate high-quality programming; insuffi-
> cient performance programming by the private sector in
> English Canada, insufficient attention paid to information
> and public affairs programming in the private sector in Que-
> bec; and a general reluctance to give priority to the social
> goals of the broadcasting system.

The reasons for these problems are equally clear: the public sector, which must be the chief purveyor of quality Canadian programming, is inadequately scaled and funded; the private sector, which should complement the public sector at least to the extent of contributing to the fulfillment of the social objectives of the Broadcasting Act, is not contributing enough. (Caplan and Sauvageau, 1986, p. 691).

After additional consideration, the co-chairs called for a redefinition of Canadian broadcasting which would promote a partnership between the private sector and public sectors, and they also called for greater definition concerning the social and cultural objectives within a new Broadcasting Act. They conclude by saying:

> In the end, decisions must be made by those who form public policy: the CRTC, provincial governments and, above all, the government of Canada. It is those bodies that must gauge the extent of the commitment of Canadians to a Canadian broadcasting policy. They must determine how serious they themselves are about demanding a substantial contribution from the private sector to the goals of the new Broadcasting Act that we hope to see introduced. They must decide the proper level of government spending on broadcasting. They must determine, for example, whether Canadians are prepared to pay higher cable fees or sales taxes to pay for a new public sector broadcasting network. We do not underestimate how difficult it will be to make these decisions; but it is perhaps not excessive to assert that a great deal of the future of this country, and the kind of country we will be in the future, rests on those decisions. (Caplan and Sauvageau, 1986, p. 699)

The Caplan-Sauvageau Task Force contributed a great deal to the public debate on Canadian sovereignty as it relates to television broadcasting, but no eminent new broadcasting act was forthcoming. Instead, the problems identified clearly in the Caplan-Sauvageau report were exacerbated.

Despite years of attempts to promote indigenous television fare in the Canadian system, there continues two major problem areas. The first is cultural; namely, there have not been sufficient high-quality Canadian shows attracting large Canadian audiences which deal basically with Canadian history, Canadian folklore, or

Canadian drama. The second major problem is economic; namely, with the fragmentation of the television viewing audience, created by the dual forces of cable and the proliferation of television stations. These forces ultimately resulted in the creation of a 1990 Task Force on the Economic Status of Canadian Television.

This task force was established by the minister of communications with a two-fold mandate. The first was: "to examine the underlying financial structure of the Canadian television system with a view to making recommendations which will insure the on-going strength and dynamism of both public and private Canadian broadcasters."

The second mandate was to make recommendations specifically dealing with the following four areas:

1. The role of advertising.
2. The economic impact of new television services/channels.
3. A general investigation of the operation of the Canadian Broadcast Program Development Fund.
4. An examination of alternative television programming services. (Canada, 1991b, p. 11).

Before beginning to review the results of this task force, it is important to note that a large proportion of the problems which forced the creation of the 1990 task force directly related to the adverse actions of the Mulroney Conservative government during the 1980s. In law, the CBC has a strong mandate to provide Canadian programming, but this role is drastically affected by its ability to finance new Canadian programming. The Mulroney government, almost since its first electorial victory in 1982, had systematically decreased public funds being allocated to the CBC. The net result was a further Americanization of the Canadian broadcasting system under the Mulroney administration. In addition, a number of Conservative Members of Parliament, particularly those from Western Canada, were well known, via their public statements, for their detestation of the national public broadcasting network, mainly the CBC. Unfortunately, these political Neanderthals routinely sought to not only diminish, but in some cases, to close down CBC television outlets in a few Canadian cities during the Mulroney administration.

Even noted British scholar, Anthony Smith, has also identified the Canadian conundrum. He puts it this way:

The culturally and politically debilitating effects of media dependence are perhaps most eloquently illustrated by taking an example not from the non-aligned or developing countries but from within the developed world itself. Canada has always been obliged to struggle to maintain a thriving indigenous culture because of the proximity of the United States with its enormous output of information and entertainment. To all intents Canada has been treated as part of a large North American market for films, television programmes and other media products. . . . Many Canadians treat the phenomenon today as a kind of running national crisis. No country in the world probably is more completely committed to the practice of free flow in its culture and no country is more completely its victim. (Smith, 1980, pp. 52–54).

To claim it is a "running national crisis" is at times an understatement. For the last decade, the Conservative party systematically reduced the funding for the CBC, thus leaving the option, and in some cases, the necessity for greater imports of U.S. software for Canadian television outlets.

At the heart of the problem in terms of producing Canadian indigenous television fare are the programming costs. Clearly, it is cheaper and easier to import U.S. sitcoms. But even in this particular case, the competition among Canadian television stations has driven up the costs for such programming. During the 1980s, for example, the cost of importing foreign programming increased twelve percent yearly, and the Task Force reports: "Bids by one network to raid the property of another network, whether or not they were successful, often resulted in significant inflation in the costs of purchase of a program. After such attempts, the cost of "Cheers," "Empty Nests," "China Beach," and "Head of the Class" climbed up to 40 percent in one year" (Canada, 1991b, pp. 37–38).

The problem of importing foreign programming is further exacerbated by the costs of replacing that programming. In other words, if Canadian networks do not purchase U.S. sitcoms, then they have to provide their own materials in that time-slot, and that is simply expensive. The Task Force refers to this situation as follows:

The CTV network claims the opportunity costs of Canadian entertainment programming has also increased. By opportunity costs, CTV means the profit-margin differential between one hour of Canadian programming and one hour of even a low-rated U.S. show. CTV contends each hour of Canadian entertainment now represents a $5 million loss in annual profit margin. (Canada 1991b, p. 39)

The economic determinism for private television broadcast, as reflected in the above opportunity-cost situation, certainly works in an adverse fashion against promoting Canadian programs. One does not have to be a mathematical genius to realize that if each hour of indigenous programming represents an annual $5 million loss, than it would not take many hours in prime time to bankrupt a private network. Many private broadcasters seek out low-cost U.S. sitcom entertainment shows as a matter of economic survival, with little priority being given to the cultural and social consequences of importing such shows as "Roseanne" or "The Simpsons", of violent or sexist genre.

FRAGMENTATION

There are major problems created by the expansion of television stations in Canada. For example, according to the latest available figures, in 1989 the audience share for Canadian television programmings was thirty-two percent; in essence, this means that sixty-eight percent of the shows were foreign, mostly American sitcoms. This problem is compounded with the recent introduction of new Canadian television services. For example, in 1982, pay-TV networks, like HBO, featuring first run feature movies were introduced. In 1984, a very successful specialty music channel and a popular sports channel were introduced, along with two ethnic channels. In the latter part of the 1980s, a health channel, additional pay movie channel, plus nine specialty services were introduced; and finally in 1991, a new pay-per-view service, known as Viewer's Choice Canada, was established. Although on the surface this appears to be an aggressive list of new Canadian initiative, the history of Canadian broadcasting has shown that every time a new channel is introduced, it ultimately creates further inroads for U.S. programming. U.S. stations and U.S. produced entertainment shows dominate Canadian television, despite legislative and regulatory attempts to counter this cultural invasion.

RADIO

Although the thrust of this chapter deals with television development and communication, clearly the CRTC has Canadian Content Rules for radio as well. A recent example of the problem of rating audio materials as Canadian or not involves a leading Canadian musician and artist, Bryan Adams. He wrote his international best-seller "Waking up the Neighbors," with a British colleague, and it thus failed to meet the CRTC Canadian Content (Radio) Regulations. Thus, it may not be played more than 18 times a week on Canadian FM radio stations. This has Adams and others concerned. Adams, himself, criticized CRTC bureaucrats for failing to understand that the music industry is a global industry, just as McLuhan labeled the world a "global village." (Toronto Star Feb. 8, 1992).

Adams most telling attack on the Canadian Content Regulations is, indeed, bitter. Referring to the system as it now stands, he says, ". . . mediocrity is its biggest by-product, and mediocrity will never be raised by penalizing excellence. It is my belief that real talent will always win out, whether or not it is supported by the government." He continues: "It's time to shut off the government tap as it relates to music, and direct its largess with taxpayers' money to programs that are much more important than whether or not some musician gets a chance to make his ninth album. Especially if there was not demand for the first eighth." (Toronto Star Feb. 8, 1992).

Although Canadian radio stations have a requirement to play thirty percent Canadian content, by virtue of the CRTC's regulations, there are now some, in addition to Adams, who are questioning the wisdom of this system. Over time, artists, writers, and producers learn to provide what will qualify as Canadian content for radio exposure with less regard for artistic talent or merit. Ultimately, the international market has less and less to do with those who take the easier path of hiding under and qualifying solely for Canadian Content radio approval. Whereas, international stars, ranging from Bryan Adams to Neil Young to Anne Murray prefer to extend their talents and sales off-shore, even at the risk of being labeled "Un-Canadian" by the parochial regulations.

NEW BROADCASTING ACT (1991)

The 1968 Broadcasting Act was replaced in 1991 by a new federal act. The act is extremely detailed and runs some fifty-seven pages in length. This discussion will limit itself to select sections which deal with nontechnical aspects of the act.

One of the major sections is entitled "Broadcasting Policy for Canada." This section provides a detailed outline of how development communication is applied in practice.

It declares:

3. (1) It is hereby declared as the broadcasting policy for Canada that
(a) The Canadian broadcasting system shall be effectively owned and controlled by Canadians;
(b) the Canadian broadcasting system operating primarily in the English and French languages and comprising public, private and community elements, makes use of radio frequencies that are public property and provides, through its programming, a public service essential to the maintenance and enhancement of national identity and cultural sovereignty,
(c) English and French language broadcasting, while sharing common aspects, operate under different conditions and may have different requirements;
(d) the Canadian broadcasting system should
(i) serve to safeguard, enrich and strengthen the cultural, political, social and economic fabric of Canada,
(ii) encourage the development of Canadian expression by providing a wide range of programming that reflects Canadian attitudes, opinions, ideas, values and artistic creativity, by displaying Canadian talent in entertainment programming and by offering information and analysis concerning Canada and other countries from a Canadian point of view,
(iii) through its programming and the employment opportunities arising out of its operations, serve the needs and interests, and reflect the circumstances and aspirations, of Canadian men, women and children,

including equal rights, the linguistic duality and multicultural and multiracial nature of Canadian society and
the special place of aboriginal peoples within that society, and

(iv) be readily adaptable to scientific and technological
change;

(e) each element of the Canadian broadcasting system shall
contribute in an appropriate manner to the creation and presentation of Canadian programming;

(f) each broadcasting undertaking shall make maximum use,
and in no case less than predominant use, of Canadian creative and other resources in the creation and presentation of
programming, unless the nature of the service provided by
the undertaking, such as specialized content or format or the
use of languages other than French and English, renders that
use impracticable, in which case the undertaking shall make
the greatest practicable use of those resources;

(g) the programming originated by broadcasting undertakings
should be of high standard;

(h) all persons who are licensed to carry on broadcasting
undertakings have a responsibility for the programs they
broadcast;

(i) the programming provided by the Canadian broadcasting
system should

(i) be varied and comprehensive, providing a balance of
information, enlightenment and entertainment for men,
women and children of all ages, interests and tastes,

(ii) be drawn from local, regional, national and international sources,

(iii) include educational and community programs,

(iv) provide a reasonable opportunity for the public to be
exposed to the expression of differing views on matters
of public concern and

(v) include a significant contribution from the Canadian
independent production sector;

(j) educational programming, particularly where provided
through the facilities of an independent educational authority, is an integral part of the Canadian broadcasting system;

(k) a range of broadcasting services in English and in French
shall be extended to all Canadians as resources become available;

(l) The Canadian Broadcasting Corporation, as the national public broadcaster, should provide radio and television services incorporating a wide range of programming that informs, enlightens and entertains;

(m) the programming provided by the Corporation should
  (i) be predominantly and distinctively Canadian,
  (ii) reflect Canada and its regions to national and regional audiences, while serving the special needs of those regions,
  (iii) actively contribute to the flow and exchange of cultural expression,
  (iv) be in English and in French, reflecting the different needs and circumstances of each official language community, including the particular needs and circumstances of English and French linguistic minorities,
  (v) strive to be of equivalent quality in English and in French,
  (vi) contribute to shared national consciousness and identity,
  (vii) be made available throughout Canada by the most appropriate and efficient means and as resources become available for the purpose, and
  (viii) reflect the multicultural and multiracial nature of Canada;

(n) where any conflict arises between the objectives of the Corporation set out in paragraphs (1) and (m) and the interests of any other broadcasting undertaking of the Canadian broadcasting system, it shall be resolved in the public interest, and where the public interest would be equally served by resolving the conflict in favour of either, it shall be resolved in favour of the objectives set out in paragraphs (1) and (m);

(o) programming that reflects the aboriginal cultures of Canada should be provided within the Canadian broadcasting system as resources become available for the purpose;

(p) programming accessible by disabled persons should be provided within the Canadian broadcasting system as resources become available for the purpose;

(q) without limiting any obligation of a broadcasting undertaking to provide the programming contemplated by paragraph (i), alternative television programming services in English and in French should be provided where necessary to ensure that the full range of programming contemplated by that paragraph is made available through the Canadian broadcasting system;

(r) the programming provided by alternative television programming services should

(i) be innovative and be complementary to the programming provided for mass audiences,

(ii) cater to tastes and interests not adequately provided for by the programming provided for mass audiences, and include programming devoted to culture and the arts,

(iii) reflect Canada's regions and multicultural nature,

(iv) as far as possible, be acquired rather than produced by those services, and

(v) be made available throughout Canada by the most cost-efficient means;

(s) private networks and programming undertakings should, to an extent consistent with the financial and other resources available to them,

(i) contribute significantly to the creation and presentation of Canadian programming, and

(ii) be responsive to the evolving demands of the public; and

(t) distribution undertakings

(i) should give priority to the carriage of Canadian programming services and, in particular, to the carriage of local Canadian stations,

(ii) should provide efficient delivery of programming at affordable rates, using the most efficient technologies available at reasonable cost,

(iii) should, where programming services are supplied to them by broadcasting undertakings pursuant to contractual arrangements, provide reasonable terms for the carriage, packaging and retailing of those programming services, and

(iv) may, where the Commission considers it appropriate, originate programming, including local programming, on such terms as are conducive to the achievement of the objectives of the broadcasting policy set out in this subsection, and in particular provide access for underserved linguistic and cultural minority communities. (Canada, 1991a, pp. 3–7).

This, in essence, is the development communication material within the overall act. It is also worth noting that this is a substantial elaboration of rather brief sections relating to cultural
objectives in the previous 1968 act. Also, from a comparative point
of view, this represents, internationally, one of the most detailed
statements concerning the application and goals for television in
terms of a nation-state establishing objectives which are of a non-
commercial nature. This preceding is a model statement of development communication as applied to television.

Two additional items are worth noting in the new act. The
first is the direct statements concerning the role of the regulatory
commission to provide and encourage Canadian programs. In addition, the act provides the federal cabinet with override power
which provides an avenue of appeal from the final decision of the
regulatory commission, the CRTC. Some critics have difficulty
with this, but the federal government maintains that they are the
elected representative of the people, whereas the regulatory com-
missioners themselves are appointed, and thus, it is the Minister
of Communication who has the ultimate responsibility for the
activities of both the regulatory agency, the CRTC, as well as the
major national television network, the CBC.

In closing, the act also spends several pages discussing specific activities and the makeup of the Canadian Broadcasting Corporation, including its appointed board of directors. This is important
since the corporation, the CBC, receives substantial funds from
the federal government and requires those funds in order to operate a national system. The reader should also be aware that there
are other national, or quasi-national television systems which are
privately owned or controlled. For example, the CT Network, the
Global Network and several strong independent private television
stations exist in major cities across Canada. Thus, it is a combination of both the public (CBC) and the private television stations
which constitutes the overall Canadian television broadcasting
system.

The new 1991 act, as it affects the television industry during
the balance of this decade, possibly will have major repercussions.
For example, if the mandate to provide culturally diverse or region-
ally diverse programming becomes a major influence in terms of
the production agenda, then one may see production funds being
allocated to regional areas, such as the Maritimes, or subgroups,
such as Eskimos. If this is the case, funds will not be available or
directed to national programming or will not go to finance produc-

tions which serve a broad cross section of Canadians in terms of national or international issues. This has been the case since the introduction of television in Canada, but with the new act, it could change. Some critics maintain that this is, indeed, a moot point since there is such little funding available, that new programming, whether it be regional or national, is not likely to come about in any substantial fashion. Rather, more closings of CBC outlets or greater utilization of foreign, mostly U.S. software, will likely increase across Canadian television stations until fiscal difficulties are resolved.

CANADIAN BROADCAST DEVELOPMENT FUND (CBDF)

The CBDF fund was established to create quality Canadian television productions which would attract large Canadian television audiences and focus primarily on Canadian themes and issues. The CBDF 1991 policy statement states that its goal is to stimulate the production of all types of Canadian television, ranging from children's programming to entertainment programming, to documentaries. The productions are to be of sufficiently high quality to be shown in prime time, and these productions should also be used to stimulate an independent Canadian television production sector. The broadcast fund came into existence in 1983, and now has existed for a decade. It annually allocates about $50 million a year to generate English language prime time productions.

The fund has been moderately successful in at least stemming the slide of Canadian program viewing, but also, about fifty percent of the productions are undertaken by the CBC, leaving a relatively small pool of development funds available for either the commercial television broadcasting networks or the smaller independent stations.

QUEBEC: AN ALTERNATE MEDIA MODEL

It is important to recall that Canada is not a monolithic nation-state. For example, the people of Quebec, who constitute approximately one-quarter of the population of Canada, speak French as their first language and in some cases, as their only language. Thus, much of what is described in this chapter deals with what is referred to as English-Canada, or the other nine English-speaking provinces, and of course, they are the sites where New York or Hollywood productions, because of the English language, are viewed almost in unison, whether on television or in movie theaters. But in the province of Quebec, there was frequently a time delay as these productions had to be either translated or subtitled in French. But this, of course, aided in protecting the French culture, and allowed the opportunity for French media personalities, French soap operas, and French public affairs programming to achieve major ratings and produce media superstar personalities, some of whom were better known, in terms of the cultural industries, in France, than they were in the rest of Canada, or indeed, the English-speaking world.

Beginning as early as the 1920s, Quebec officials realized the importance of control over broadcasting, and sought provincial, rather than federal, control. This attempt at provincial control in order to protect indigenous French cultural industries failed. The ultimate court of appeal at that point in time, was Westminster in London, England, since Canada was a colony of the British Empire. This not only reflected the demeaning colonial status of Canada as a whole, but also the antipathy toward French culture. The entire issue of Quebec media was debated by English-speaking parliamentarians in England, and this clearly grated the Quebecois.

From a cultural perspective, Quebec never fit well into either English-speaking Canada or English-speaking North America. They are an island of French-speaking individuals who happen to be geographically located and surrounded by about 250 million English-speaking North Americans. Yet, they have always had the significant insight to attempt to maximize their linguistic and cultural initiatives, in essence, promote and protect their cultural and communication industries. Although it is not the specific purpose of this chapter to deal in detail with the Quebec situation, the authors are of the opinion that it represents a classic case study of development communication. Because of their language, in the first instance, Quebecers were protected to a considerable extent against the influx of U.S. media. As a result, it is the other nine provinces of Canada which are dealt with in greater detail via federal activities in this chapter.

CONCLUSIONS

Canadians are still attempting to find a proper place in the modern video world. Development communication activities, although well-articulated, well-studied, and well-intentioned over many decades, have still failed to produce the type of television programming which is made by Canadians, for Canadians, and about Canadians. Instead Canadians, in large numbers, either continue to watch American networks available in Canada via cable or satellite dish, or else watch U.S. sitcoms on Canadian television stations, particularly in prime time.

Some of the problems stem from the failure of the national regulatory agency, the CRTC, to separate and deal systematically with the mandates and appropriate public policies for the different systems, namely the public (primarily the CBC) or the private (primarily CTV). Instead the CRTC has attempted to regulate both under the same set of rules and laws with the same set of vaguely worded objectives. In addition, no strong punitive decision has ever been taken by the CRTC for any broadcast undertaking that has failed, in some cases miserably, to achieve Canadian content goals or quotas.

Another weakness is the lack of economic support for the overall system. Canada, with its relatively small population, cannot generate the type of advertising revenue needed on a broad scale to sustain prime time indigenous programming. In terms of the public network, CBC, the federal government for the last decade has systematically reduced its funds, in some cases actually closing CBC television outlets, and in other cases ensuring weakened Canadian production schedules.

Despite the above difficulties, there may be a solution. Namely, to abandon the 24-hour model of TV on-air systems, and in its place, restrict the number of hours to essentially day and prime time evening hours. In these time slots, concentration on high quality, first-rate Canadian productions makes more sense. These productions could range from popular entertainment shows, including well-known Canadian artists, or miniseries specials dealing with major events in Canadian history. In addition, expanded public affairs programming from a Canadian perspective makes a lot of sense. In this way, development communication goals of presenting a positive indigenous model will be realized. Now the situation is of such nature that when solid Canadian programming is produced, it is frequently lost among U.S. imported sitcoms. Also there is the additional problem that every time a new television station is licensed or a new cable outlet is approved, this has a direct negative co-relation with Canadian programming availability. Although the intentions of the licensees at the time of application are indeed honorable and well-articulated, the economic reality, unfortunately, sets in quickly. The end result is simply another Canadian system being put into place which carries a token amount of underfinanced Canadian shows and serves, essentially, as a front for providing more American programming in Canadian living rooms.

Over the decades, the Canadian laboratory as a development communication model has achieved mixed results in the final analysis. On the one hand, there are clearly positive indications of the success of public policy strategies developed by the federal government. CBC radio is world class, and Canadian documentary films are outstanding. Canadian recording artists and musicians are known worldwide. Some of the Canadian television productions on both the public and private television systems are highly rated and viewed by a substantial number of Canadians, and finally, an occasional Canadian feature film becomes an international commercial success. Yet on the other hand, the development communication strategy has resulted in a dismal picture, particularly with regard to overall television viewing patterns. Today, most Canadians watch American television. They either watch directly on American channels brought into Canadian homes via cable or they watch American sitcoms on Canadian television stations which tend to place Hollywood sitcoms in prime time viewing hours. Canadian children watch such dubious programming as "Roseanne," "The Simpsons" or wrestling in mass numbers. This, in spite of decades of major public policy initiatives, licensing renewals, and substantial tax revenue being aimed at presenting a Canadian option in the media spectrum. These initiatives have simply failed.

In the future, things are likely to get worse before they get better. Consider, for example, that by the turn of the century, we will probably have thousands of movies available on demand in some type of pay-per-view system, whether it is by cable or satellite-delivered. This means that Canadian films will be further marginalized. In addition, there could be over 100 television channels of all varieties available, mostly from the United States. This will further damage the very fragile audience picture as well as the advertising revenue base for many Canadian television broadcasting outlets. Some critics have said no country has tried so hard as Canada to promote development communication yet failed so miserably to deliver in terms of the actual representation of Canadian history, culture, politics, and ideas to young Canadian minds. The current Canadian political malaise and lack of public will for a strong national government and solution to its constitutional problems is likely associated with the failure to imprint a Canadian stamp on its broadcasting systems over time.

NOTES

1. A good example of this personality phenomena from a political perspective, is former Quebec premier Rene Levesque. He began his career as a highly-respected commentator on French television, and thus became very well known across the province, much as Walter Cronkite or Peter Jennings are well known in the United States. In the 1960s, during what is termed the "quiet revolution", he left the broadcast industry and became a politician. He broke with the Liberal party, which had strong federalist ties, to eventually head the Parti Quebecois, a provincial political party whose aim was to separate from the rest of Canada. (Saywell, 1977). Levesque was eventually leader of the opposition in Quebec City, and finally, premier, after 1976. I can still recall the evening of the election when I was based at the School of Journalism at Carleton University in Ottawa, the nation's capital. I and many other media types were at the National Press Club watching the returns, and there was substantial glee at the Press Club, which one might have predicted. This is in large measure a tribute to Levesque's personality, because he was such a decent hard-working individual, that those of us who had met him, were truly touched by not only his sincerity, but also by his vision. His vision was an embodiment of development communication ideals extending to the political arena. What he succeeded in doing was to understand and apply development communication strategies at the same time his federal counterparts were at an almost total loss in terms of what to do with the national media systems.

2. The history of the Canadian satellite program is interesting. Canadian engineers and scientists aided in the development of many important components of today's satellites. In the 1960s, Canada undertook two major research satellite initiatives, entitled "Isis" and "Alouette." In the 1970s, a prototype DBS entitled "Hermes" was also put into space. Following this, a series of broadcasting satellites was launched, known as the "Anik" series. (McPhail and Judge, 1983). The major problem was that both Canadian scientists and substantial revenue were being concentrated on the hardware and technical aspects of satellite transmission. Little, if any, thought was given to what was going to be sent via these advanced broadcasting systems. When Anik and other satellites began broadcasting, it represented a quantum step forward in terms of the amount of foreign programming available in Canada. Whereas traditionally much of the broadcasting had been limited to those areas either close to

the U.S. border or with cable systems, now, almost anywhere in Canada, a satellite dish can pick up the CBC from the Anik satellites. But the problem was and still is that the CBC carries shows such as "The Dukes of Hazard" and "Dallas," as even the most remote Eskimo village in Canada's north or isolated fishing communities on the coast of Newfoundland are able to pull in the CBC's satellite signal, or just as likely, switch the satellite to pick up CNN out of Atlanta, Georgia, or WGN out of Chicago, Illinois.

The basic point is that although Canadians may lament the demise of their broadcasting sovereignty in the age of television, clearly some of the blame should be directed at Canadian policymakers and engineers in the 1960s and 1970s who directed an inordinate amount of funds into the hardware side, with little, if any, concern about the software, social and cultural consequences of what they were designing or promoting.

REFERENCES

Babe, R. 1975. *Cable Television and Telecommunications in Canada.* East Lansing: Michigan State University Press.

Canada. 1936. *Canada's Broadcasting Act 1936.* Ottawa: King's Printer.

Canada. 1951. *Royal Commission on National Development in the Arts. Letters, and Sciences. 1949–51.* Ottawa: King's Printer. Referred to as Massey Commission.

Canada. 1957. *Royal Commission on Broadcasting.* Ottawa: Queen's Printer. Referred to as Fowler Commission.

Canada. 1958. *Broadcasting Act 1958.* Ottawa: Queen's Printer.

Canada. 1968. *Broadcasting Act 1968.* Ottawa: Minister of Supply and Services.

Canada. 1983. CRTC Public Notice, 1983–18. *Policy Statement on Canada Content in Television.* Ottawa: Minister of Supply and Services.

Canada. 1991a. *Broadcasting Act 1991.* Ottawa: Minister of Supply and Services.

Canada. 1991b. *The Economic Status of Canadian Television.* Ottawa: Minister of Supply and Services.

Caplan, G., and Sauvageau, F. 1986. *Report of the Task Force on Broadcasting Policy.* Ottawa: Minister of Supply and Services.

Collins, R. 1990. *Culture. Communication and National Identity: The Case of Canadian Television.* Toronto: University of Toronto Press.

Descrambling the Logic. May 18, 1991. *Globe and Mail*, p. C–3.

Downey, B. 1985. *Regulation, Politics. and Public Policy: The Case of Canadian Content Regulations, 1959–1984.* Unpublished master's thesis, University of Calgary, Calgary, Alberta.

Fowler. See Canada. 1957.

Globerman, S. 1983. *Cultural Regulation in Canada.* Montreal: Institute for Research on Public Policy.

Habermann, P. 1978. *Development Communication: Rhetoric and Reality.* Singapore: AMIC.

Hughes, E. 1943. *French Canada in Transition.* Chicago: University of Chicago Press.

Massey. See Canada. 1951.

McPhail, T. 1976. The Future of Canadian Broadcasting: Proposed Revision of Regulatory Mechanisms and Policies. *The Crisis in Canadian Broadcasting.* Ottawa: Canadian Broadcasting League.

McPhail, T. 1978. Interactive Cable Communication Services: The Duplex Society Problem. *Canadian Journal of Communications* 4, (4): 1–7.

McPhail, T., and Barnett, G. 1980. An Examination of the Relationship of United States Television and Canadian Identity. *International Journal of Intercultural Relations,* 4, 2, 1980, pp. 219–32.

McPhail, T. 1982. Aspects of the NWIO: A Canadian Perspective. *Media Information Australia* 26, pp. 69–72.

McPhail, T. 1983. The Future of Canadian Communications. In B. Singer (ed.), *Communications in Canadian Society,* pp. 73–82. Toronto: Addison-Wesley.

McPhail, T., and Judge, S. 1983. Direct Broadcast Satellites: The Demise of Public and Commercial Policy Objectives. In I. Singh (ed.), *Telecommunications in the Year 2000: Nation and International Perspectives,* pp. 72–79. Norwood, New Jersey: Ablex Publishing Corporation.

McPhail, T. and Downey, B. 1984. Community Broadcasting: High Technology Represents a New Twist. In *Canadian Journal of Communication,* Vol.10, Summer pp. 47–64.

McPhail, T. 1986. Contemporary Canadian Communication Issues: An Alternative Plan. *Culture and Communication: Methodology Behavior. Artifacts. and Institutions.* pp. 262–78. New Jersey: Ablex Publishers.

McPhail, T. 1987. *Electronic Colonialism: The Future of International Broadcasting and Communication.* (2nd edition revised). Beverly Hills, Calif.: Sage Publications.

McPhail, T. and McPhail, B. 1987. The International Politics of Telecommunication: Resolving the North-South Dilemma. *International Journal,* XLII, (Spring), pp. 289–319.

McPhail, T., and McPhail, B. 1988 Canada: Broadcasting Issues. In P. Rosen (ed.), *International Handbook of Broadcasting Systems.* pp. 47–60. Westport, Conn.: Greenwood Press.

McPhail, T. 1988. Canadianization of European Broadcasting: Is an Electronic Berlin Wall the Answer? *Broadcasting and Research Experiences and Strategies.* pp. 15–30. Amsterdam: ESOMAR publishers.

McPhail, T. 1989. Inquiry in International Communication. In W. Gudykunst (ed.), *Handbook of International and Intercultural Communication.* pp. 47-66. Sage Publications.

McPhail, T., and McPhail, B. 1990. *Communication: The Canadian Experience.* Toronto: Copp Clark Pitman, Ltd.

Ostry, B. 1978. *The Cultural Communication.* Toronto: McClelland and Stewart.

Peers, F. 1979. *The Public Eye: Television and the Politics of Canadian Broadcasting. 1952–68.* Toronto: University of Toronto Press.

Prang, M. 1965. The Origins of Public Broadcasting in Canada. *Canada's Historical Review,* 46 (1):1–31.

Saywell, J. 1977. *The Rise of the Parti Ouebecois 1987–1976.* Toronto: University of Toronto Press.

Servaes, J. 1990. Rethinking Development Communication: One World, Multiple Cultures. *Journal of Development Communication.* 1 (2):35–45.

Smith, A. 1980. *The Geopolitics of Information: How Western Culture Dominates the World.* New York: Oxford University Press.

Starowicz, M. 1984, Nov. *Slow Dissolve, How Canada will Lose Its Broadcasting Sovereignty.* Address to the Graduate Programme in Communication Studies of the University of Calgary, Alberta.

Toronto Star. Feb. 8, 1992. Real Talent Will Always Win Out. p. J-1.

Weir, A. 1965. *The Struggle for National Broadcasting in Canada.* Toronto: McClelland and Stewart.

11

Communicating Knowledge of Immunization for Development: A Case Study From Nigeria

INTRODUCTION

This chapter focuses on the specific role of communication in the management of a development program, using Nigeria's program of mass immunization for young children as a case study. The chapter is based on research conducted in 1989 on the Expanded Programme on Immunization (EPI), Nigeria's massive attempt to eliminate six major childhood diseases: measles, whooping cough, tuberculosis, diphtheria, polio, and tetanus. The United Nations estimated about seven million cases of these killer diseases by 1985, about six percent of which resulted in either death or permanent disability for children under the age of five years (UNICEF, 1986).[1]

Focus on the role assigned communication in the implementation of Nigeria's program of immunization derives from three reasons. One, there was a presumption by managers of the EPI program in Nigeria that communication was an integral part of the strategy to mobilize communities for the acceptance of vaccination services. This position was shared by the UNICEF, one of the principal sponsors of Nigeria's EPI (UNICEF, 1986:11). Given the prominence assigned communication in the dissemination of vaccination messages, it is necessary to study both the structure and content of mass media messages directed at nursing mothers.

Two, past surveys on the acceptance of vaccination services in both Nigeria and other developing countries concluded that shortcomings in communication partly account for the failure to achieve high vaccination coverage and the inability to lower dropouts from vaccination series. The factors most frequently discussed by public health scholars include lack of information (Blum, 1986; Belcher, 1978), ignorance of mothers (Ogunmekan, 1982), inadequate publicity, and poor communication between government departments (Jinadu, 1983). Because high dropouts from vaccination series and low coverage threaten the success of immunization programs, the response of policy makers and EPI managers was to invest more resources in communication, mass media channels in particular, to boost vaccination coverage. Unfortunately, this strategy has not always worked, judging by the persistently low coverage of vaccine acceptance (Ogundimu, 1991; United Nations, 1989).

Three, the low coverage and high dropout rates from vaccination series, despite intensive mass media campaigns and mass mobilization exercises, raise questions about the efficacy of communication in the service of development. Hornik (1988) addresses the failures of development programs utilizing communication approaches by making distinctions between "program failures" and "theory failures," suggesting that knowledge of the conditions under which communication can effect development is important. This observation is, of course, not new. It goes to the heart of the debate among communication scholars on the nature of communication effects, and in a broader context, the diffusion of innovations (Rogers, 1983).

The literature on communication effects is expansive, extending beyond the scope of this chapter. But broadly, communications scholars have long debated the nature of communication effects, the distinctions to be made between mass communication and interpersonal communication, and the conditions under which mass media messages in particular affect individuals. Since EPI managers devote considerable attention to mass media, for the mobilization of mothers whose children need vaccination services, I will ignore the literature on media effects and specifically address how assumptions of media effects relate to Nigeria's program on immunization. Two aspects of Nigeria's mass media campaign are specifically examined, radio and television jingles used for promoting immunization services, and use of posters to publicize the program. Limiting the chapter's emphasis to these two forms of mass media campaign was dictated by the need to narrow the focus of the mass media campaign in this chapter.

HISTORICAL BACKGROUND OF NIGERIA'S IMMUNIZATION PROGRAM

Nigeria's attempt to immunize children from childhood diseases has a long history, beginning with the smallpox campaigns of the 1960s and the measles eradication program of the 1970s. Smallpox was successfully eradicated in 1970 but measles persisted. The poor results of the measles eradication program led to the first Expanded Programme on Immunization (EPI), launched in 1976 by the Nigerian federal government. But the program never got off the ground, resulting in the immunization of only about 15 percent of children by 1983 (UNICEF, 1986). Consequently, the impact on the disease was minimal. Following this earlier failure, the Nigerian government revitalized the program in 1984 as part of a primary health care scheme that focused on immunization, oral rehydration therapy (ORT), and nutrition. The immunization phase of the program pledged to achieve at least 80 percent coverage against the six target diseases—measles, whooping cough, tuberculosis, diphtheria, polio, and tetanus—for children under the age of two years by the year 2000.

FUNDING IMMUNIZATION IN NIGERIA

The program to revitalize EPI was allocated about $103.6 million for the period 1986 to 1990. For this initial funding, state governments in Nigeria provided 72 percent of the money, the federal government 10 percent, and the United Nations Children's Fund (UNICEF), another 10 percent. The rest of the money was given by the Canadian International Development Agency (CIDA), 4 percent; United States Agency for International Development

(USAID), 2 percent; and Rotary International, 2 percent (UNICEF, 1986). Since this initial funding, the UNICEF alone spent an additional $19 million on the project between 1989 and 1991. The additional UNICEF funding was 47 percent of the agency's expenditure in Nigeria for that period (UNICEF, 1986:11).

USING MASS MOBILIZATION AS KEY STRATEGY

The decision by Nigeria's health policy managers to adopt a strategy of intensive mass media use to promote immunization services was part of the social advocacy perspective sponsored by the UNICEF and previously used in many other developing countries. The heart of the strategy was to court political commitment and sustain support for the immunization program through national and local political leaders. Once political commitment was established, the program then mobilized local administrative capacity, including the involvement of health, professional, and civic groups, as well as mass media (Obadina, 1988; United Nations, 1989).

By 1989, the social mobilization perspective was fully established and EPI had gained high visibility. But the program continued, however, to face serious problems of inadequate coverage and high dropouts from completion of vaccination series. A national coverage survey conducted by the UNICEF and the Federal Ministry of Health at the end of 1988 found only 38 percent of the children under two years completed vaccination series (United Nations, 1989:6). Similarly, my surveys in Lagos and Kano states in 1989 found only 31 percent of children under the age of three years completed the DPT (diphtheria, pertussis, tetanus) series of vaccination, and only 25 percent completed all five trips required for full immunization (Ogundimu, ibid).

Protection against the six EPI target diseases requires a minimum of 14 doses of vaccines for children—given at five intervals—and two doses of tetanus toxoid vaccines for pregnant women. The World Health Organization and the UNICEF recommend that the bulk of the vaccines—the oral polio vaccine (OPV) and DPT series vaccine—be given at three different occasions for children; and the tetanus toxoid (TT) vaccine be given twice to pregnant women. Additionally, the BCG vaccine—for protection against tuberculosis—is given at birth, and the measles vaccine is given when a child is nine months old. The minimum interval for injecting vaccines requiring more than one dose (OPV and DPT series) is four weeks (*W.E.R*, 1979:389; WHO/UNICEF, 1985:7–8).

In 1988, Nigeria's EPI vaccines were given on three consecutive "National Immunization Days" (NIDs) during March, April, and May.[2] This mass immunization exercise was designed to boost coverage and lower the dropout rates. Great emphasis was placed by health officials administering the immunization program on voluntary compliance by mothers who were expected to take children to vaccination clinics. To reach mothers, massive publicity campaigns were staged, typically in the preceding week before an immunization days exercise. The primary vehicles for the campaigns were radio, television, mobile vans outfitted with loudspeakers, and handbills and other kinds of illustrated posters displayed in public places. Aside from mass media campaigns, local community action groups and religious leaders were used to publicize the program. The concept of mass immunization has since been applied at the state level, in 1989 under a program known as "State Immunization Days" (SIDs). And in 1990, the program was known as "Local Immunization Days" (LIDs), under the auspices of local government authorities.

PRIORITY ASSIGNED MASS MEDIA IN NIGERIA

I have mentioned that the concept of mass mobilization for mass immunization was a key strategy adopted by managers of the EPI in Nigeria, originating from the social advocacy perspective of the UNICEF, prime sponsor of the program to immunize children against diseases in developing countries. A critical part of this social mobilization perspective involves intensive use of mass media, with particular emphasis on radio and television messages.

In the case of Nigeria, radio and television were so accorded prominence in the dissemination of vaccination messages that a tripartite agreement was signed between three key agencies handling the immunization program. The agreement provided for the UNICEF to supply broadcasting equipment, transportation, and funding to the Federal Radio Corporation of Nigeria (FRCN), and the Nigerian Television Authority (NTA), in return for the production and dissemination of child survival messages (including EPI promotional messages) on Nigerian radio and television stations. The Federal Ministry of Health, the government agency coordinating the primary health care scheme, acted as a third party to the agreement, its chief responsibility to provide technical expertise in the design of vaccination messages and in the coordination of training workshops for mass media producers of those messages.[3]

The priority the Nigerian government accords mass media, radio and television especially, has deep historical attachment. First, these media are seen as prestige media essential to the country's security and development. Hence only government owns broadcasting in Nigeria.

Second, broadcasting enjoys very high profile, judging by the money government spends on radio and television in comparison to other social welfare programs such as health. For example, in 1987 federal grant to radio and television was 63 percent of the entire budget of the Ministry of Information and Culture. Or to put it another way, the allocation to both media was 76 percent of the budget for grants, contributions, and subventions made by the information ministry to 34 operational agencies, including the Nigerian Cultural Troupe, the National Theatre, and Federal Information Centers (*Nigeria Approved Budget*, 1987:Schedule 11).[4] Furthermore, whereas federal support for information services was cut by 23 percent between 1986 and 1987, cutbacks from the budget of the Ministry of Health was 40 percent. And in years when the economy got a boost, such as in 1987–1988 fiscal year, the increase in federal allocation to information (32 percent) was almost as large as that for health (56 percent) (*Nigeria Approved Budget*, 1988).[5]

The potential of the mass media to mobilize the masses for development is the principal reason frequently given by government spokespersons for the large sums of money spent on radio and television in Nigeria. This, despite evidence that the penetration of these mass media may be exaggerated. Nigeria's Federal Office of Statistics show that by 1980 only one-half of the households in the country owned radio, and only 12 percent owned television (F.O.S., 1983:27). These data reinforce the observations of other Nigerian scholars that the mass media are not the most important channels for communicating information in the country. For example, a survey of an education program, a food production program, and a local government reform program in Nigeria's Bendel state found that radio and newspapers ranked lowest as sources of information. Ranking ahead of these media were the school, market social forum, and town crier (Moemeka 1981:45–46).

The problems of Nigeria's mass media are symptomatic of what other scholars have identified about the African media. Doob (1961) highlights infrastructure constraints; Mytton (1983) mentions political control and domination of the mass media by an urban elite; McLellan (1986) points to the unfulfilled potential of television to serve as an instrument for the diffusion of development messages, and Moemeka (1981) blames media ineffectiveness on organizational constraints of urban-based elite.

NOTION OF MASS MEDIA EFFECTS AND NIGERIA'S EPI

I have already shown that the mass media were accorded high priority by both government and the UNICEF, two key agencies seeing to the implementation of vaccination services in Nigeria. I have also argued that the emphasis on the use of communication resources to mobilize the population for participation in the immunization of young children draws support from public health literature.

Most communication scholars do not doubt the potential of mass media to mobilize populations for development programs, including programs that involve the adoption of vaccination series such as health behavior. What they doubt is if much credence can be attached to the effect of mass media messages on individuals, or if the effects of communication on individuals are as simple as usually conceived. Over the years, debate has focused on the nature of mass media effects, the thinking being that the mass media have either powerful, direct, indirect, or limited effects on individuals. This debate led in the past to the formulation of models to explain social reality (McQuail, 1981:42). But preoccupation with mass media effects is no longer an overriding concern, although some scholars continue to study the nature of communication effects (Piotrow, 1990; Davison, 1987; Schoenbach, 1985).

The tendency to blame low vaccination coverage and high dropouts from vaccination series in Nigeria on "mothers' ignorance" underscores what Rogers (1983) calls pro-innovation bias of diffusion programs. By this, he means the tendency to blame the adopters of innovation for the failure to adopt new ideas. In the Nigeria EPI case, the failure of mothers to grasp the concept and practice of immunization was neither the fault of policymakers who used mass media to diffuse vaccination messages, even when it was clearly inappropriate to do so, nor was the fault due to the failure of vaccination messages to convey information that could help mothers understand both the concept and practice of vaccination. This failure to address both the structure and content of mass media messages dealing with immunization, in respect of the Expanded Programme on Immunization in Nigeria, becomes the focus of the remainder of this chapter.

FRAMEWORK FOR STUDY OF VACCINATION MESSAGES

This chapter reports data collected during research on Nigeria's immunization program in 1989. The research involved cluster sampling of households, resulting in the survey of 465 mothers of children under the age of three years. The households were located in fifty-three clusters, in eighteen towns, four villages, and four local governments (counties) of Lagos and Kano states of Nigeria.

Aside from household surveys, the research also involved field observation of vaccination exercises, focus studies, research at newspaper archives, and collection of administrative data, as well as analysis of samples of mass media messages used for promoting the EPI program in Nigeria.[6] Apart from news coverage in all mass media, broadcasting's campaign to get Nigerian mothers to immunize their children depended on promotional jingles of between 30 seconds and 90 seconds, broadcast in English and several local languages on radio and television stations. Also, child survival themes were inserted, occasionally, in the plots of a few popular television drama programs. Health officials said the campaign was broadcast in fifty-seven local languages.

This chapter will now focus primarily on the mass media campaign to immunize children in Nigeria, using data collected from focus studies and content analysis of communication messages as evidence. Five key elements will be examined, in respect of the attempt to communicate knowledge of immunization to nursing mothers in Nigeria. First, the structure and content of radio and television jingles used for promoting vaccination services in Nigeria will be examined. Second, I will discuss the shortcomings of the jingles. Third, the publicity posters used in the campaign will be examined. Fourth, newspaper coverage of the EPI program will be analyzed. And five, I will discuss how Nigerian mass media scholars and media practitioners perceived the campaign to immunize children.

RADIO AND TELEVISION JINGLES

I collected several samples of radio and television jingles broadcast in English and Yoruba and used on the network service of the Nigerian Television Authority, as well as on radio stations in Lagos, Abeokuta, Ibadan, and Ondo states of western Nigeria for content analysis. I was interested in both the thematic structure of the messages and their idiomatic characterization. My interest in idiomatic representation was motivated by the need to establish cultural relevance or some such similar symbols to EPI messages. As for thematic structure, I examined how the media relate to established facts or knowledge about immunization. To help with this analysis, the media messages were compared to seventeen facts on immunization published by the WHO and UNICEF. The two organizations identified the seventeen facts as being important to mothers understanding of both the concept and principles of immunization. (See Appendix.)

The three jingles discussed below are typical of promotional messages broadcast on radio and television to publicize the immunization program. Jingle 1 is an English language production that opens with a mellow song about EPI, composed and vocalized by a famous Nigerian female singer. The song lasts for 90 seconds and is set in the jazzy rhythm and blues format preferred by Nigeria's younger generation. The song contains the following key messages: (1) EPI will save the lives of the younger generation; (2) strong children start out as EPI babies, they are free from all diseases; (3) EPI babies sleep well; (4) Nigerian mothers love their babies; (5) EPI allows for a healthy life.

Jingle #2 is a Yoruba-language production that lasts for about 50 seconds. It features a man and his wife engaged in dialogue. No songs or musical embellishment accompany this particular jingle. The dialogue is depicted as follows: (1) the man calls out to his wife and admonishes her for not taking vaccinations despite her advanced pregnancy. He uses a proverbial saying to warn that not taking immunization is a serious health hazard. (2) The woman responds by rejecting the advice and questioning the value of vaccinations. (3) The man tells the woman about the functions of the EPI vaccines and adds that he is aware the woman is ignorant of immunization. He identifies several of the diseases the vaccines protect against. Several times during the man's harsh monologue, the woman interjects to ask if what she is being told is true. To this, the man replies in the affirmative, adding sarcastically that the woman is a nonbeliever and an ignoramus. Finally, the woman asks for directions to the nearest vaccination center, and the husband gives the direction, along with the dates of vaccination. The jingle ends with both husband and wife telling everyone to take advantage of vaccinations immediately.

Jingle #3 is narrated in Nigeria's pidgin English, the form of the English language widely spoken throughout the country. This production is of 85 seconds and opens with a foreign musical interlude. Then two male characters begin to speak to one another. The format is basically a question and answer dialogue depicted as follows: (1) Speaker #1 asks Speaker 2 if he knows that the immunization program is still ongoing. (2) Speaker #2 feigns ignorance of immunization and asks for clarification. (3) Speaker #1 tells who immunization is meant for; the diseases the vaccines protect against; the place of vaccination; and the dates of vaccination. (4) Both speakers conclude with a joint statement calling for the mobilization of all nursing mothers who may benefit from the program. They say it s free, and its a civic duty to have a child immunized.

SHORTCOMINGS OF EPI JINGLES

Comparison of the EPI jingles with facts on immunization published by the WHO/UNICEF shows there was little relevance between the three jingles and the facts on immunization. Jingle 1 speaks to no specific knowledge of immunization and provides no specific information about what the vaccinations were for; the schedule of the vaccinations; where to obtain them; and so forth. The emphasis of the production was its acoustic and musical elements, which sounded pretty good but were probably meaningless and uninteresting to a majority of local women.

Jingle #2 contains some basic information on the immunization program but the message is extremely sexist. It blatantly insults the intelligence of women by assuming they generally are ignorant and unaware of what is good. The message implies that women, in general, need men in order to be educated about the good things of life. Furthermore, it implies that a woman was more likely to take action if a man was sarcastic and demeaning.

As with Jingle #2, Jingle #3 is also an informational production except that it is less condescending. But again, it is men who address a predominantly female audience about the utility of immunization. The jingle assumes that men know better when it comes to knowledge of such things as immunization and men would be better at organizing women for vaccination exercises.

Although it is difficult to attach anthropomorphic character-istics to communication messages by themselves, my own experi-ence with Nigerian broadcasting stations was that it was common for men to dominate decision-making in production processes and that this sometimes affected the quality of production. In this par-ticular case, it is unlikely that knowledgeable female producers would approve productions such as those featured in Jingles #2 and #3.[7]

To summarize the shortcomings of EPI jingles, all three lack some of the key facts needed for understanding both the concept and practice of immunization. The omissions in the vaccination jingles include: (1) information about the side effects of vaccina-tions; (2) information about the sources of infection for the EPI dis-eases; (3) information about the consequences of failure to com-plete vaccination series; (4) information about the specific dangers posed by some of the diseases; and (5) information about the ages at which children needed to be vaccinated.

A common property of all three jingles, moreover, is that each favors a top-down approach to communication, one in which producers decide what information and which approaches they thought were best in communicating vaccination information to women—without prior research. The point was not lost on Tuluhungwa whose agency, UNICEF, helped train Nigerian broad-casters about appropriate production techniques in broadcasting. Audience research is not part of the culture of production at Nige-rian radio and television, Tuluhungwa said. At Nigerian television, "Planning for production is not done: you do the picture first, then you do the script, is the way the NTA goes about its production," he said.

EPI PUBLICITY POSTERS

Aside from jingles used for promoting vaccinations, samples of publicity posters were collected for examination of content. These posters were produced in a variety of languages, but they usually featured the same themes and similar artistic illustrations. The posters were examined for their relevance to the

WHO/UNICEF facts on immunization. Additionally, the posters were examined for information about the operational aspects of the vaccination program, information thought by many health experts as essential for completing vaccination series. These are: (1) if the source of the message was identified; (2) if the target of the message was stated; (3) if the purpose of the message was given; (4) if the importance of the message was explained; (5) if specific action was required of the receiver; (6) if the message had any cultural significance; (7) if the vaccination site was given; (8) if dates of vaccinations were given; (9) if age for child's vaccination was stated; (10) if the names of the vaccines were given; (11) if the notion of repeated vaccination was conveyed; (12) if side effects of vaccination was discussed; and (13) if the costbenefit of vaccination was discussed.

Six posters were obtained for analysis. Three of them (#1, #2, and #3) were productions of the Lagos state Ministry of Health; poster #4 was a Rotary Club handbill; and the last two posters (#5 and #6) were productions of the Federal Ministry of Health, Lagos. Poster #1 featured an illustration of a pregnant mother pictured with the famous EPI needle-and-child logo. The poster reminds pregnant women to take the tetanus toxoid vaccine in the fourth and fifth months of pregnancy. Poster #2 shows the illustration of a healthy-looking child beside the needle-and-child logo of the EPI. The poster tells parents to get children immunized against the six EPI diseases. The poster stresses that the diseases are preventable. Poster #3 is an illustration of a big healthy child holding aloft the vaccination card on which are displayed the six EPI diseases and the months the vaccinations are to be given. The poster tells parents that delaying vaccination could be dangerous to the health of children. Poster #4, the Rotary Club poster, features the child-and-needle logo of the EPI and presents detailed information about the 1988 NID campaign. This poster tells mothers why they should vaccinate children, the dates and venues of vaccination exercises, and gives a 10-point explanation of why the message is important. Posters #5 and #6, the Federal Health posters, both feature the pictures of pregnant women being injected by a female nurse with EPI vaccines. In poster #6, only the pregnant woman and the nurse are featured. In poster #5, a nursing mother, a pregnant nurse, and a nursing father, are also shown in the background awaiting their turns to receive vaccination injections.

Because all six posters were similar in many ways—in terms of the thirteen categories outlined earlier—emphasis will be placed on the key differences among the posters and on their perceived shortcomings. Unlike the broadcast messages, the posters in general contained many more important vaccination facts which ought to be featured in vaccination campaigns. However, there was the noticeable absence from all the posters of information about the side effects of vaccination, the sources of infection of EPI diseases, the grave consequences of not immunizing a child, explanation of why it is safe to immunize even a sick child, and why breast feeding provides additional source of immunization for the child. All this information was prominently highlighted in the WHO/UNICEF fact book on immunization.

True, one might argue that it is not necessary to highlight the side effects of vaccinations or the sources of infection of EPI diseases; such information could be discussed once mothers are attracted into vaccination clinics with simple, easy-to-grasp messages. This would make sense only if negative information such as rumors about the adverse side effects of vaccinations are not prevalent in the information environment of the mothers. But if such negative information persists, then there may be problems in even getting mothers to attend vaccination clinics in the first place. As it turns out, there was widespread belief among women in Nigeria at the time of my study, and beginning with the 1988 national immunization days campaign that the tetanus toxoid vaccination program was meant for the sterilization of women. Evidence is presented elsewhere to show that this problem should not have been discounted lightly in 1989 (Ogundimu, ibid).

Furthermore, only three of the posters clarified the importance of the vaccination message. One poster did not mention that some specific action was required on the part of the message receiver. Only two of the six posters attempted to convey cultural relevance. The Rotary Club poster attempted to do so by translating the importance of EPI into the Yorba language, splicing the information with proverbial wise sayings of the Yoruba people. Similarly, poster #6 attempted to attach cultural significance to the message by showing the picture of a nursing mother in fine traditional clothing. Furthermore, only three of the six posters specifically mentioned where vaccinations could be obtained or the dates on which the vaccinations were given; and two of them neither mentioned the age at which vaccinations should be given nor said the vaccination was repetitive.

ASSUMPTIONS ABOUT MOTHERS' KNOWLEDGE
OF IMMUNIZATION

Communication practitioners and scholars interviewed at focus studies during my research in Nigeria listed poorly designed vaccination messages on radio and television as a major factor responsible for the low coverage of the vaccination exercise. They mentioned five specific communication-related factors they thought were the most problematic for mass media's coverage of the immunization program.

One, they said the campaign was too narrowly conceived, that men, too, could be targets of immunization campaigns. Two, they mentioned the overemphasis (by EPI officials) of mass media as primary channels of access when mass media were only accessible to the urban literate. Three, they said message content was poor, particularly the failure to dispel fears of side effects despite widespread belief among would be mothers that the vaccines could trigger adverse reactions. Four, they thought local languages often misrepresented the meaning and concept of immunization, and that this was critical for appropriately conveying technical information such as the concept and practice of immunization. Five, they said too much of the news coverage relating to vaccination exercises was about personalities involved in the program rather than about more substantive issues affecting the program.[8]

The debate among media practitioners and communication scholars in Nigeria raises some questions about the extent of use of mass media as sources of vaccination information, and about the kinds of knowledge Nigerian mothers have of vaccination or the EPI program. The content analysis of media messages and newspaper coverage of the EPI program I have presented shows that Nigeria's mass media overall did a poor job of communicating vaccination messages. This supports many of the assumptions stated by focus group participants drawn from the media and academic community. Indeed my study in 1989 showed that the mass media were not the most important sources of communicating vaccination information. In both Lagos and Kano states, radio and television trailed far behind clinic-health person as sources of vaccination information. In Rano, the top three choices mentioned by mothers were "clinic-health person" (65.9 percent), "older woman" (14.1 percent) and "radio" (10.3 percent). In Lagos, the top three choices of respondents were "clinic-health person" (74.6 percent), "radio" (12.1 percent) and "television" (4.3 percent). (See

Table 11.1.) These numbers call into question the decision to spend the bulk of the social mobilization or communications budget on mass media agencies.

Table 11.1
First Source of Vaccination Information by Mothers' Place of Residence in Lagos and Kano states, Nigeria.
(Household Survey, 1989. Percent Distribution)

	Place of Residence	
	Kano state (n=185)	Lagos state (n=232)
Source Mentioned (Percent)		
Clinic-health person	65.9	74.6
Radio	10.3	12.1
Television	0.0	4.3
Newspaper	1.1	0.0
School	1.6	2.2
Older Woman	14.1	3.4
Other	7.0	3.4
Total	100.0	100.0

Chi-Square=28.82, Df=6, Significance=.00.
Cramer's V=.26, p=.00.

Whereas the mass media trail badly as prime sources of vaccination information among nursing mothers in Nigeria, the impotence of mass media was not exactly unknown to senior policy advisers who oversaw the management of the immunization program. For example, Tuluhungwa, the UNICEF regional director, admitted that the potential of the mass media to bring about dramatic improvement in awareness of immunization services was all the agency had to show for its investment, as at the time of my study.

Media performance on the diffusion of immunization messages in Nigeria may also have led to a reevaluation of thinking at senior policymaking levels, considering the admission in late 1989 by Tuluhungwa that there was an awareness that the mass media were limited in convincing people to accept immunization. He said the mass media were best at promoting awareness. That the job of convincing people to accept immunization was that of interpersonal channels. That may be so. But that evidence was nonexistent at the time of my study.

I have argued elsewhere that whereas knowledge of immunization services and mother's education were the most important factors explaining the acceptance of vaccination series in Nigeria (Ogundimu, ibid), no communication factor—whether interpersonal or mass media—contributes anything to the completion of vaccination series. The communication of basic awareness information, for which the mass media are usually credited, cannot even be regarded as a positive force in the Nigerian case study. This is because of the finding that even knowledge of basic awareness information among nursing mothers in Nigeria was very poor. When asked to name some basic facts of the Nigeria EPI program, less than 4 percent of mothers were able to identify all seven facts for which knowledge of basic immunization services was being tested (see Table 11.2).[9] For both Lagos and Kano combined, the majority of mothers (25.8 percent) were able to identify only four of the seven basic facts. The proportion identifying four basic facts in Lagos state was 31.5 percent. In Kano state it was 20 percent (Table 11.2).

The harsh review of mass media performance in communicating vaccination messages in Nigeria should not be regarded, however, as evidence that the potential of the mass media to communicate knowledge of immunization is totally without merit. This is because of the finding that there is limited support for a high correlation between exposure to radio and knowledge of whooping cough.[10] In establishing a link between knowledge of whooping cough and frequency of exposure to radio, I found that although there was some relationship in the Nigeria case I studied, this cannot be overstated. (See Table 11.3.) The relationship was curvilinear. As seen in Table 11.3, regardless of the amount of knowledge displayed, the two largest pools of respondents belong to those who "never listen to radio and those who listen every day." Indeed there are more non-listeners than every day listeners (see Table 11.3). But among respondents identifying all three correct answers, 35.2 percent "never listen" to radio and 39.8 percent "listen to radio every day." The proportion of those making the same correct choices remains flat, 12.5 percent, for those who either listen "1–3 days a week," or "4–6 days a week." The latter pool of respondents was considerably smaller than the every day listeners and non-listeners, however (Table11.3). Hence, the conclusion that whereas non-exposure to radio does not necessarily preclude knowledge of whooping cough, infrequent exposure to radio does not automatically guarantee more knowledge either.

Table 11.2
Vaccination Attendance Record 0–to–3 Year Old Children
Taking EPI Vaccines in Lagos and Kano State of Nigeria.[a]
(Household Survey, 1989)

	Percent Making Vaccination Trips				
	Combined (n=459)	Rural (n=234)	Urban[b] (n=225)	Kano (n=225)	Lagos[c] (n=234)
No trip	27.9	33.3	22.2	32.4	23.5
One trip	11.5	6.8	16.4	7.1	15.8
Two trips	14.4	14.5	14.2	13.3	15.4
Three trips	11.3	12.4	10.2	12.4	10.3
Four trips	10.2	11.5	8.9	12.0	8.5
Five trips	24.6	21.4	28.0	22.7	26.5
Total[d]	*100.0*	*100.0*	*100.0*	*100.0*	*100.0*

Notes
a. Computed with SPSS-X, based on acceptance of any combination of BCG, DPT1, DPT2, DPT3 or measles vaccine. Five vaccination trips refers to fully vaccinated children—BCG + DPT1 + DPT3 + measles.
b. Cramer's V=.20, p=.00 (Rural-Urban difference). Chi-Square=17.57, df=5, p=.00.
c. Cramer's V=.17, p=.02 (Lagos-Kano difference). Chi-Square=13.65, df=5, p=.02.
d. Total percent may not equal 100 exactly due to rounding.

CONCLUSION
IMPLICATIONS OF MASS MEDIA FAILURE

This chapter has highlighted the shortcomings of the Nigerian mass media campaign for the immunization of young children. The campaign was directed at mothers who bore the responsibility for getting children to vaccination centers where series vaccines were given to young children and pregnant women. The vaccines protect both children and pregnant women against six deadly child killer diseases: diphtheria, whooping cough, tetanus, measles, polio, and tuberculosis. I have provided both the historical and contemporary context of the Nigeria immunization program to show that the use of mass media has always been accorded prominence in the delivery of services or development programs, such as the Expanded Program on Immunization.

Table 11.3
Knowledge of Whooping Cough by Frequency of Radio Listening
in Lagos and Kano, Nigeria.
(Household Survey, 1989. Percent distribution)

	Knowledge of Whooping Cough Number of Correct Answers (Percent)				
	None Right	*One Right*	*Two Right*	*Three Right*	
Frequency of Radio Listening Weekly					
Never	58.8	43.4	36.3	35.2	n=197
1–3 days	7.8	23.0	22.3	12.5	n= 80
4–6 days	3.9	4.4	3.2	12.5	n= 25
Every day	29.4	29.2	38.2	39.8	n=158
					N=460

Cramer's V=.15, p=.00.
Chi-Square=32.84, df=9, p=.00.

The priority accorded the mass media for the promotion of Nigeria's immunization program notwithstanding, I have tried to show in this chapter that the expectations of the program sponsors have not always been met. This is because of both theory failures regarding the role of communication in immunization campaigns and because of program failures in the management of the communications component of the Nigeria mass media campaign. The shortcomings of the mass media campaign to immunize children in Nigeria were conceived of as both structural failures and content failures.

On paper, federal broadcasting stations had good plans for promoting EPI, but performance was lacking in many ways. For example, not enough EPI messages permeated existing programs at the time of this study. Also, no new program specifically directed at child survival themes had been broadcast, several months after the idea was conceived.

Two, producers trained for the production of EPI messages on radio and television were often deployed to other assignments before they had a chance to implement what they learned at EPI workshops.

Three, on both radio and television, immunization messages lacked crucial information needed for mothers' understanding of both the concept and practice of immunization. I mentioned that both the WHO and UNICEF—two international agencies concerned with immunization—had published information which could be included in vaccination messages in mass media. The WHO/UNICEF "Fact" book made available to the mass media contained the kind of information which many health experts say would help with the acceptance of vaccination series. One criticism of radio and television was that preproduction planning was lacking, hence the tendency to produce messages that had little or no relevance for mothers understanding of immunization services. Critics say this is a top-down approach to communication.

Four, I suggested that vaccination messages should highlight the side effects of vaccines and the sources of infection of EPI diseases, since many mothers were concerned about the side effects of vaccines. Also, it was necessary to counter widespread suspicions of the vaccination program, considering that the true purpose of the vaccination exercise was misunderstood. This was evident from the thinking by many mothers that the vaccination program was linked to the government s population control policy and that the program was therefore a back-door attempt to sterilize women.

Five, most officials responsible for EPI favored the mass media as channels of communicating vaccination information to mothers, even when there was limited access by the mothers to the mass media. However, it was also stated that EPI program managers were not completely unaware of the limitation of mass media in communicating vaccination messages. At the UNICEF, in particular, there was strong awareness that the mass media were most effective in communicating basic awareness information and that the job of convincing mothers to accept immunization services was to be accomplished through interpersonal channels. At the time of this study elaborate plans for more intensive use of interpersonal channels had not been implemented.

A final comment or recommendation I would like to make concerns the need for the mass media—radio, television, and newspapers in particular—to encourage listener and reader interest in Nigeria's immunization program by sponsoring promotional activities associated with the vaccination exercise. This can be in the form of contests and coupons, aimed at rewarding mothers who identify key immunization facts, or who show evidence of attendance or completion of vaccination series. The almost total absence of such media promotional activities in Nigeria at the time of my study was a graphic demonstration of the lack of media marketing expertise. It denied the mass media opportunities to expand their audience base. And at a more strategic level, the lack of active promotion of development concepts in Nigeria's media is further evidence of the lack of social responsibility. For an institution which enjoys tremendous public support, the poor awareness or lack of capacity to engage in meaningful promotion of a vital development concept such as the need to immunize children speaks volumes for the capacity of media practitioners to act as active promoters of development.

APPENDIX

Excerpts of Facts on Immunization Used for Judging
Knowledge of Immunization Services and Content Analysis
Mass Media Messages
(Cf: UNICEF, WHO, UNESCO. *Facts for Life: A Communication Challenge.* New York, N.Y.: UNICEF, n.d.; pp. 33–38)

Item No.   *Category Theme*

1. Immunization offers protection against most diseases.

2. Non-immunized child could get measles, whooping cough; could suffer death; survival results in weakened child plus threat of malnutrition and other illnesses.

3. Measles causes malnutrition, mental retardation, blindness.

4. Non-immunized child could be infected with polio; 1 in 200 get paralyzed for life.

5. Tetanus germs grow in dirty cuts, kill most infected persons if not immunized.

6. Breast feeding offers immunization against most diseases; mother's resistance is passed on to child in her breast milk, especially in first few days after birth.

7. Vital for infants to complete full course of immunizations, otherwise vaccines may not work.

8. Parents must know a child should be taken for immunization five times in the first year of a child's life.

9. Schedule of Immunization: (a) birth: tuberculosis and polio in some countries); (b) six weeks: DPT1, OPV1; (c) 10 weeks: DPT2, OPV2; (d) 14 weeks: DPT3, OPV3; (e) nine months: measles (12–15 months in more developed countries).

10. Measles is one of the most dangerous of childhood diseases. For first few months of life, the child has some natural protection against measles, inherited from the mother. This interferes with the measles vaccine. But after about 9 months, this natural protection comes to an end. Child now at risk and should be immunized.

11. If child not fully immunized by end of first birthday, important to have child immunized as soon as possible thereafter.

12. It is safe to immunize a sick child. Fever, cough, diarrhea, cold, or some other mild illness does not interfere with immunization.

13. After injection, the child may cry, develop a fever, a rash or a small sore. As with any illness, a child should be given plenty of fluid food. Breast-feeding is particularly helpful. If problem persists for more than three days, contact a health center.

14. Every woman between the ages of 15 and 44 should be fully immunized against tetanus. If the mother is not immunized against tetanus, then 1 in 100 babies will die from tetanus.

15. Remember, tetanus germs grow in dirty cuts. Avoid using unsterilized knife to cut umbilical cord, or putting anything unclean on the stump of the cord. To sterilize, first clean object, then boil or heat in flame, then allow to cool.

16. Mothers can protect themselves and newborn babies against tetanus by making sure they are immunized before or during pregnancy.

17. If a woman is not already immunized, a first dose of tetanus vaccine should be given as soon as pregnancy is known. The second dose can be given four weeks after the first, and should be given before the last two weeks of the pregnancy. A third

dose should be given six to twelve months after the second dose or during the next pregnancy. These three tetanus vaccinations protect mother and newborn baby for five years. All infants should be immunized against tetanus during the first year of life.

NOTES

1. One estimate put the numbers of death and disability from measles alone at 100,000 for children under 24 months (United Nations, 1989:4). Nigeria's Infant Mortality Rate of 105 per 1,000 live births for 1985–1990 was higher than Africa's average of 101 per thousand or the mean of 79 per thousand for less developed countries. By comparison, more developed countries have an IMR of 14 per thousand. The lowest figures recorded for Africa are for Reunion, 11 per thousand, Mauritius 23 per thousand and Madagascar 59 per thousand (UN, 1986).

2. These NIDs were held on the last Tuesdays, Wednesdays, and Thursdays of those months. These were work days, ordinarily. Although no special work-free days were given to women, this did not appear to be problematic for women employed in the public sector. The culture of the Nigerian bureaucracy was such that allowing women time off to attend to the health of a child was ordinarily considered a legitimate excuse for missing work. Those employed in the private sector might have experienced the most difficulty because taking time off usually meant loss of wages. And many women interviewed as part of focus studies for this research said a major reason why many self-employed women failed to show up for subsequent immunization schedules was because of the opportunity cost—expressed in lost business—of taking a child to an immunization clinic.

3. Information based on interviews with regional director of UNICEF, R.N. Tuluhungwa. Interview held at UNICEF office, Lagos, Nigeria, August 24, 1989. The UNICEF director did not say exactly how much was spent on technical support for radio and television equipment and training in Nigeria. But the social mobilization and technical support budget in the past was a high as 50 percent of total expenditure on EPI and ORT programs.

4. This pattern has been constant over the year. In 1988, the federal grant to radio and television was 79 percent of the Ministry of Information budget (*Nigeria Approved Budget*, 1988).

5. In 1987-1988, defense expenditures accounted for the biggest share of total recurrent spending (6.1 percent) followed by education (2.2 percent), health 1.9 percent), and information (1.1 percent).

6. I am grateful for the support provided by the Rockefeller Foundation which funded the research. For providing initial funding for the project, I am also indebted to: the William and Flora Hewlett Foundation; the Population Institute for Research and Training, Indiana University, Bloomington; and the African Studies Program, Indiana University, Bloomington.

7. The identity of the producers of the promotional jingles was not revealed. But it is noted that the director of the programs division at the Nigerian Television Authority at the time was a woman, Ezeokoli. The head of the Child Survival Unit (NTA) responsible for the production of Jingle #1 was a man—Aiten Ahua. Jingles #2 and #3 were radio promotional tapes. The heads of those production units were unknown.

8. Participants at the focus group discussion from which these observations are summarized are: Andrew Moemeka, Ralph Akinfeleye, Agboola, Adidi Uyo, Idowu Sobowale, Delu Ogunade, Segun Oduko, and Olatunji Dare. Dare represented the *Guardian* newspaper; Agboola, FRCN. All the others were professors at the University of Lagos. Eleven other persons representing mass media, the UNICEF, and the health ministries, failed to show up at the last minute because of bad weather. Alternative arrangements were made to record interviews with several of them separately.

9. Knowledge of basic immunization services was computed by means of factor analysis. The proportion of variance explained by factor scale following varimax rotation was 28.4 percent n = 457). The alpha reliability of the computed factor scale was 0.98.

10. Knowledge of whooping cough was also determined by factor analysis of respondents answers to three questions: (1) awareness that whooping cough is deadly; (2) awareness that whooping cough spreads other than by coughing; and (3) awareness of the side effects of whooping cough. Following varimax rotation, the proportion of variance accounted for by this factor scale was 4.3 percent (n = 460). The alpha reliability of the scale was 0.61.

REFERENCES

Belcher, D. W., et. al. March-April, 1978. A Mass Immunization Campaign In Rural Ghana: Factors Affecting Participation. *Public Health Reports* 93:170–176.

Blum, Deborah, and Phillips Magaret. 1986. *An Assessment of the Expanded Programme on Immunization in Nigeria.* UNICEF.

Davison, Phillips W. 1987. A Linkage Theory of Communication Effects. *Mass Communication Review Yearbook* 6:107–116.

Doob, Leonard W. 1961. *Communication In Africa: A Search For Boundaries.* New Haven: Yale University Press.

Federal Office of Statistics (F.O.S.). Jan. 1983. *Nigeria: National Integrated Survey of Households (June 1980–May 1981).* Lagos: F.O.S.

Hornik, Robert. 1988. *Development Communication: Information Agriculture and Nutrition in the Third World.* New York: Longman.

Jinadu, M. K. Aug. 1983. Case Study in the administration of the Expanded Programme of Immunization in Nigeria. *Journal of Tropical Pediatrics,* 29:217–19.

McLellan, Iain. 1986. *Television for development: The African experience.* Ottawa, Canada: The International Development Research Centre.

McQuail, Denis and Windahl, Sven. 1981. *Communication models for the study of mass communications.* New York: Longman.

Moemeka, Andrew A. 1981. *Local Radio: Community Education for Development.* Zaria: Ahmadu Bello University Press, Ltd.

Mytton, Graham. 1983. *Mass Communication in Africa.* London: Edward Arnold Publishers.

Nigeria. 1987. *Approved Budget. 1987 Fiscal Year.* Lagos: Federal Government Printer.

Nigeria. 1988. *Approved Budget. 1988 Fiscal Year.* Lagos: Federal Government Printer.

Obadina, Elizabeth. 1988. Making Immunization Work. *West Africa,* July 11, 1988:1250.

Ogundimu, Folu. 1991. Communication and Structural Determinants of Vaccine Acceptance among Nursing Mothers in Northern and Southern Nigeria. Ph.D. dissertation, Bloomington: Indiana University.

Ogunmekan, Dorothy A. 1982. Utilization of Health Services. In E.O. Akeredolu-Ale (ed.), *Social Development in Nigeria: A Survey of Policy and Research.* Ibadan, Nigeria: NISER, University Press Ltd.

Piotrow, Phyllis T., Jose G. Rimon II, Rim Winnard, D. Lawrence Rincaid, Dale Huntington, and Julie Convisser. Sept./Oct. 1990. Mass media planning promotion in three Nigerian cities. *Studies in Family Planning.* 21 (5):265–74.

Rogers, Everett. *Diffusion of Innovations.* 1983. Third Edition. New York: The Free Press.

Schoenbach, Klaus, and Weaver, David H. 1985. Finding the unexpected: cognitive bonding in a political campaign. In Sidney Kraus and Richard Perloff (eds.), *Mass media and political thought.* Beverly Hills, Calif.: Sage.

UNICEF. 1986. *Protecting Nigeria's Children: the vaccine cold chain.* Lagos, Nigeria: UNICEF.

United Nations. 1989. Economic and Social Council (Unicef Programme Committee) Document No. E/ICEF/P/L.8 of 30 March 1989.

W.E.R. 1979. Intervals Between Successive Doses of Killed Vaccines: The Persistence of Immunological Memory and Implications for the Expanded Programme on Immunization. *Weekly Epidemiological Record* 50:388–89.

W.H.O./UNICEF. 1985. *Planning Principles for Accelerated Immunization Activities.* Geneva: World Health Organization.

12

Communication and Family Planning Campaign: An Indian Experience

> We must now act decisively and bring down the birth rate speedily to prevent the doubling of our birth rate in a mere 28 years. We should not hesitate to take steps which might be described as drastic.
>
> Indria Gandhi
Inaugural Address, A.P.I.

The strategy and content of two-thirds-world[1] development communication campaigns have been dictated, in large measure, by reference to indirect and direct international influences: program *strategy* is shaped by theoretical approaches taught in Western universities; and program *content* is shaped by reference to the current dictates of international funding agencies for agriculture, public health, and family planning. Moreover, even program *evaluation* falls to Western-educated methodologists, who influence the design of development efforts to assure that the result of campaigns will be more readily measurable. Variables, such as social structure, that do not lend themselves to ready measurement, and which too seldom concern those who propose changed agricultural or health practices, are factored out of change program designs.

Since international influence has been viewed, to date, chiefly in terms of the linearity of development models, cultural hegemony, or the failure to determine "need" in terms of indigenous knowledge, a study is required to (1) identify some of the strategies that evolved under Western influence as they are tailored to a given two-thirds-world context; (2) assess the reception of messages that derive from these strategies for rural populations; and (3) derive lessons from how these messages were introduced and processed for future communication campaigns. Such an analysis follows for the case of India, particularly for three localities in Himachal Pradesh in North India.

EXTERNAL ORIGIN OF CHANGE STRATEGIES FOR FAMILY PLANNING

Development of Domestic Family Planning Strategies in India

During India's first Five Year Plan, family planning (FP) was recognized as an eventual need for the nation. The sum of 1.5 million rupees was budgeted chiefly to determine whether any organized groups or entrenched attitudes were prevalent which would oppose FP in India. Since no particular pockets of resistance were disclosed, planners assumed that the provision of contraceptives and clinics would suffice to permit a public favorable to contraception to choose a suitable method of family limitation and spacing. The 22 million rupees allocated by the second Five Year Plan sought to build primary centers and to generally increase availability of services.

Planners uncritically adopted the perception of international development agencies to the effect that: (1) the products being offered were good products; (2) they were being offered at a subsidized rate; (3) attitudes were favorable or neutral toward the use of contraceptives; and (4) product awareness would be tantamont to adoption. Available clinics, it was reasoned, would be fully utilized once the public learned of the availability of services in their vicinity. By analogy to agricultural models, a good idea would diffuse among adopters, requiring only timely information and availability of supplies and inputs. Questions of public perceptions received little attention: (1) would FP messages be suitable for mass media broadcast? (2) Were group meetings so public as to place overt pressure on potential adopters to discontinue contraception? (3) Were extension communicators and physicians sufficiently convinced of the merits of FP to risk their standing by publicly supporting the program? (4) Was profitability of FP obvious, i.e., was asserted "happiness" a sufficient reason to forego additional earning potential? (5) Could person-to-person doubts be assuaged by an urbanized outsider? and (6) Was information merely lacking, or was attitude change likewise involved?

By the time of the Third Five Year Plan, over 240 million rupees were allocated for family planning. The agricultural extension approach lacked conspicuous success, and further differences between agricultural and health campaigns became apparent: (1) an intensive effort in a few districts might be suitable for increased agricultural productivity, but population control touched all corners of the subcontinent; (2) socioeconomic differences and religion played a more prominent role in determining family planning message approval than it did for agriculture; (3) while women might have favorable attitudes toward bearing fewer children, it was men who largely dictated the fertility rate, posing gender considerations unfamiliar to agricultural campaigns; (4) for agricultural messages, profitability is so obvious as to speak for itself, whereas, for FP, social costs are more visible than profitability; (5) gains for agriculture are direct and immediate, while for FP they are remote and often abstract, phrased in terms of national imperatives; (6) the field of application for FP is the self, leading to greater ego-involvement for FP than for agriculture; (7) agricultural decisions are, within certain parameters, reversible, and can be tried in small quantity, while sterilization is generally forever; (8) social norms enter into play more directly in FP than for agriculture; (9) the demonstration technique that worked so well for agriculture was all but useless for FP; (10) local informal leaders were more likely to support agricultural innovation than to support FP; (11) FP techniques generated real and imagined client complaints which, if left unattended, worked against message acceptance elsewhere more often than for agricultural matters; (12) money could compensate a loss of crops, but what could compensate the loss of children following tubectomy or vasectomy? (13) messages involving agriculture were considered a matter of expertise, and the worker was granted credibility, whereas for FP, workers were ridiculed, their expertise was placed second to that of neighbors and relatives, and little credibility was accorded the worker; (14) fewer communal issues were raised for agriculture, such as the perception that a community which did not contracept might grow relative to one's own community; and (15) for a variety of reasons, "adoption" was harder to measure for FP than for agriculture.

The Transition to "Motivation"

Fifty houses would be assigned; twenty would be visited; ten would have the decision-maker at home; two would give a sympathetic hearing; one might seek additional information. The report of the worker would indicate fifty families contacted for family planning purposes.

Indian family planning official

Treatments such as Everett M. Roger's *Communication Strategies in Family Planning* indicate a general pattern for the evolution of worldwide family planning efforts which fits the Indian experience quite closely. In the early stages of the FP effort, clinics were opened to provide a wide range of health services. One of these services was FP, but doctors were not motivated to offer this service for various reasons: (1) as a type of preventive medicine, FP was given second priority to restorative medicine such as vaccinations, setting of bones, and the prescription of drugs; (2) FP measures such as sterilization placed the repercussions of any side effects or personal tragedies (the death of one or more of the planned family) squarely on the physician, not on national or foreign population agencies; (3) a tubectomy, as one example, required follow-up visits (and "treatment like a VIP") for any complaint, physical or psychosomatic, expending precious time and depleting small stocks of medicines available to rural doctors; (4) physicians were very wary of the use of some contraceptive techniques such as the loop; and (5) many physicians were not themselves convinced of the urgency of having a small family, externally generated messages to the contrary notwithstanding.

Public attitudes were anything but supportive of a FP campaign. Some persons were unaware that families could be planned, or took suggestions that children be disavowed as an affront to God. Others feared, by various accounts, promiscuity, medical complications, the complete removal of the male organ or its being rendered impotent, societal derision, marital strife, and the like.

Communication specialists first turned to the only successful information programs they knew, which invariably were agricultural campaigns. The agricultural approach, with few exceptions, operated vertically, whereby an extension worker was directed to screen a certain number of films, to canvas a certain number of households, or to talk with village leaders and to enlist their support. Spurred in part by government-sponsored entertainers' insertion between acts of a puppet show or songs by traveling singing troupes that "a small family is a happy family," the rural public gained awareness of the *praiwaaar niyojan nigam kendra* and its internationally diffused red triangle symbol. During early campaign years, awareness of at least one means of limiting family size grew impressively. But the technical, or "how to," aspects of the application of contraceptive technology lagged behind the awareness level. While ninety percent of the nation could respond superficially to questions probing awareness, few persons outside of the cities knew the details of any practice except abstinence from intercourse. "Rhythm" showed the least awareness of all.

The reasons for this information gap are of interest: (1) technical information contains more scientific jargon than awareness messages, it presupposes a basically scientific worldview, and it is harder to present across genders and religious differences; (2) "how to" information is embarrassing to speak about, leading to "you should practice" over "this is how to practice," (3) technical information assumes a certain degree of literacy on the part of the practitioner; (4) television and radio are too public, and print media too urban, to convincingly alter rural thinking; and (5) the village environment was quicker to reinforce negative messages of unhappy contraceptors than it was to endorse the experience of happy ones. Good news makes bad gossip, and successes of happy contraceptors tend to be private matters, anyway. The diffusion model premised upon the notion that "farmers talk to farmers" confronted a simple truth: contraceptors emphatically did *not* generally endorse their practice before other villagers.

At this stage, two notions were on the minds of family planning communicators: "motivation" and "strategies." The agricultural diffusion model assumed the self-evident worthiness of the innovation, and revolved around "information," not "motivation." But contraceptive technology was imperfect—its results, in spite of doubtful claims in the village on extension worker flannelgraphs that sterilization could be reversed, failed to convince villagers of the appropriateness of FP technology for their personal needs. Following twenty years of intensive campaigns, less than 20 million sterilizations were performed. Of 102 million targeted couples, less than 17 million known couples employed any form of contraception. Thus did the stress on "information" move increasingly toward another on "motivation," in a break from agricultural diffusion approaches.

STRATEGIES

"Strategies" is a word that crept almost unbeknownst into the vocabulary of family planning communicators. When asked by the writer to elaborate on the notion, respondents pointed to India's many religions, languages, and other sociolinguistic variables. Individual agencies sought authority from the Center to adapt messages to local environs, posters employed local idioms or native dress; or media were coordinated such that mass media and interpersonal communicators reinforced each other. The inevitable trend of the development of strategies was to try to speak the local idiom and to converse with the local mind on an increasing level of sensitivity and awareness.

Early efforts at "motivation" appeared in one of three forms: mass motivation camps, offering of incentives and disincentives, and the creation of mini-sterilization camps. "Targets" is a notion central to each of these approaches, and deserves a moment's attention. Each motivator, physician, clinic, midwife, village-level worker, or FP functionary was set a numerical quantity of expected adopters for the currently favored practice. Pressures to reach a numerical target led to a failure on the part of the communicator to fully explain a recommended practice, and to a commensurate drop in the quality of adopter. Some clients were misled or coerced, others were almost past reproductive age. Even so, targets seldom were reached, and positive incentives for the public to plan families began to dissolve into disincentives and threats.

Along these lines, the efforts at setting up festival-type mass vasectomy camps, coupled with material or monetary rewards, rarely induced a much higher level of public commitment to family planning: incentives did not differentiate by quality of adopter; records were easily falsified to show programmatic success at meeting program targets; and explanations of contraceptive procedures to clients were minimal or nonexistent, amplifying public discontent and fear of sterilization, and fostering rumors about the abuses of the FP efforts. Instead of thinking of maternal health, a visit to a health center became synonymous with sterilization. The public shifted its expectations from fertility counseling and health care to a widespread fear of health workers.

The above impressions stem largely from interviews by the writer over six months of officials from India's Ministry of Health and Family Planning, Central Institute for Family Planning, National Institute for Health Administration and Education, and National Institute for Community Development, plus published materials from various other agencies.[2]

THE RECEPTION OF FAMILY PLANNING MESSAGES IN VILLAGE NORTH INDIA

Knowledge, Attitude, and Practice (KAP) studies which proliferated over the years measured awareness levels of potential family planners. Nearly the entire population of the two-thirds world reported at least a skeletal knowledge of the existence of family planning: to the horror of parents, young school children were coming home to say "they wanted a loop." But a "KAP gap" remained apparent between convincing levels of awareness, and abyssmal levels of contraceptive practice. In a like manner, a cognitive model occupied the minds of Indian government officials during the first three Five Year Plans. The conceptualization of the "population problem" abroad and within India stood at the same stage: if the public knows, they will contracept. Knowledge, from the standpoint of methodologists, was conveniently measurable.

The "motivation" chapter of the FP effort moved from a belief in the need for "information" to a view based on "affect": it now appeared possible for a person who "knew" about contraception to hold negative attitudes toward it, and to be ill-disposed to practice some means of family planning. Slogans evolved from "two or three children, enough! Take the advice of your doctor" through "We are two, ours are two" to "We two are one; We have one." The thread that tied the campaign together was that "A small family is a happy family."

Indeed, a small family might be a happy family. But could happiness be quantified, as the urban sloganizer implies, and is the result of that quantification plain before a family has reached, say, eight children? Will a difference in happiness then be clear? Is such happiness for the self or for the nation? Is the abstraction "nation"

of much motivational significance for a villager? And is it a *fact* that a smaller family is a happier family, or only an *opinion*? If an opinion, is it more valid for expensive urban settings than for rural areas? It indicates an emphasis on sender over receiver to suggest that such conclusions are "self-evident."

The writer performed a 1976 study of rural attitudes toward family planning in three villages in the North Indian state of Himachal Pradesh during the most intensive moment of India's family planning campaign. Since the study centered on receptivity to the messages regarding family planning on the part of the subjects, and on perceptions of the validity of some of those messages, the results document the (in)effectiveness of the shift from "providing information" to "providing inducements" upon a defined Indian population. The study also marks motives that are drawn from international agencies as they are used to convince rural, two-thirds-world minds.

The Study

1. Subjects. One hundred and forty-nine (149) subjects were interviewed from three locations in the North Indian state of Himachal Pradesh. The subjects were to be somewhat equally divided between male and female subjects, subject to availability. Any adult of reproductive age could be interviewed as available in a target village or neighborhood.

2. Interview conditions. The interview team comprised six persons trained in sociology or social work to conduct rural interviews, and was divided into three teams of two persons, one man and one woman. Each team contained at least one worker who was fluent in the local Hindi dialect. The workers used an instrument that was developed, back-translated, and pretested on a sample group of villagers from the general area in which the study would be conducted. Workers were told to talk their way into the interview informally, with no time limit placed upon an interview. The workers practiced using the instrument, questioned items that got unpredictable responses, and were told to mark on the interview schedule afterwards whether, in their joint impression, the subject seemed to them to be cooperative and forthright. Three interviews "seemed wrong" to the field workers, and two others lacked coherence. Results are based upon the remaining 144 interviews.

3. Details of study. The study was designed to determine whether three groups of persons (villagers, slum dwellers, and

lower middle class persons from a city neighborhood) knew reasons for having fewer children, from which sources (mass media or interpersonal) they learned them, whether they believed any of these reasons, and whether knowledge of some or all of these reasons predicted contraceptive practice. Various demographic data were also gathered to permit cross-correlations. This paper reports only the quantity and type of motives known and whether these motives struck the subjects as credible.

Of the subjects, 56 (38.9%) were from a village setting, 58 (40.3%) were from a slum, and 30 (20.8%) were lower middle class city dwellers (hereafter, "the city"). Women were interviewed more frequently than men (85, or 59%, versus 59, or 41%, respectively) due to their being more readily available when the interviewers could be present. Interview teams arranged times to meet with some males in order to increase their percentages in the study, whereas women were generally more easily reached for interviews. Of the subjects, 59 (41%) had at least three living children, while 85 (59%) had two or fewer children.

Measurement of motives to limit family size. Subjects were brought around, in the course of the interview, to the subject of family planning. They were asked if they had ever heard, or if they could come up with on their own, any reasons that could be offered to have smaller families. If, without prompting, the subject came up with a reason, that reason was given two points of weight. The workers would than suggest other reasons that had not been volunteered by the subject, asking whether the subject had ever heard any of these other reasons. In the case where the subject said she remembered hearing that motive also, the motive was weighted one point. If the subject wanted to comment on any reason that was under discussion, the interviewers allowed him or her to comment, and kept notes of the remarks for future reference.

Subjects were then allowed to tell whether they agreed with any of the motives or not. Those persons who disagreed with three or more motives were considered to be "alienated" from family planning. Such persons who disagreed with three or more reasons to limit families were disinclined to practice family planning: An apparent correlation arises between subjects who reject multiple motives and those who do not endorse sterilization, with 88.3% of those most alienated who did not consider the idea of sterilization, versus 51.7% of persons who did not contest more than one motive who did not consider the possibility of sterilization. Only two persons who quarreled with three or more motives still said they would consider sterilization, as opposed to fifteen such persons who rejected the idea.

Table 12.1
Level of Alienation and Inclination Toward Sterilization

Alienation Level	Inclined to Sterilize	Disinclined to Sterilize
High	2 (11.7%)	15 (88.3%)
Medium	12 (32.4%)	25 (67.6%)
Low	29 (48.3%)	31 (51.7%)

MOTIVES

The subjects were familiar, in at least one instance, with fourteen reasons that could be offered to plan a family. These include:

1. Cost. A child is expensive. He or she constitutes a drain on family resources. Education is costly. Contrarily, a child may represent an economic profit, and may bring money to the family. If the family has enough children, a few will find jobs and bring money back to care for the parents in their older years.

2. Happiness. "A small family is a happy family." No contrary position was offered, but the perception of "small family" varied drastically between urban planners and the rural subjects of the study. The planners regarded "about two kids" to be a "small" family, while villagers were inclined to estimate "six or seven children" to be a "small" family.

3. Penalties. Subjects had heard of pressures at the workplace which could be used against persons who had too many children. They could sometimes cite specific disincentives or penalties for persons with three or more children who could not produce a sterilization certificate. No contrary position was offered, but the observation is in order that disincentives promoted negative rumors, and that disincentives applied mostly to persons who were government employed.

4. Mother's health. The bearing of children wears down the mother's body. It subjects her to the possibility of infection. It exposes her to possible death in childbirth. This motive was more likely to be noted in the slums or the city than in the villages. The UN declaration of a decade for women prompted the use of this motive.

5. Child's health. It is easier to provide for fewer children and to see they are healthy than to care properly for many children. The contrary position is that, without health facilities nearby, the health of children is unrelated to numbers.

6. Dividing property among many children fragments holdings. When the parents die, the children, or the sons, will divide up the property. Smaller pieces of land will no longer support the children, or only the eldest will inherit anything of importance.

7. Rewards or incentives. The community might receive a tube well or a paved road, schools might get new supplies, workers might get time off from work or bonuses, or persons might be moved up on various waiting lists, as examples of possible incentives to reach individual or community sterilization decisions. The contrary position is that such incentives were likely to be awarded fraudulently, and that a sterilization certificate could be gained without being sterilized.

8. Education. Fewer children would mean the family would have a better chance of educating their children, of buying their children school uniforms and pencils or books. The children would go farther, and make more of themselves. Perhaps this would enable them to better care for their parents.

9. Survival. In the old days, children often died in infancy. But now, with increased availability of rural medical facilities, children survived to adulthood. It is no longer necessary to have many children to compensate for high levels of infant mortality. the contrary position is that children still frequently die in infancy, and that things have not changed much since the "old days." Rural health facilities are too few, are too distant, and cannot prevent infant deaths anyway.

10. The good of the nation. Overpopulation is ruining the nation. Children cannot be fed, clothed, or schooled. The nation's resources are being used to care for children, when they might be going to make the nation strong. Contrarily, the nation is strengthened by having many children. Many people makes a nation mighty.

11. Spacing. It is good to put space between children, to give them more room to grow. Children are like plants: when crowded too closely together, they keep each other from growing properly. Contrarily, whether a person will have a child is up to God. It is nonsense to talk of deciding how closely together to have children.

12. Quality versus quantity. It is better to lavish attention and resources onto a few children, and to give them a quality life,

than to spread resources out thinly over many children. Quality children will go farther, make a name for the family, and support their parents properly. The contrary position is that only if a family has enough children might one or two make enough of themselves to support their parents. Too few children is a guarantee of a poverty-stricken later adulthood.

13. Boys and girls are equal. Whatever a boy can do, a girl can do. There is no need to keep trying for a son. Contrarily, "one keeps a son, but the girl goes to another family at marriage." Boys are needed to perform Hindu funeral rights. Boys inherit property, and take responsibility for the well-being of the family if the father dies. (Only one family in 114 stopped bearing children without having a son, and this after seven daughters.) This motive, too, was inspired by the UN decade for women.

14. Give more *dyaan* to the children. Dyaan has no exact English translation, but it connotes attention, support, caring, and loving.

Table 12.2 reports the frequency with which respondents reported encountering or considering the above motives. The table combines results for subjects who volunteered the motive without prompting, and who recognized it when it was raised by a fieldworker.

DISCUSSION

Most Familiar Motives. A motive which was raised without prompting would likely be more important and salient for the subject than another which was familiar only once it was raised by the researcher. As noted in Table 12.2, this makes the more salient motives for planning families to be "cost," "happiness," "education," and "giving more *dyaan* to the children." FP workers and campaigners who were to stress these motives would probably meet with little resistance on the part of the subjects, since these motives resonate with the experience of the subjects themselves.

Motives Familiar after Prompting. Matters of the health of the mother or the child, the nation's might, fragmenting of property, the equivalence of boys and girls, incentives, disincentives, or the need to space children either were not familiar, or they were relatively non-salient. They might be recognized as possible motives for planning families, but primarily if they were first mentioned by the fieldworker.

Table 12.2
Familiarity with Motives for Planning Families by Contraceptive Status

Motive	Sterilized	Want Operation	Some Method	Unprotected
cost	39 (1)	16 (1)	43 (1)	33 (2)
happiness	32 (7)	13 (2)	38 (7)	29 (4)
penalties	29 (28)	16 (13)	31 (27)	19 (17)
mother health	28 (18)	16 (13)	39 (27)	22 (15)
child health	29 (15)	16 (12)	35 (16)	33 (23)
property	14 (11)	9(9)	19 (16)	17 (13)
incentives	30 (28)	13 (12)	30 (29)	16 (16)
education	33 (4)	15 (2)	41 (6)	33 (4)
infant mortality	10 (9)	6 (6)	13 (12)	1 (0)
nation's good	17 (13)	13 (12)	25 (13)	15 (8)
spacing	10 (8)	5 (4)	15 (11)	4 (2)
plus quality	1 (1)	0 (0)	5 (2)	3 (2)
boys/girls same	12 (11)	4 (40	12 (12)	6 (5)
dyaan	23 (4)	10 (1)	12 (2)	22 (1)

Legend: Numbers represent how often the motive was known. The parentheses contain how many of these were given only after prompting.

Table 12.3
Disagreement with Motives for Planning Families
by Contraceptive Status

Motive	Sterilized	Want Operation	Some Method	Unprotected
cost	1	0	1	2
happiness	0	1	1	2
penalties	0	0	2	2
mother health	2	1	0	2
child health	1	1	1	2
property	1	0	1	0
incentives	1	1	3	2
education	0	0	1	0
mortality rate	7	2	6	11
nation's good	5	0	4	4
spacing	3	0	0	0
quality	0	0	0	0
boys/girls same	7	6	7	12
dyaan	0	0	0	0

Perceptual Differences. Further analysis of "happiness" that stems from a "small" family, recalls to mind the fact that rural and urban perceptions about the meaning of "small" may vary by a factor of three to four: city residents may regard two children as a small family, whereas rural persons may think of six or eight as a small family. Cost, education, and giving *dyaan* seem the most self-evident reasons for the subjects to consider limiting the size of families.

Resistance to or Unfamiliarity with International Motives. As for the motives inspired by the UN declaration of a decade for women, "mother's health" and "the equality of boys and girls" may be derived from this international source. The health of the mother was not an especially critical concern of the subjects, either male or female. Six motives are reported among those who are sterilized as of greater weight than concern for the mother's health. Eighteen of those twenty-eight persons who were sterilized recognized the motive only as an afterthought, indicating a low degree of salience as a reason for action.

The presumed equality of boys and girls, the second internationally inspired motive, appeared to have even lower motivational force. Ten other reasons seemed to carry greater recognition and, by inference, motivational force than the equality between the sexes. Adding data from Table 12.3, no single motive attracts so much disagreement as the equality of boys and girls. In terms of rhetorical theory, it is easier to persuade from an object analysis of the analysis, i.e., what means something to the audience, than from a subjective one, i.e., what means something to the persuader. The reliance on international motives to reach local minds invites distortion and rejection of messages, and stands to close the rural mind to appeals from sources that do not recognize truth from the local perspective.

Indigenous Motives. The offering of more *dyaan* to children offers a contrasting case. Not only is it a widely recognized reason to limit the number of children, but it is an indigenous reason. Its personal salience is attested to by the fact that in only eight of sixty-seven cases did the fieldworker have to prompt the subject before the motive was offered. Nor did any subject contest the motive.

Abstract Motives. Abstractions such as "the good of the nation" appear to mean more to the planners than they do to the subjects of the study. Not only is this motive unfamiliar to many in the study, but it is recognized largely only after prompting. In fact, a sizable number of subjects have reached exactly the opposite conclusion from that posited to be true by planners.

Spacing of children or the argument between quality and quantity of children seemed to pass over the heads of most of the subjects entirely.

Motives Untrue to Experience. The survival of more children now than in years past may or may not be a statistical truth, and it may or may not be true for the region under study. Clearly, though, it is not a reason that leaps to the mind without prompting as a rational for having fewer children. Subjects in the study could provide numerous instances of children who died in infancy. Twenty-four persons offered this as a motive to limit families without being prompted, whereas twenty-six gave it as a reason that more children were required.

The fragmentation of property was neither heavily endorsed, nor was it heavily disputed. Nor had motives based on incentives or disincentives come to mean much to the population under study, except upon prompting. The health of the child had more apparent motivational value than did the health of the mother.

IMPLICATIONS FOR FUTURE CAMPAIGNS

Policy Considerations

With the realization that India's family planning communication efforts have been received in a manner inconsistent with their conception, and that they probably cannot enable India to reach her stated population goals, a rethinking of policy occurred in government circles. The outlines for a revised FP communication program included:

1. Vertical versus horizontal. Health services which are offered topically inherently waste effort, and serve to turn a client against the nth worker to call on her. Health services must be consolidated and combined. The result, a multiservice Integrated Health Service worker, can better minister to the uppermost client need.

2. Agency versus client. The client must be given greater voice in defining his own needs, which implies, among other points, that the quota system should give way to a system more responsive to local perception and definition. A private advertising agency approach that brought results in Sri Lanka was tried on a

trial basis in three villages in an effort to implement a health package approach.

3. Reducing physician apathy. A National Institute of Health Administration and Education study disclosed that physicians who offer a patient seeking pregnancy care a three-minute talk about combined health centers (including family planning) produced quantifiable results. Policy should more fully draw on the credibility of physicians.

4. Motivation. The meaning of "motivation" must be rethought. While this notion will not be completely discarded, the addition of health care benefits for mother and child, work incentives for government workers, and educational benefits could serve to improve the persuasiveness of appeals, at least for villagers who are close to becoming involved in the local economy through employment.

5. Research base. More and more, FP communication materials should reflect the input of researchers and social scientists, on the one hand, and of groups of villagers of the region involved, on the other. A needs-based strategy begins with soliciting statements and opinions from local villagers, and then using own-categories sorting to determine a definition of need in terms of local perceptions. The social scientist involvement is that of process facilitator and inquirer more than as omniscient knower.

6. Project support communication. Context, ecological environment, and public attitudes and perceptions increasingly must come to the attention of, and be taken seriously by, planners. No FP attempt can be expected to succeed without the assistance of a multimedia campaign to prepare a psychological context for each message. This campaign would not center on those ideas that were attractive to international agencies, but rather on points that made sense within the local context. The relative stress on nonsterilization aspects of the FP package should lead to increasing acceptance of the program.

7. Continuing priority. With occasional changes of government within a parliamentary democracy, a sense of importance should be maintained. A motivational program can be undermined by shifts of sentiment with the change from one governing coalition to another. "Priority" is used deliberately in place of "urgency," since too-intensive pressures by an agency serve to turn the public against the agency and its priorities.

8. Climate for economic development. The use of mass media outlets to promote support for a broad range of economic

development activities should bear directly on the population growth rate. Past Health and Family Planning minister Dr. Karan Singh found international acceptance for his Bucharest conference position that "development is the best contraceptive." Fieldwork connected with this paper confirmed his impressions to be true for the subjects under study.

9. Diffusion of responsibility. The stress on mass communication should give way to another which renders every rural agent and functionary, even bus drivers, a channel of communication. The goal of "face-to-face" communication, which is more aware of the positions and needs of the other party, and which is likely to be presented in a local dialect and idiom, may best be so realized.

The nine elements listed above constitute building blocks for the construction of a new multiservice, client's perception-centered communication policy which should improve upon earlier generations of strategies. If, as Mrs. Gandhi believed, "for every man-made problem there is a man-made solution," the prospects could be bright for development communication programs.

NOTES

1. "Two-thirds world" is used in preference to alternatives such as "underdeveloped" (backward?) nations, "transitional" (in transition toward what?) societies, "Third World" (is the world any longer bi-polar or nonaligned?), or "developing" (on a linear path?) nations. "Two-thirds" signifies a numerical proportion of all nations, diminishing the centrality of the major economic powers in national development equations.

2. Opinions here presented were culled from thirty semi-structured personal interviews of media officials concerned with agriculture, health, and family planning. Names are deleted to allow officials greater freedom to express their concerns without negative consequence. The synthesis of their views remains, of course, the author's. I have taken editorial liberty in framing their views in a manner that corresponds to my own perceptions. The interviews took place between January 12 and February 20, 1976. The author acknowledges receipt of a Senior Fellowship from the American Institute for Indian Studies for the period during which the interviews were conducted.

Contributors

Godwin C. Chu a Senior Research Associate of Program on Cultural Studies, East-West Center. His publications include *Radical Change through Communication in Mao's China; Moving a Mountain—Cultural Change in China; China's New Social Fabric; Cultural Change in Rural Taiwan; Social Impact of Satellite Television in Rural Indonesia; The Great Wall in Ruins—Communication and Cultural Change in China; and Modernization vs. Revolution—Cultural Change in Korea and China*. His current research focuses on modern communication technologies and social-cultural change in Asia. He was formerly the director of the Communication Institute, East-West Center.

Donald P. Cushman is a Professor of Communication at the State University of New York at Albany. Dr. Cushman has been named a Senior Research Fellow by the Ford Foundation, NEH, NIMH, Warrnambool Institute for Advanced Education in Australia, and the East-West Center in Hawaii, and a Distinguished Research Scholar by ECA, Fulbright Commission, Canberra College of Advanced Education in Australia, Fudan University in the People's Republic of China, and the World Academic Conference of the Seoul Olympiad in Korea. Dr. Cushman has co-authored or edited three books including *Organizational Communication: Issues, Problems, and Trends; Communication in Interpersonal Relationships; and Message-Attitude-Behavior Relationships*. He also has to his credit over one hundred published journal articles and over forty book chapters.

Sarah S. King is a Professor and the Dean of the Division of Communication the Arts at Marist College, Poughkeepsie. Dr. King has been the recipient of $326,550 in grants from such agencies as NEH, NIMH, University of Hawaii, East-West Center, and the state of Connecticut for work with Hispanic organizations in Connecticut, stress and coping behavior among ethnic groups in Hawaii, high-technology development in the United States (with emphasis on Hawaii and Connecticut), and communication policy and planning. Dr. King has participated in curricular and research development in Australia, Yugoslavia, Thailand, and the People's Republic of China at the request of universities and government organizations in those countries. Dr. King was former Chair of the Department of Communication at two universities—the Central Connecticut State University, and the University of Hawaii. She has also served as Fellow or Research Associate at the University of Chicago, Ohio State University, Harvard University and at the East-West Center, Hawaii. Dr. King was a Fulbright Scholar to Yugoslavia.

Brenda M. McPhail is a Visiting Assistant Professor at the University of Missouri-St. Louis in the departments of Political Science and Communication. She has undertaken research on Canadian and American media and telecommunications, and she published, with Thomas L. McPhail, *Communication: The Canadian Experience.* Her current research interest focuses on the impact of the North American Free Trade Agreement (NAFTA) on communication policy.

Thomas McPhail is the Chair of the Department of Communication at the University of Missouri-St.Louis. He has published one of the landmark books of international communication—*Electronic Colonialism: The Future of International Broadcasting and Communication* (Sage Pub.). In addition, he has co-authored with Brenda McPhail, *Communication: The Canadian Experience.* His current research interests deal with international communication, focusing on global broadcasting issues.

Andrew A. Moemeka is Professor of Communication at the Central Connecticut State University, New Britain. Dr. Moemeka has been involved with the theory and practice of the use of the mass media in fostering development purposes for more than two decades. He has taken part in various UNESCO and other international conferences and seminars on Development Communication, and has written one book, fifteen book chapters, and numerous journal articles. Dr. Moemeka is a consultant to many international and national organizations, on communication and development and was a member of UNESCO's experts group on the "Right to Communicate," and of the African Council on Communication Education's Experts on Teaching and Training Materials on Development Communication. He is at present editing another book titled *Development (Social Change) Communication: Building Understanding and Creating Participation.*

Ikechukwu Nwosu is a Senior Lecturer (Communication) in the Department of Marketing at the University of Nigeria, Enugu Campus. He is the Co-ordinator of Public Relations Programs in the department. Dr. Nwosu—a prolific writer—has published extensively. He has to his credit more than thirty scholarly journal articles and book chapters, as well as six co-published books. His latest books are *Mass Communication and National Development* and *Public Relations.* He is an accredited editor to the African Council on Communication Education, and was the head of the publicity department of the office of the governor of Anambra State, Nigeria. Dr. Nwosu is also a member of the experts committee on Teaching and Training Materials on Development Communication of the African Council on Communication Education.

Folu Ogundimu is an Assistant Professor at the School of Journalism, Michigan State University. He teaches International Communication, Broadcasting and Research Methods. Dr. Ogundimu has extensive professional media experience in Nigeria and the United States, including working for the Nigerian Television Authority, the *St. Petersburg Times*, Fla., and the *Portland Oregonian*, Ore. He has been awarded many research fellowships, among which are the Rockefeller Foundation, New York; the Hewlett Foundation and the Population Institute for Research and Training, and the *St. Petersburg Times*, Florida. Dr. Ogundimu's research involves the mass media and communication processes in both developing and developed countries. He also teaches and publishes in these areas.

Scott R. Olson is an Associate Professor of Communication at the Central Connecticut State University. A young and gifted academic, Dr. Olson speaks with authority on Devolution and Broadcasting and their impact on development and international relations. He has to his credit book chapters and journal articles on these and other areas of intellectual pursuit. His most recent publications have been in the *Journal of Communication, Critical Studies in Mass Communication*, and in the book: *Human Communication As A Field of Study* (ed. Sarah S. King). Dr. Olson is at present the acting chair of the Department of Communication at Central Connecticut State University.

Cornelius Pratt an accredited member of the Public Relations Society of America, is an Associate Professor in the Department of Advertising at Michigan State University. He holds a Bachelor of Science degree from the University of Lagos, Nigeria, and a Masters' and a Ph.D. degree from the University of Minnesota. His research interests include ethics in Third World development programs and in Public Relations. His research has been published in such journals as *The Journal of Modern African Studies, The Journal of Media Planning, The Journal of Business Ethics, Public Relations Review, Journalism Quarterly, Public Relations Journal,* and *Public Relations Quarterly.*

William J. Starosta is a Graduate Professor of Rhetoric and Intercultural Communication at Howard University. His research interests include social change communication in two-thirds world settings, inter-ethic communication, and cultural influence on rhetoric. Dr. Starosta founded the *Howard Journal of Communications*—a scholarly quarterly on culture and communication. He has conducted sponsored research dealing with extensive study of development and communication in Sri Lanka and India.

Author Index

Subject Index

A

Access, sufficient citizen, 14
ACPO, 132, 136
Activities
  decentralization of, 14
  stages of, 54–55
Advantage, comparative
  antecedents of, 146–147
Advancement, economic, vii;
  material, 10, 26
  socioeconomiceconomic, 11
Africa, 30, 34, 35, 106, 115, 168,
  180
African Economic Community, 18
African Unity, Organization of, 18
Alaska, 78, 89
Algeria, 106
Alternatives, emergent, 8
America
  United States of, viii, 30, 34,35,
    41, 50, 147, 148, 170
  Latin, 34, 42, 102, 110, 115, 131,
    180, 182
Analyses, historical, 45–47
  individual and structural modes
    of, 48
Animation, radio and, 133–134,
  135–136
Approach, one-dimensional, 9
  multi-dimensional, 9
  basic, 55–63
Argentina, 26
Asia, 18, 34, 37, 41, 102, 110, 115,

168, 180
southeast, 110
Asian Development Corridor, 28,
  29, 147
Aspiration, raising of, 15
Atmosphere, enhancing, 13
Audience, participation, x
  socio-cultural contexts of, x
  target, x

B

Bangladesh, 168
  development of newspaper in,
    105
Belgium, 147
Benefits, social and cultural, 18
  organizational in high-speed
    management system, 151
Benin, 56, 133
Blocks, economic trading, 147
Bolivia, 181
Brazil, 148, 149, 161, 183
Broadcasting, Open, 127–128, 135
  in Mexico, the Philippines, and
    Nigeria, 127
  weakness of, 128
  Canadian Act 206–209
  development fund (CBDF), 211
Brunei, 18
Britain, Great, 34, 147
Burma, 105
Burundi, 181